SpringBoard®

Level 2

English Textual Power™

CollegeBoard
inspiring minds™

THE COLLEGE BOARD
inspiring minds™

About the College Board

The College Board is a mission-driven not-for-profit organization that connects students to college success and opportunity. Founded in 1900, the College Board was created to expand access to higher education. Today, the membership association is made up of more than 5,900 of the nation's leading educational institutions and is dedicated to promoting excellence and equity in education. Each year, the College Board helps more than seven million students prepare for a successful transition to college through programs and services in college readiness and college success — including the SAT® and the Advanced Placement Program®. The organization also serves the education community through research and advocacy on behalf of students, educators and schools.

For further information, visit www.collegeboard.com.

ISBN: 0-87447-913-4
ISBN: 978-0-87447-913-3

3 4 5 6 7 8   13 14
Printed in the United States of America

Acknowledgments

The College Board gratefully acknowledges the outstanding work of the classroom teachers and writers who have been integral to the development of this revised program. The end product is testimony to their expertise, understanding of student learning needs, and dedication to rigorous but accessible language arts education.

Susie Challancin
English Teacher
Bellevue School District 405
Bellevue, Washington

Paul De Maret
English Teacher
Poudre School District
Fort Collins, Colorado

Suzie Doss
District English/ Language Arts
    Coordinator
Hobbs Municipal Schools
Hobbs, New Mexico

John Golden
English Teacher
Grant High School
Portland, Oregon

Nancy Gray
English Teacher
West Shore Junior/Senior High School
Melbourne, Florida

Ellen Greig
English Teacher, Consultant
Charlotte, North Carolina

Karen Hanson
Exceptional Student Teacher
Volusia Public Schools
DeLand, Florida

Cheryl Harris
English Teacher Consultant
Bedford, Texas

Susie Lowry
English Teacher
Volusia Public Schools
DeLand, Florida

Julie Manley
Middle School Language Arts
    Tech-Curriculum Coach and
    Humanities Teacher
Bellevue School District 405
Bellevue, Washington

Joely Negedly
Secondary Reading and
    Language Arts Specialists
Volusia Public Schools
DeLand, Florida

JoEllen Victoreen
Instructional Specialist,
    SpringBoard
San Jose, California

Douglas Waugh
Administrative Coach,
    SpringBoard
Bellevue, Washington

Nina Wooldridge
Instructional Specialist,
    SpringBoard
Los Angeles, California

Advisors, Reviewers, Special Feature Writers

The following teachers and writers provided invaluable assistance in creating special features and reviewing manuscript. We gratefully acknowledge their contributions to this revised edition.

Gary Cowan
English/Language Arts Coordinator
Metro Nashville Public Schools
Nashville, Tennessee

Nicki Junkins
Administrative Coach,
    SpringBoard
DeLand, Florida

Jeanneine Jones
Professor, Departments of Middle,
    Secondary, and K-12 Education
University of North Carolina
Charlotte, North Carolina

William McBride
Emeritus Professor of English
Colorado State University
Fort Collins, Colorado

Daniel Millet
English Teacher
Weld county School District
    Re-8
Fort Lupton, Colorado

Melanie Sangalli
English Teacher
Irving Public Schools
Irving, Texas

Special Acknowledgments

The College Board wishes especially to acknowledge the writers of the original *Pacesetter* program. Much of their work continues in use today. The result of their efforts was a program that helped both teachers and students succeed. With its roots in Pacesetter, the current program had an excellent foundation on which to build.

Willie Mae Crews
Educator
Birmingham, Alabama

R. Steven Green, Ed.D.
Educator
Kansas City, Missouri

Ellen Greenblatt
University High School
San Francisco, California

Alice Kawazoe
Educational Consultant, California Academic
    Partnership Program
San Carlos, California

Jenny Oren Krugman
Vice President, Southern Region
College Board
Miami, Florida

William McBride, Ph.D.
Emeritus Professor of English
Colorado State University
Fort Collins, Colorado

Robert Scholes, Ph.D.
Research Professor, Brown University
Providence, Rhode Island

In addition, we wish to acknowledge the educators and writers whose work on prior editions helped to continue the *Pacesetter* excellence and to establish the high expectations for which the College Board's SpringBoard program is known.

Lance Balla
Bellevue, Washington

Bryant Crisp
Charlotte, North Carolina

Nancy Elrod
Atlanta, Georgia

Ann Foster
Melbourne, Florida

Ana Gandara
Edinburg, Texas

Alex Gordin
Portland, Oregon

Kenyatta Graves
Washington, DC

Don Keagy
Poultney, Vermont

Don Kirk
Poultney, Vermont

Dana Mebane
Baltimore, Maryland

Bob Messinger
Providence, Rhode Island

Debi Miller
Miami, Florida

Melanie Ross Mitchell
Atlanta, Georgia

Lisa Rehm
DeLand, Florida

Penny Riffe
Palm Bay, Florida

Rick Robb
Clarksville, Maryland

Sue Rodriguez
Miami, Florida

Research and Planning Advisors

We also wish to thank the members of our SpringBoard Advisory Council, the SpringBoard Language Arts Trainers, and the many educators who gave generously of their time and their ideas as we conducted research for the program. Their suggestions and reactions to ideas helped immeasurably as we planned the revisions. We gratefully acknowledge the teachers and administrators in the following districts:

Broward County Public Schools
Fort Lauderdale, Florida

Cherry Creek School District
Cherry Creek, Colorado

Chicago Public Schools
Chicago, Illinois

DeKalb County School System
DeKalb County, Georgia

Duval County Public Schools
Jacksonville, Florida

Guilford County Schools
Greensboro, North Carolina

Hillsborough County Public Schools
Tampa, Florida

Hobbs Municipal Schools
Hobbs, New Mexico

Indianapolis Public Schools
Indianapolis, Indiana

Miami-Dade County Public Schools
Miami, Florida

Metropolitan Nashville Public Schools
Nashville, Tennessee

The City School District of New Rochelle
New Rochelle, New York

Orange County Public Schools
Orlando, Florida

School District of Palm Beach County
Palm Beach, Florida

Peninsula School District
Gig Harbor, Washington

Pinellas County Schools
Largo, Florida

San Antonio Independent School District
San Antonio, Texas

Spokane Public Schools
Spokane, Washington

Volusia County Schools
DeLand, Florida

Editorial Leadership

The College Board gratefully acknowledges the expertise, time, and commitment of the language arts editorial manager.

Betty Barnett
Educational Publishing Consultant

Level 2 Contents

Grammar Handbook 347

Resources

To the Student

Welcome to the SpringBoard program. We hope you will discover how SpringBoard can help you achieve high academic standards, reach your learning goals, and prepare for success in your study of literature and language arts. The program has been created with you in mind: the content you need to learn, the tools to help you learn, and the critical-thinking skills that help you build confidence in your own knowledge and skills.

The College Board publishes the SpringBoard program. It is also the publisher of the PSAT/NMSQT, SAT, and Advanced Placement exams—exams that you are likely to encounter in your late middle school and high school years. Preparing you to perform well on those exams and to develop the language, reading, and writing skills needed for high school success is the primary purpose of this program. SpringBoard maps out what successful students should know and be able to do at each grade level as they prepare to succeed in college-level work.

What Is the Foundation for SpringBoard?

The foundation of SpringBoard is the College Board Standards for College Success, which set out the knowledge and critical-thinking skills you should acquire to succeed in high school and in future college-level work.

The standards are divided into five categories:

1. Reading
2. Writing
3. Speaking
4. Listening
5. Media Literacy

Your success as a **reader** depends on many factors, including your interest and motivation to read, the amount of time you spend reading, understanding the purpose for reading, knowledge about a topic, and knowledge about how to read different kinds of text.

Your success as a **writer** depends on learning many words and how to use those words effectively to communicate a story or information for others to read and understand. Successful writers determine their purpose for writing, such as to explore, inform, express an opinion, persuade, entertain, or to share an experience or emotion. As they write, they also consider their audiences and choose the language that will help them communicate with that audience. Writing is a process that involves several steps, and you will have many opportunities in this program to learn the process and to improve your own writing.

Your success as a **speaker** is based on how well you communicate orally. What is your message, what words will best communicate it, how do you prepare, or rehearse, for a speech? Good speakers also consider the audience and what they know about a specific topic. They can then deliver a message that uses a shared understanding, or develops one based on common knowledge, with their listeners.

Being a good **listener** is the other part of effective communication. Communication includes the speaker, listener, message, feedback, and noise (the conditions surrounding the communication). You'll have opportunities throughout the program to practice both your speaking and listening skills.

Finally, being **media literate** means that you can interpret, analyze, and evaluate the messages you receive daily from various types of media. Being media literate also means that you can use the information you gain to express or support a point of view and influence others.

As you complete the activities in this text, you will develop your skills and knowledge in all of these areas.

How Is SpringBoard Unique?

SpringBoard is unique because it provides instruction with hands-on participation that involves you and your classmates in daily discussions and analysis of what you're reading and learning. The book is organized into multiple activities that invite participation by providing adequate space for taking notes and writing your own thoughts and analyses about texts you're reading or questions you're answering. Among the key features that make SpringBoard a unique learning experience are:

▶ Activities that thoroughly develop topics, leading to deep understanding of the concepts and enabling you to apply learning in multiple situations.

▶ Extensive opportunities to explore connections between your own life and the world around you by reading a variety of texts—both fiction and nonfiction—that introduce you to many different ways of thinking, writing, and communicating.

▶ Questions that help you examine writing from the perspective of a reader and a writer and the techniques that good writers use to communicate their messages effectively.

▶ Built-in class discussions and collaborative work that helps you explore and express your own ideas while integrating the ideas of others into your base of knowledge.

▶ Integrated performance-based assessments that give you practice in showing what you know and can do, not just repeating what you've read.

▶ Assessments that help you decipher tasks and plan how to accomplish those tasks in timed situations like those for standardized tests.

Strategies for Learning

As you complete the activities in this text, you will work on many reading, writing, and oral presentation assignments. You will often work in groups and pairs. To help you do your best, you and your teacher will use a variety of reading, writing, and collaborative learning strategies.

Reading strategies give you specific tools to help you improve your skills in reading and making meaning from text. These strategies will help you improve your ability to analyze text by developing skills in using context clues, finding meaning for unfamiliar words, or organizing your responses to what you read. As you learn to use different reading strategies, it's important to think about which ones work best for you and why.

Writing strategies help you focus on your purpose for writing and the message you want to communicate to your readers. Using writing strategies will help you analyze your own writing for specific purposes and identify how to improve that writing using better word choices or punctuating differently or using sentence structure in different ways.

You and your classmates will use ***collaborative strategies*** to explore concepts and answer text-related questions as you work in pairs or in groups to discuss the work you're doing and to learn from each other.

Performance Portfolio

You will learn to use language in both written and spoken forms in this course. You are encouraged to keep your work in a Working Folder from which you can choose examples to show where you started and how you are growing in your skills and knowledge during the year. Presenting your best work in a Portfolio not only helps you evaluate your own work and improvement, but also helps you explore your unique style and analyze how your work can best represent you.

Presenting yourself through a portfolio also provides direction as you revisit, revise, and reflect on your work throughout the year. Your teacher will guide you as you include items in your portfolio that illustrate a wide range of work, including examples of reading, writing, oral literacy, and collaborative activities. As you progress through the course, you will have opportunities to revisit prior work, revise it based on new learning, and reflect on the learning strategies and activities that help you be successful. The portfolio:

▶ Gives you a specific place to feature your work and a means to share it with others.
▶ Provides an organized, focused way to view your progress throughout the year.
▶ Allows you to reflect on the new skills and strategies you are learning.
▶ Enables you to measure your growth as a reader, writer, speaker, and performer.
▶ Encourages you to revise pieces of work to incorporate new skills.

As you move through each unit, your teacher will instruct you to include certain items in your portfolio. Strong portfolios will include a variety of work from each unit, such as first drafts, final drafts, quickwrites, notes, reading logs, audio and video examples, and graphics that represent a wide variety of genre, forms, and media created for a variety of purposes.

Your teacher will also instruct you about preferences for your portfolio. For example, your portfolio may:

▶ Be organized in a 3-ring binder with dividers to separate the work for each unit in your text.
▶ Remain in the classroom at all times (if your teacher chooses).
▶ Be arranged chronologically, beginning with the first unit and moving to the last.
▶ Include periodic reports on assessments with your reflections on your progress.
▶ Include multiple drafts of an activity (where applicable).
▶ Contain a table of contents that lists each activity in your portfolio.

We hope you enjoy using the SpringBoard program. It will give you many opportunities to explore your own and others' ideas about becoming effective readers, writers, and communicators.

How to Use This Book

English Textual Power, Level 2, focuses on the theme of choice—linking the personal choices you make to the influences on those choices. This year, you will examine how the choices people make affect their lives and those of the people around them. You'll have the opportunity to reflect on your own choices and how you make decisions. Finally, you'll explore the deliberate choices behind actions that people take.

Preview the Unit

Essential Questions pose questions to help you think about the "big ideas" and make connections between what you learn and how you apply that learning.

Unit Overview sets the stage by:

▶ Providing a bridge from what you know to what you'll be learning in the unit.

▶ Outlining the big ideas in the unit and how the book's theme is connected from unit to unit.

Unit Contents give a snapshot of the unit activities and identify the texts and genres you'll explore in the unit.

▶ **Goals**—skills and knowledge you'll learn in the unit.

▶ **Academic Vocabulary**—key terms to use in the unit and to help you gain the vocabulary needed for AP courses and college.

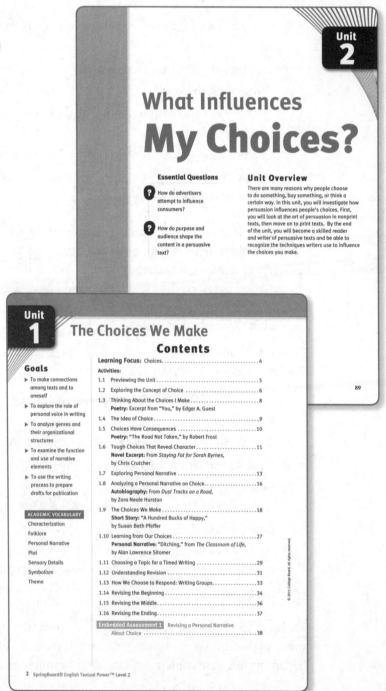

Preparing for Learning

Learning Focus
Learning Focus connects what you already know with what you'll learn in the unit and why it's important.

▶ Highlights key terms.

▶ Connects learning from unit to unit.

▶ Introduces concepts for the unit.

Previewing the Unit
Previewing the Unit helps you identify the expectations for knowledge and skills you'll need to learn in the unit by asking you to read and respond to:

▶ **Essential Questions**

▶ **Unit Overview–Learning Focus**

▶ **Embedded Assessment and Scoring Guide**

Starting with the End in Mind
Graphic organizer helps you:

▶ Map out the skills and knowledge you'll need for the Embedded Assessments.

▶ Read the assignment and the Scoring Guide (see page xvi) and outline what you'll need to do.

▶ Identify skills and knowledge to be assessed.

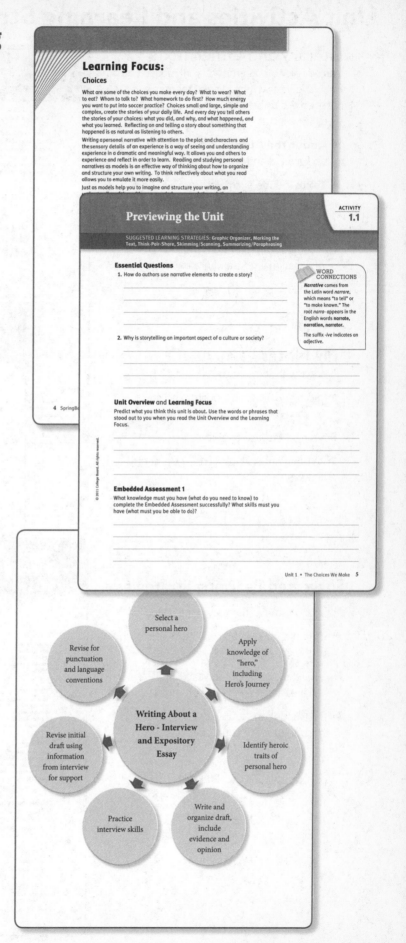

Unit Activities and Learning Strategies

Literary and Other Texts

from classic to contemporary introduce you to a variety of writers, stories, themes, and perspectives to help you interact with all types of writing.

▶ **About the Author** provides author's background and insights about the text.

▶ **Texts** include examples from a variety of genres, including poetry, film, autobiography, essay, print and online articles, folk tales, myths, fables, memoir, short stories, novel excerpts, interviews, Informational text, and drama.

My Notes provides space for you to interact with the text by:

▶ Jotting down your thoughts and ideas as you read.

▶ Using the space to analyze text.

▶ Writing notes about literary elements in texts.

Suggested Learning Strategies

▶ Clearly listed at the top of the page.

▶ Suggest strategies that are most appropriate for the activity.

▶ Over the course of the year, you'll learn which strategies work best for you.

▶ You'll find these strategies consistent with those used in AP courses.

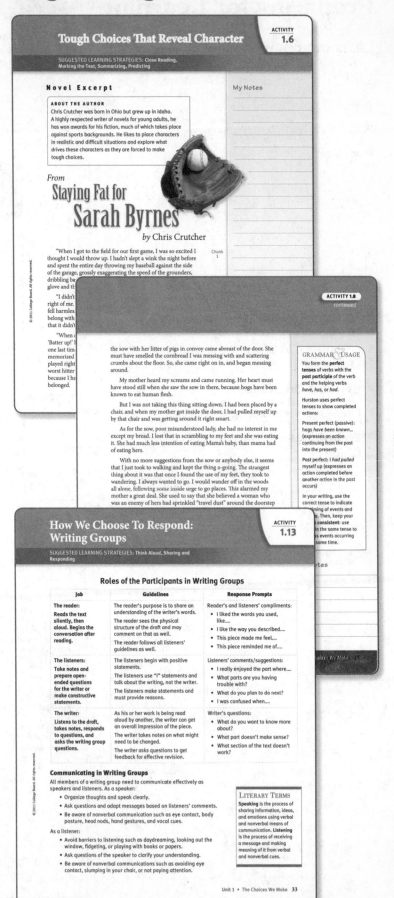

Integrated Language Skills

Vocabulary and Word Study

▶ **Academic Vocabulary** highlights key words you'll need to know for the unit and to expand your vocabulary for AP and college.

▶ **Literary Terms** define key words as you encounter them in your reading and analysis of text.

▶ **Word Connections** help you use context clues from Latin and other roots, understand analogies, and identify words with multiple meanings.

Grammar & Usage

▶ Offers tips about points of grammar and how to avoid common errors.

▶ Shows how writers use various grammatical constructions to clarify their text and to convey meaning for readers.

▶ Helps both speakers <u>and</u> writers use grammar to make their text or message more effective.

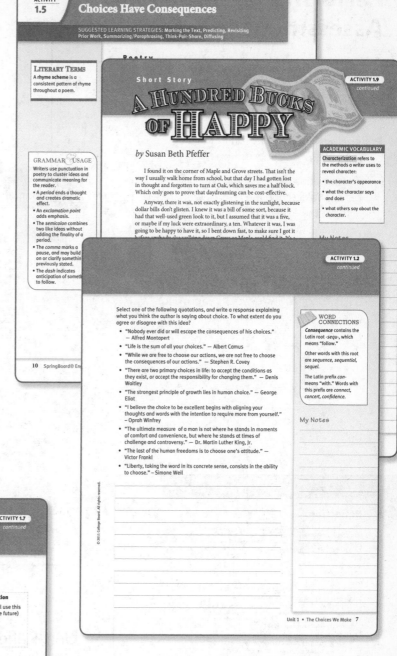

Writing

▶**Writing Process** is defined and practiced through opportunities to draft, revise, edit, and prepare publishable writing.

▶ **Writing Prompts & Timed Writings** provide practice in identifying specific writing tasks and writing under timed conditions.

▶ **Portfolios** are encouraged to collect your writing throughout the year to show your progress.

Performance-Based Assessment

▶ **Embedded Assessments** provide opportunities to demonstrate your knowledge and your skills in applying that knowledge in a variety of assessments.

▶ **Scoring Guide** walks you through the expectations for performance.

• Descriptions under Exemplary, Proficient, and Emerging describe the level of work required and set the expectations for what you need to know and do <u>before</u> you start the Embedded Assessment.

• Using the descriptions for Exemplary, Proficient, and Emerging, you decide what you'll do and take responsibility for your performance.

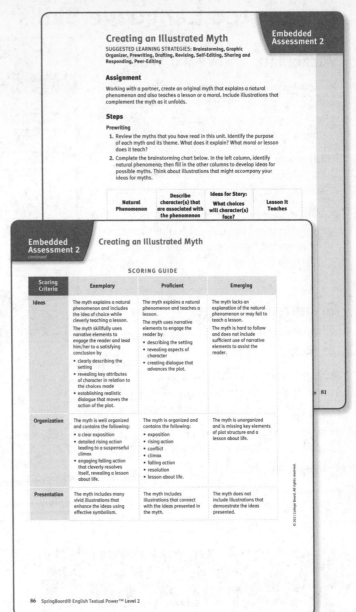

Creating an Illustrated Myth
Embedded Assessment 2

SUGGESTED LEARNING STRATEGIES: Brainstorming, Graphic Organizer, Prewriting, Drafting, Revising, Self-Editing, Sharing and Responding, Peer-Editing

Assignment

Working with a partner, create an original myth that explains a natural phenomenon and also teaches a lesson or a moral. Include illustrations that complement the myth as it unfolds.

Steps

Prewriting

1. Review the myths that you have read in this unit. Identify the purpose of each myth and its theme. What does it explain? What moral or lesson does it teach?

2. Complete the brainstorming chart below. In the left column, identify natural phenomena; then fill in the other columns to develop ideas for possible myths. Think about illustrations that might accompany your ideas for myths.

Natural Phenomenon	Describe character(s) that are associated with the phenomenon	Ideas for Story: What choices will character(s) face?	Lesson It Teaches

Embedded Assessment 2 *continued*

Creating an Illustrated Myth

SCORING GUIDE

Scoring Criteria	Exemplary	Proficient	Emerging
Ideas	The myth explains a natural phenomenon and includes the idea of choice while cleverly teaching a lesson. The myth skillfully uses narrative elements to engage the reader and lead him/her to a satisfying conclusion by • clearly describing the setting • revealing key attributes of character in relation to the choices made • establishing realistic dialogue that moves the action of the plot.	The myth explains a natural phenomenon and teaches a lesson. The myth uses narrative elements to engage the reader by • describing the setting • revealing aspects of character • creating dialogue that advances the plot.	The myth lacks an explanation of the natural phenomenon or may fail to teach a lesson. The myth is hard to follow and does not include sufficient use of narrative elements to assist the reader.
Organization	The myth is well organized and contains the following: • a clear exposition • detailed rising action leading to a suspenseful climax • engaging falling action that cleverly resolves itself, revealing a lesson about life.	The myth is organized and contains the following: • exposition • rising action • conflict • climax • falling action • resolution • lesson about life.	The myth is unorganized and is missing key elements of plot structure and a lesson about life.
Presentation	The myth includes many vivid illustrations that enhance the ideas using effective symbolism.	The myth includes illustrations that connect with the ideas presented in the myth.	The myth does not include illustrations that demonstrate the ideas presented.

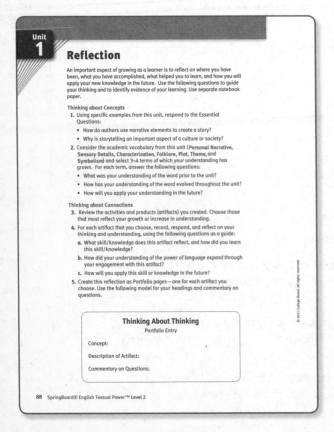

Unit 1

Reflection

An important aspect of growing as a learner is to reflect on where you have been, what you have accomplished, what helped you to learn, and how you will apply your new knowledge in the future. Use the following questions to guide your thinking and to identify evidence of your learning. Use separate notebook paper.

Thinking about Concepts

1. Using specific examples from this unit, respond to the Essential Questions:
   • How do authors use narrative elements to create a story?
   • Why is storytelling an important aspect of a culture or society?

2. Consider the academic vocabulary from this unit (**Personal Narrative, Sensory Details, Characterization, Folklore, Plot, Theme,** and **Symbolism**) and select 3–4 terms of which your understanding has grown. For each term, answer the following questions:
   • What was your understanding of the word prior to the unit?
   • How has your understanding of the word evolved throughout the unit?
   • How will you apply your understanding in the future?

Thinking about Connections

3. Review the activities and products (artifacts) you created. Choose those that most reflect your growth or increase in understanding.

4. For each artifact that you choose, record, respond, and reflect on your thinking and understanding, using the following questions as a guide:
   a. What skill/knowledge does this artifact reflect, and how did you learn this skill/knowledge?
   b. How did your understanding of the power of language expand through your engagement with this artifact?
   c. How will you apply this skill or knowledge in the future?

5. Create this reflection as Portfolio pages—one for each artifact you choose. Use the following model for your headings and commentary on questions.

> **Thinking About Thinking**
> Portfolio Entry
>
> Concept:
>
> Description of Artifact:
>
> Commentary on Questions:

Unit Reflection helps you to take ownership of your learning by stopping at regular points to think about:

▶ What you've learned.

▶ What strategies and tools helped you learn.

▶ What you still need to work on in the future.

The Choices
We Make

Essential Questions

? How do authors use narrative elements to create a story?

? Why is storytelling an important aspect of a culture or society?

Unit Overview

This unit introduces the yearlong focus on "choices," using a variety of genres to investigate this thematic concept. You will examine texts that present characters who, for personal or cultural reasons, have made choices about the way they live their lives. You will analyze fiction and nonfiction texts and create and present original works that express your own connections to the texts in relationship to the choices you face.

Contents

Goals

▶ To make connections among texts and to oneself

▶ To explore the role of personal voice in writing

▶ To analyze genres and their organizational structures

▶ To examine the function and use of narrative elements

▶ To use the writing process to prepare drafts for publication

ACADEMIC VOCABULARY

Characterization

Folklore

Personal Narrative

Plot

Sensory Details

Symbolism

Theme

Learning Focus:

Choices

What are some of the choices you make every day? What to wear? What to eat? Whom to talk to? What homework to do first? How much energy you want to put into soccer practice? Choices small and large, simple and complex, create the stories of your daily life. And every day you tell others the stories of your choices: what you did, and why, and what happened, and what you learned. Reflecting on and telling a story about something that happened is as natural as listening to others.

Writing a **personal narrative** with attention to the **plot** and **characters** and the **sensory details** of an experience is a way of seeing and understanding experience in a dramatic and meaningful way. It allows you and others to experience and reflect in order to learn. Reading and studying personal narratives as models is an effective way of thinking about how to organize and structure your own writing. To think reflectively about what you read allows you to emulate it more easily.

Just as models help you to imagine and structure your writing, an understanding of the writing process helps you work through the creative process.

Remember, the writing process consists of these steps:

▶ Brainstorming or prewriting

▶ Drafting

▶ Revising

▶ Editing and proofreading for publication

All writers need practice in these areas until they become second nature, an automatic part of your personal writing process.

Revision is often a part of the writing process that is challenging for writers because it is sometimes difficult to evaluate your own writing to see where it can be improved. Writing groups or partners can help you in the art of "revisioning" your writing through the careful sharing of and responding to early drafts of writing. Even more importantly, you can be a more thoughtful and deliberate reviser of your own work when you have specific strategies to help you with this important aspect of the writing process. Think of revising as the art of playing with words and sentences and paragraphs until you have shaped and molded them into the exact form you know will convey your ideas to others. It takes time and effort, but in the end the improvement is exhilarating.

Independent Reading: In this unit, you will read folk literature, including myths. Folk literature gives the reader an "inside look" at the people of a culture and their beliefs. For your independent reading for this unit, choose a collection of folklore from a culture that interests you.

Previewing the Unit

Essential Questions

1. How do authors use narrative elements to create a story?

_____

_____

_____

_____

2. Why is storytelling an important aspect of a culture or society?

_____

_____

_____

> **WORD CONNECTIONS**
>
> *Narrative* comes from the Latin word *narrare*, which means "to tell" or "to make known." The root *narra-* appears in the English words **narrate, narration, narrator.**
>
> The suffix *-ive* indicates an adjective.

Unit Overview and Learning Focus

Predict what you think this unit is about. Use the words or phrases that stood out to you when you read the Unit Overview and the Learning Focus.

_____

_____

_____

_____

Embedded Assessment 1

What knowledge must you have (what do you need to know) to complete the Embedded Assessment successfully? What skills must you have (what must you be able to do)?

_____

_____

_____

Exploring the Concept of Choice

Choice Chart

Create a brainstorming web of words, phrases, images, or quotes that
you associate with the idea of choice.

CHOICE

Select one of the following quotations, and write a response explaining what you think the author is saying about choice. To what extent do you agree or disagree with this idea?

- "Nobody ever did or will escape the consequences of his choices." — Alfred Montapert

- "Life is the sum of all your choices." — Albert Camus

- "While we are free to choose our actions, we are not free to choose the consequences of our actions." — Stephen R. Covey

- "There are two primary choices in life: to accept the conditions as they exist, or accept the responsibility for changing them." — Denis Waitley

- "The strongest principle of growth lies in human choice." — George Eliot

- "I believe the choice to be excellent begins with aligning your thoughts and words with the intention to require more from yourself." – Oprah Winfrey

- "The ultimate measure of a man is not where he stands in moments of comfort and convenience, but where he stands at times of challenge and controversy." — Dr. Martin Luther King, Jr.

- "The last of the human freedoms is to choose one's attitude." — Victor Frankl

- "Liberty, taking the word in its concrete sense, consists in the ability to choose." – Simone Weil

WORD CONNECTIONS

Consequence contains the Latin root *-sequ-*, which means "follow."

Other words with this root are *sequence, sequential, sequel*.

The Latin prefix *con-* means "with." Words with this prefix are *connect, concert, confidence.*

My Notes

Thinking About the Choices I Make

My Notes

ABOUT THE AUTHOR

Edgar A. Guest was 13 when he started working for the *Detroit Free Press* newspaper. He stayed there for more than 60 years and never missed a deadline. Guest lived from 1881 to 1959 and was nicknamed the "Poet of the People."

"You are the person who has to decide,
whether you'll do it or toss it aside;

You are the person who makes up your mind,
whether you'll lead or will linger behind.

Whether you'll try for the goal that's afar
or just be contented to stay where you are."

Excerpt from "You," by Edgar A. Guest

Read and discuss the poem above. Then brainstorm a list of the choices you make regularly in life. Use the cluster diagram below, the My Notes space, or separate paper. You will share this brainstorming with a partner and select one choice that is significant to you.

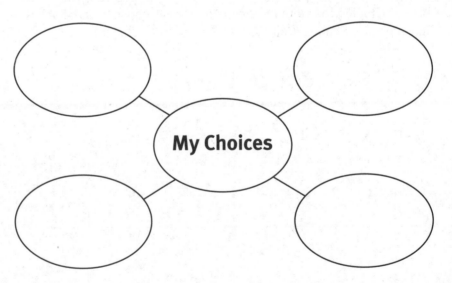

My Choices

Quickwrite Using your brainstorming cluster, write about a significant choice you had to make. Describe the factors that went into making that decision.

The Idea of Choice

SUGGESTED LEARNING STRATEGIES: Vocabulary Notebook,
Word Map, Think Aloud

Definition

Visual

Word

Example

Example

Example

Word in Context

Choices Have Consequences

LITERARY TERMS

A **rhyme scheme** is a consistent pattern of rhyme throughout a poem.

GRAMMAR & USAGE

Writers use punctuation in poetry to cluster ideas and communicate meaning for the reader.

- A *period* ends a thought and creates dramatic effect.
- An *exclamation point* adds emphasis.
- The *semicolon* combines two like ideas without adding the finality of a period.
- The *comma* marks a pause, and may build on or clarify something previously stated.
- The *dash* indicates anticipation of something to follow.

Poetry

ABOUT THE AUTHOR

Robert Frost (1874-1963) was one of America's most popular twentieth-century poets. For much of his life, he lived on a farm in New Hampshire and wrote poems about farm life and the New England landscape. His apparently simple poems, however, have many layers of meaning.

The Road Not Taken

by Robert Frost

Two roads diverged in a yellow wood,
And sorry I could not travel both
And be one traveler, long I stood
And looked down one as far as I could
5   To where it bent in the undergrowth;

Then took the other, as just as fair,
And having perhaps the better claim,
Because it was grassy and wanted wear;
Though as for that the passing there
10 Had worn them really about the same,

And both that morning equally lay
In leaves no step had trodden black.
Oh, I kept the first for another day!
Yet knowing how way leads on to way,
15 I doubted if I should ever come back.

I shall be telling this with a sigh
Somewhere ages and ages hence:
Two roads diverged in a wood, and I —
I took the one less traveled by,
20 And that has made all the difference.

Tough Choices That Reveal Character

Novel Excerpt

ABOUT THE AUTHOR
Chris Crutcher was born in Ohio but grew up in Idaho.
A highly respected writer of novels for young adults, he
has won awards for his fiction, much of which takes place
against sports backgrounds. He likes to place characters
in realistic and difficult situations and explore what
drives these characters as they are forced to make
tough choices.

From

Staying Fat for Sarah Byrnes

by Chris Crutcher

My Notes

"When I got to the field for our first game, I was so excited I thought I would throw up. I hadn't slept a wink the night before and spent the entire day throwing my baseball against the side of the garage, grossly exaggerating the speed of the grounders, dribbling back as I snapped them into the merciless trap of my glove and threw the runner out.

Chunk 1

"I didn't catch one ball in warm-ups. They dropped to the right of me. They dropped to the left of me. They hit my arms and fell harmlessly to the grass. But I was just so happy to be there, to belong with these other kids with 'Junior Oilers' across their chests, that it didn't matter.

"When coach called us into a huddle before the umpire yelled, 'Batter up!' he went over our positions and the batting order one last time, but he didn't need to for my sake because I had memorized those things from the first practice. I batted ninth. I played right field. I knew what that meant. I knew I was the very worst hitter on the team and the very worst fielder. But I didn't care, because I had a new glove and a green-and-gold uniform and I belonged.

Tough Choices That Reveal Character

GRAMMAR & USAGE

A *dash* is used in prose:

- to mark a parenthetical thought
- to indicate an unfinished sentence
- to show an abrupt change in thought, when a period is too strong and a comma is too weak.

My Notes

Chunk 2

"We were the home team and batted the bottom half of the inning, so we touched our gloves together in the middle of the huddle and yelled, 'Go Oilers!' and broke to take our position. I was *so* proud. But before I got even to the baseline, Coach's hand was on my shoulder, and when I turned around, Ronnie Callendar stood next to him. And he said, 'I want you to give Ronnie your glove.'

"I said, 'What for?'

"He said, 'He doesn't have one.'

"Coach watched my face fall — I know he did — and I think he knew how I felt because he was very kind, but he said, 'Cindy, if we're going to win this, Ronnie has to have a mitt. A shortstop has to have a mitt, that's just all there is to it.' I looked at the glove on my hand; I bit my lower lip while I read Warren Spahn's name, and I handed it over. Coach told me to play as far back in right field as I could so no balls could get over my head — that I could run faster forward than backward — and sent me on my way. I walked so far back I almost disappeared into the playground swings beyond the field.

Chunk 3

"Just that quick I *didn't* belong, and I remember thinking something always has to spoil it. I was hurt and embarrassed and I wanted to go back to being invisible me again, but I couldn't because I had on the green shirt and cap, and all of a sudden that uniform was my enemy. I remember hating Ronnie Callendar for being poor, and I hoped his father never got a job and they'd have to move away.

"Every game after that was miserable. I couldn't quit because we would have only eight players and all the kids would hate me. Coach didn't always take my glove; in fact, I don't know that he ever took it again. But each time I walked down that hot, dusty summer road toward the playing field, I knew he *might*, that I didn't really belong because they could take my glove."

Exploring Personal Narrative

Complete the graphic organizer below to explore your knowledge about personal narratives. Then share your responses with a partner.

Exploring Personal Narratives

1. With what kinds of narrative texts are you familiar?

2. What are some of your favorite types of narratives? Explain what makes them enjoyable.

3. What are the elements of a good story?

4. What can a good story do for a reader?

Exploring Personal Narrative

> **LITERARY TERMS**
> An **incident** is a distinct piece of action, as in an episode of a story or a play. An incident is made up of a sequence of events.

Brainstorm a list of 7–8 important incidents that involved choices in your life. An incident may have included a major or minor choice that you made, or it could be about choices that were made for you. After you finish listing the incidents, fill in some details about the events that made up the incident. Then, put the events in chronological order.

Incident	What choices were involved? (Who, what, where, when, why, and how)	Sequence of Events in Chronological Order
1.	1.	
2.	2.	
3.	3.	
4.	4.	
5.	5.	
6.	6.	
7.	7.	
8.	8.	

Writing About an Event from Your Choices Chart

As your teacher explains, take notes on the key components of a personal narrative.

Incident	Response	Reflection	Reflection
(what happened)	(feelings and thoughts of people involved)	(lesson you learned from this experience)	(how you will use this lesson in the future)

Definition: A personal narrative is...

_____

_____

Oral Story Telling: With a partner, share an incident orally from your Choices Chart. Use the 5 Ws to guide your storytelling:

1. **When** and where did the incident take place?

_____

2. **Who** was involved?

_____

3. **Why** is it a memorable incident?

_____

4. **What** happened and **why**?

_____

5. **How** did the people involved respond?

_____

Writing Prompt: Write about an incident listed on your Choices Chart. You may use the same one you used in your oral retelling. Use the 5 W's that you used in your storytelling to generate ideas for your writing.

Analyzing a Personal Narrative on Choice

LITERARY TERMS

Tone is a writer's or speaker's attitude toward a subject

My Notes

GRAMMAR & USAGE

Verb **tenses** (present, past, and future) show time. You form the **progressive tenses** with a form of the verb *be* and the **present participle** of the verb.

Hurston uses the past progressive tense to indicate an ongoing action in the past:

Everything *was going* along all right...

...I *was messing* with...

In your writing, use progressive tenses when you want to describe a continuing action.

Autobiography

ABOUT THE AUTHOR

Born in 1891, Zora Neale Hurston was an American anthropologist and writer who wrote her best-known works during the time period known as the Harlem Renaissance. Growing up in Florida, Hurston lived in the small town of Eatonville, the first incorporated black township. Hurston's idyllic childhood was interrupted by the death of her mother when Hurston was only 13. She struggled to finish high school, which she still had not accomplished by age 26. Despite her early struggles, Hurston went on to graduate from Barnard College in 1928. She wrote several short stories and novels. *Their Eyes Were Watching God* is considered her master work. She died in 1960.

From

Dust Tracks on a Road

by Zora Neale Hurston

But nine months rolled around, and I just would not get on with the walking business. I was strong, crawling well, but showed no inclination to use my feet. I might remark in passing, that I still don't like to walk. Then I was over a year old, but still I would not walk. They made allowances for my weight, but yet, that was no real reason for my not trying.

They tell me that an old sow-hog taught me how to walk. That is, she didn't instruct me in detail, but she convinced me that I really ought to try.

It was like this. My mother was going to have collard greens for dinner, so she took the dishpan and went down to the spring to wash the greens. She left me sitting on the floor, and gave me a hunk of cornbread to keep me quiet. Everything was going along all right, until the sow with her litter of pigs in convoy came abreast of the door. She must have smelled the cornbread I was messing with and scattering crumbs about the floor. So, she came right on in, and began messing around.

My mother heard my screams and came running. Her heart must have stood still when she saw the sow in there, because hogs have been known to eat human flesh.

But I was not taking this thing sitting down. I had been placed by a chair, and when my mother got inside the door, I had pulled myself up by that chair and was getting around it right smart.

As for the sow, poor misunderstood lady, she had no interest in me except my bread. I lost that in scrambling to my feet and she was eating it. She had much less intention of eating Mama's baby, than mama had of eating hers.

With no more suggestions from the sow or anybody else, it seems that I just took to walking and kept the thing a-going. The strangest thing about it was that once I found the use of my feet, they took to wandering. I always wanted to go. I would wander off in the woods all alone, following some inside urge to go places. This alarmed my mother a great deal. She used to say that she believed a woman who was an enemy of hers had sprinkled "travel dust" around the doorstep the day I was born. That was the only explanation she could find. I don't know why it never occurred to her to connect my tendency with my father, who didn't have a thing on his mind but this town and the next one. That should have given her a sort of hint. Some children are just bound to take after their fathers in spite of women's prayers.

GRAMMAR & USAGE

You form the **perfect tenses** of verbs with the **past participle** of the verb and the helping verbs *have, has,* or *had.*

Hurston uses perfect tenses to show completed actions:

Present perfect (passive): hogs *have been known...* (expresses an action continuing from the past into the present)

Past perfect: I *had pulled* myself up (expresses an action completed before another action in the past occurs)

In your writing, use the correct tense to indicate the timing of events and actions. Then, keep your tenses **consistent**: use verbs in the same tense to express events occurring at the same time.

My Notes

The Choices We Make

Quickwrite: Write a description of how you would spend $100 you found on the street.

_____

_____

_____

_____

_____

What do you think your choices reveal about you?

_____

_____

_____

_____

_____

_____

ABOUT THE AUTHOR

Susan Beth Pfeffer writes for children and teens and loves to write about families. In an interview, she said she likes to start her stories and novels with a "what if..." situation and then figure out the characters and plots. Born in New York City in 1948, she grew up in the city and suburbs. She published her first novel while she was in college. Since then she has written more than 60 books.

A Hundred Bucks of Happy

by Susan Beth Pfeffer

I found it on the corner of Maple and Grove streets. That isn't the way I usually walk home from school, but that day I had gotten lost in thought and forgotten to turn at Oak, which saves me a half block. Which only goes to prove that daydreaming can be cost-effective.

Anyway, there it was, not exactly glistening in the sunlight, because dollar bills don't glisten. I knew it was a bill of some sort, because it had that well-used green look to it, but I assumed that it was a five, or maybe if my luck were extraordinary, a ten. Whatever it was, I was going to be happy to have it, so I bent down fast, to make sure I got it before anybody else walking down Grove or Maple could find it. It's a well-walked intersection.

I bent down, scooped the money up, and started walking away fast, with that heartbeating sensation of having done something exciting and wrong, even though as far as I know, there's no crime in finding money on the street. I've read about people who do that for a hobby, jog with their heads down, collecting the nickels and dimes they find as they run. Whatever this was, it wasn't a dime, and I didn't feel like taking any chances. So I bent, swooped, and increased my pace until by the time I reached Elm I was half running. Not that anybody cared. The rest of the world kept on walking toward whatever their lives were propelling them to. The money was as much mine as if it had been left to me by some munificent great aunt.

I was three doors away from my house before I took the bill out of my jacket pocket, to check its denomination. As I did, I noticed there was a hole in my pocket and the money had slipped into the lining. It took a bit of searching before I found it, but eventually my fingers made contact, and I found what I was looking for.

It was a hundred-dollar bill. I had never seen one before, so I wouldn't have recognized it, but it was clearly labeled. Ben Franklin stared at me—and I swear he winked—as I turned his bill over and over, not believing it could be real, not believing my luck.

Once I knew what I had, I ran like the devil the three houses to mine. My fingers shook as I searched for the front-door key, and I dropped my schoolbooks all over the front stoop, I was clutching onto the money so hard.

ACADEMIC VOCABULARY

Characterization refers to the methods a writer uses to reveal character:

• the character's appearance

• what the character says and does

• what others say about the character.

My Notes

The Choices We Make

LITERARY TERMS
Transitions are words or phrases that connect ideas, details, or events in writing.

My Notes

I got everything together, using what little strength I had left in me, and let myself into the house. Mom was at work, and Danny, my kid brother, was sitting in front of the TV, watching Dance Dynomite and finishing up a bag of potato chips I suspected he'd started not that long ago.

Things hadn't always been like this. For starters, it wasn't until this year that Danny had given up superheroes in exchange for girls dancing on TV. And it used to be that Mom stayed at home, making wholesome and nutritious snacks for us to eat when we got back from school, instead of letting us shove potato chips into our mouths. Or at least into Danny's. He ate them so fast, there were never any left by the time I got home.

Those golden days of nutritious snacks ended when Dad moved out. I have an MIA father. You know the sort. He sends a few bucks every Christmas with a note to Mom telling her to buy herself and the kids something nice, and the rest of the year he's missing in action. He's not one for halfway measures, though. When he finally did leave, after threatening to often enough, he moved six hundred miles away. His address is a post office box, and if for some reason you have to call him, his machine answers for him and swears he'll call right back. Don't hold your breath waiting.

So Mom, not wanting us to starve, got a job and became a statistic. They do studies about people like her. They call it the feminization of poverty, but I've got to tell you Mom looked a lot more feminine before she got poor. Danny looked better in those days too, but maybe the fat and the pimples would have come anyway, once he became aware of girls, and have nothing to do with his potato chip diet.

I went up to my room, thinking about how many bags of potato chips a hundred dollars could buy, threw my books down, and stared at the money a while longer. Ben Franklin had the nicest face. He looked great in green.

We ate frozen for dinner that night, each of us picking our own dinner, which Mom then threw into the oven at 350. She cooks everything at 350 these days, for half an hour, regardless of what the box says to do. As far as I can tell, it doesn't make a difference, so she's probably right going with a single system for everything frozen.

"So," she said, as we each took our trays out of the oven and spread them on the kitchen table. "Anything interesting happen at school today?"

You have to give her points for trying. Nothing interesting has happened in school for the past seven years, but she asks regularly anyway. Seven years ago the goat got loose in the cafeteria, but that's a whole other story.

"I got an 83 in science," Danny announced. "And Michelle Grain got sick in English and practically puked all over everybody."

"No puking talk over dinner," Mom said automatically. She's ended a lot of really neat conversations with that rule. "Chris? What's new with you?"

It was the moment I'd dreaded. I mean, you can hardly deny that finding a hundred-dollar bill is newsworthy, even if, technically speaking, it didn't happen in school and therefore wasn't covered by her original question.

I would have kept the news to myself, except there was no way I could come home from having spent the hundred dollars without Mom noticing. And I didn't want her to think I'd entered into a life of crime. Mom watches a lot of sitcoms, so she worries about things like shoplifting and bank robberies.

"I found some money on the corner of Maple and Grove," I said, trying to sound real casual about it.

I shouldn't have bothered. Mom's eyes lit right away, and even Danny stopped inhaling his frozen dinner.

"How much?' they both asked. It was eerie how fast they got the words out.

There are people in this world who can lie. I'm not one of them. "A hundred dollars," I said. "I found a hundred-dollar bill."

"A hundred bucks!" Danny breathed. "Wow!"

"A hundred dollars," Mom said. "Well you certainly can't keep it."

"Why not?" I asked.

"It isn't yours," she replied. "You have to find its owner."

"How am I supposed to do that?" I asked. Actually, it was a question I'd been asking myself ever since I checked the denomination. "Advertise in the paper? Ask its owner to describe what the money looks like? Does Ben Franklin wear glasses, or does he have his contacts in? Is he wearing a wedding ring? Mom, there's no way to find

My Notes

out who lost it."

"What if it belonged to some poor person?" she asked, but I could see she was weakening.

"Poor people don't carry hundred-dollar bills," I replied.

"I bet it's mob money," Danny said. "And when the mob finds out it's missing, they'll hire a hit man to shoot Chris. Terrific!"

"No one's going to shoot me," I told him. "Besides, I intend to spend the money so fast, there won't be anything for the mob to collect. I thought I'd go to the mall tomorrow and pick some stuff up."

"You can't do that," Mom said. "You have to give me the money."

"How do you figure that?" I asked.

"We need it," she said.

"I sure need it," Danny said. "I want my share."

"I'm not sharing," I told him.

"Fine," Mom said. "So you can give it to me." I swear they must send mothers to school somewhere, when they're in an embryonic mother state, kind of like the pods in *Invasion of the Body Snatchers*, before they become fully formed humans. At mother school, they're taught how to ignore the obvious to go after what they want.

"If I'm not sharing, I'm not giving," I said. "The money is mine. I found it. There's a lot of stuff I need, and I intend to get myself some of it."

Mom snorted. "Wait until you see how long a hundred dollars lasts," she said.

"I look forward to finding out," I said, trying to sound dignified.

The rest of supper was kind of a drag, with Danny whining and Mom sulking and me thinking about the money sitting on my bed, waiting for the world to come and snatch it. As soon as I could, I went back to my room and shoved the bill into the toe of my boot. Then I hid both boots under my bed. No point taking any chances.

It was positively painful sitting through school the next day. Of course having a hundred-dollar bill shoved inside my boot didn't make things any more comfortable. I kept wiggling my toe around to make sure the money was still there, until my foot started cramping. It's not easy being rich.

When school finally ended, I limped my way over to the mall. I hadn't figured out just how I was going to get the money out of the boot when I started buying stuff, but I figured I could always just take the boot off, whip the money out, and become a local legend.

We have a pretty good mall, with a lot of places where you could spend a hundred dollars. I started by trying on a leather jacket. It fit perfectly, and it made me feel great. I also liked the idea of buying just one perfect thing with the money. After all, if I bought a lot of little stuff, I could buy any one of those things on my own, and it would just be a case of quantity, not quality. But I'd have to save for years to buy a leather jacket, until by the time I could afford it I probably wouldn't want it anyway.

The jacket was on sale too. It had been $120, but it was marked down to $98. I took it over to the sales register, where the woman looked me over real carefully and asked if it was cash or charge.

"Cash," I told her, feeling for the thousandth time the money in the toe.

She rang the numbers up and said "That will be a hundred and four dollars and three cents."

"No," I said. "It's ninety eight dollars. See." I showed her the price tag.

She looked at me like I had just emerged from the primordial swamp. "Sales tax," she said. "A hundred and four dollars and three cents." I didn't have a hundred and four dollars and three cents.

I had two dollars and thirty-five cents, and a hundred dollars stuffed in my boot. Add the two together, and you do not come up with a hundred and four and three cents. Believe me, I tried five different ways of adding the numbers together, and none of them worked.

"I can't afford it," I muttered.

"Kids," the saleslady said. I nearly took my boot off to throw at her, but then I decided I didn't want to buy anything that cost more than the hundred dollars anyway. It would have been cheating, somehow. So I left the store and looked for something that cost just a few dollars less. I didn't mind having a couple of bucks change left, just as long as I didn't go over my original total it was kind of like game show rules.

My Notes

_____

_____

_____

_____

_____

_____

📖 **WORD CONNECTIONS**

An analogy shows a relationship between words and is often written with colons; for example, sleeve : jacket :: shift key : keyboard. The relationship between *sleeve* and *jacket* is the same as that between *shift key* and *keyboard*. Think of the relationship between *leaf* and *tree*. Then write the word that has the same relationship to *finger*.

Leaf is to tree as finger is to _____.

The Choices We Make

I must have walked through that mall a half-dozen times, upstairs and down, trying to find just the right thing to buy. Most of the stuff I looked at I would have killed to own ordinarily, but somehow nothing was special enough to spend my hundred on. And things didn't cost what I thought they did. I finally decided to buy a Walkman, so I went into one of the department stores to price them. Only they had one on sale, AM/FM radio and cassette player for $29.95. That seemed awfully cheap to me, only there was no point spending more than that for another brand just because it wasn't on sale. So I didn't buy one, and I didn't get any cassettes either. And all the books I used to dream about owning looked like crap, and suddenly I realized there was nothing at the mall I really wanted.

I sat down then, by the fountain, to collect my thoughts. There was no water in the fountain area, because of the water shortage, and its tile floor was littered with pennies and nickels. I couldn't get over how people had just tossed their money away like that, when I couldn't even make myself take my boot off.

It occurred to me then that I could buy a car for a hundred dollars. Maybe not a great car, but a car, nonetheless. I had this entire fantasy about being behind the wheel of my very own car, driving my friends around, parking in the high school lot, going to drive-ins, moving around the way you could if you owned a car. It was a pretty picture, and I was just about ready to spend part of my $2.35 on a newspaper so I could see what cars were available for a hundred bucks, until common sense made me stop.

The problem wasn't the money for the car, or even the sales tax. I figured I could always argue the owner down the extra couple of bucks. The problem was car insurance. Somehow I didn't think I could count on finding the insurance money on the corner of Maple and Grove every six months. No insurance, no car. No car, no freedom. I still had my money, but the fun was fast going out of it.

Just to show myself that I could, I went into Woolworth's and bought some chewing gum. They were out of my brand, but I bought a package of some other brand, and broke one of my singles. The change jingled as I walked away from the mall, chewing my gum, and limping.

I found myself walking a half block out of my way, to return to the corner of Maple and Grove, but a scary thing happened once I got there. I realized I hadn't gone back to see if there was any more money there but to leave the hundred-dollar bill smack where I'd found it.

You know, I actually wanted the person whose money it was to show up, demanding that I give it back. I looked around for penniless orphans, or Mafia dons, or anybody who looked like they might be searching for a missing Ben Franklin, but the only people on Grove and Maple were the sorts of people who were always on Grove and Maple. I know, because I stood there for close to ten minutes, waiting for someone who looked a hundred dollars poorer than they had the day before.

It was then that I knew what I had to do. So I limped over to the bank. It was Friday, and they were open until five. I walked in, like it was the most ordinary thing in the world for me to be in a bank, and sat down in the section where they keep you waiting if you want to start a new account. For some reason, banks like to keep people waiting before they take their money.

I got comfortable and took my boot off. People looked at me, but there wasn't anything I could do about it. I took out the hundred-dollar bill, and a couple of people actually laughed. I grinned, but it was mostly from relief at getting my toes unjammed.

I straightened the bill out, put my boot back on, and got in line. It took a while, but eventually I got to a teller.

"I'd like a hundred singles," I said, handing her the hundred-dollar bill.

She looked at it like it must be hot, and she called some guy over to check it out. They held it to the light and crinkled it and read the serial numbers and practically asked me for its pedigree before they finally decided the money was legit. I had a bunch of lies available about how it was I happened to have a hundred-dollar bill, but they didn't ask me and I didn't volunteer. Instead the teller counted out a hundred singles, and then I counted them with her, and she gave me an envelope to put the dollars in. The envelope was pretty thick once they were all in, but the bank is only a couple of blocks from my house, and there was no way I was going to shove the money back in my boot. Instead I held on to it carefully and walked home, trying to appear inconspicuous. I probably did too.

At supper that night I handed thirty-three dollars to my mother, and thirty-three dollars to Danny. I kept thirty-three for myself, and the remaining dollar I sent to my father's post office box. I figured he could buy a Hallmark card with it, to send to himself for Father's Day.

After supper Mom drove Danny and me to the mall, and we all went shopping. I bought the Walkman with my thirty-three. Good thing it was on sale.

My Notes

The Choices We Make

Sequence of Events Using Transitions of Time	Identify the Choice Involved with This Incident	Character Traits or Attitudes the Choices Reveal	Textual Evidence for the Character Traits
In the beginning of the story, the narrator finds a $100 bill on the way home from school.	The narrator has to decide whether to pick up the money or leave it there.	Nervous Unsure	Actions: "I bent down, scooped the money up, and started walking away fast with that heartbeating sensation of having done something exciting and wrong..."
Then,			
Next,			
In the middle,			
After that,			
Later,			
Toward the end,			
In the end,			

Learning from Our Choices

Personal Narrative

ABOUT THE AUTHOR
Named California Teacher of the Year in 2007, Alan Lawrence Sitomer writes novels for young adults in addition to teaching. He writes from a part of himself, he says, that "wants to inspire other people to be the best they can be, no matter the adversity they face nor the hurdles they are forced to climb." He hopes his books encourage readers "to find the strength to battle on when times get tough."

Ditching

From The Classroom of Life
by Alan Lawrence Sitomer

"Wanna ditch today?" Geoffrey Peterson asked me. "We'll blow this place and head to my house. It'll be cool." Geoff asked me this question at 7:28 a.m. Come 7:30, the bell would ring and then adults from all over would start rushing us to class. It was a now-or-never decision.

"Sure," I said. I'd never ditched before. Sounded like fun. We walked for 45 minutes. "Man, you live far," I said.

"Relax, we're here," he said as he turned the key. "My mom's at work. She won't be home till 'bout 4:30. The place is all ours."

First thing we did was eat. But Geoff didn't really have any good food. There were no frozen pizzas or microwave burritos—just cereal, but no milk. I thought about pouring water on a bowl of Froot Loops—all he had was water and ketchup—but that seemed gross so I decided to snack on fat-free tortilla chips. That's the only thing Geoff had that I thought I'd like, a 2-pound bag of fat-free tortilla chips.

We turned on the TV. I never realized how many dumb shows

Chunk 1

Chunk 2

My Notes

Learning from Our Choices

© 2011 College Board. All rights reserved.

GRAMMAR & USAGE

Commas in prose signify a pause. Writers use commas:

- to separate items in a series
- after introductory words, phrases, and clauses in sentences
- to set off parenthetical phrases (which can be omitted from the sentence without changing its meaning)
- to separate quoted material.

My Notes

were on in the morning. Lots of shows about lots of women talking about lots of problems. Finally we decided to watch a program where old people played grocery games to win a washing machine. Dumb! I looked at the clock, it was only 8:53 a.m., and already I was bored. I still had more than six hours to go. We decided to play video games. Geoff had weak vids though, stuff I'd played over and over again about a hundred million times. After two and a half hours, I was bored again. And hungry too. But not that hungry, 'cause it seems I had eaten about a pound and three-quarters of fat-free tortilla chips. A gross, nasty taste sat on my tongue. Wow, could I have used a Pepsi. But Geoff didn't have any Pepsi, just water and ketchup. I thought about leaving, but where would I go? Back to school? No, I'd get in trouble. To the park? No, we could get caught by someone. To a friend's house? No, all my friends were at school.

I was SO bored. The only excitement in the next few hours came when the mailman showed. Geoff and I hid behind the couch, thinking he might try to bust us or something, but he never even looked in the window. He just dropped off some letters and left. One o'clock. Nothing happened. Two o'clock. Nothing happened. Three o'clock finally came. I opened the front door to his house and felt the sun for the first time that day. I had a headache and wanted to throw up. It was like I'd been trapped in a shoebox all day and I needed my toothbrush in the worst way. "How was school, honey?" my mom asked when I walked in the door. For a moment I panicked. I thought it was a trick question. "F-f-fine," I said nervously, waiting for her to explode with rage. "That's nice," she answered, folding a pile of laundry. Turns out my mom never knew the difference.

Chunk 3

The next day I found out our science teacher, Mr. Roddy, had brought a live tarantula to class and let it walk across his face. And Mrs. Ingram, the math teacher, broke her heel and fell down in front of everyone. Plus, I got an F on a pop quiz for English that I totally would have aced, and I didn't get to see Amanda Byrnes, a girl I had a huge crush on, all day. Big bummer. Later that week, when I saw Geoff at 7:28 a.m., I hustled into class before he could see me. And I never ate fat-free tortilla chips again.

Choosing a Topic for a Timed Writing

SUGGESTED LEARNING STRATEGIES: Revisiting Prior Work, Marking the Text, Think Aloud, Prewriting, Drafting

Preparing for the Timed Writing: Sample Prompt

Tip 1: Address all aspects of the prompt.

Tip 2: Plan your essay.

> **Sample Prompt:**
>
> Write a personal narrative about a significant event in your life in which you faced a major challenge and were able to overcome it. Describe the challenge, explain how you overcame it, and reflect on the impact it has had on you as a result.

Circle the key verbs in the prompt: The verbs identify what you have to do.

Underline the nouns: The nouns identify what you have to do it to.

Write the verbs next to the nouns: This list prioritizes what you have to do when you write in response to this prompt. You can use this list as a checklist to ensure that you have addressed all aspects of the prompt.

1. In this unit, you have used the following prewriting strategies to generate ideas: brainstorming, clustering, quickwrites, and 5 Ws. Which of these prewriting strategies work best for you? Explain.

_____

_____

2. What will you do to plan your timed writing essay before you write, and why?

_____

_____

3. What transition words and phrases will you use to show movement of the narrative? Consider the type of transitional words and phrases to use, such as chronological order or cause and effect.

_____

_____

_____

Choosing a Topic for a Timed Writing

Tip 3: Pace yourself.

On the day of your timed writing, you will have _____ minutes to write your essay.

How many minutes will you use for each phase?

_____ Prewrite: Plan my essay and generate ideas.

_____ Draft: Put my plan into action and get my narrative on paper.

_____ Revise/Edit: Make sure my narrative is as clear as possible for my readers.

Use this page for prewriting. Follow the same steps your teacher has modeled. Then, draft your essay on separate paper.

Writing Prompt: Write a personal narrative about a significant incident in your life in which you had to make a choice. Describe the choice, explain the consequences of that choice, and reflect on what you learned as a result of this experience.

> **GRAMMAR & USAGE**
>
> As you write your narrative, keep your **verb tenses consistent**. If you are writing in the past tense, do not shift unnecessarily to the present.

Understanding Revision

SUGGESTED LEARNING STRATEGIES: Notetaking, Think-Pair-Share, Word Map

Review what you know about **revision**. Write "Agree" or "Disagree" in each blank below.

_____ Revision and editing are the same thing.

_____ Revision is a difficult part of the writing process.

_____ I enjoy revising my work.

_____ Revision involves adding, deleting, rearranging, and substituting.

_____ Revision is focused on checking spelling and punctuation.

How often do you revise your text before you publish it? Explain.	
Explain the role of revision in your writing process.	
With what revision strategies are you most familiar?	
Describe the most effective revision technique you have used in the past. What effect did it have on your text?	
Finish this thought: **I would revise more if...**	
Define revision.	

Understanding Revision

Respond to this quotation: "I see revision as a beautiful word of hope. It's a new revision of something. It means you don't have to be perfect the first time around. What a relief!"

— Naomi Shihab Nye

Class Notes on Revision (list of revision tips)	Questions I Still Have
• • • • • • •	

Summary of What I Have Learned

_____

_____

_____

_____

_____

_____

Working Definition of Revision

_____

_____

_____

_____

_____

How We Choose To Respond: Writing Groups

Roles of the Participants in Writing Groups

Job	Guidelines	Response Prompts
The reader: **Reads the text silently, then aloud. Begins the conversation after reading.**	The reader's purpose is to share an understanding of the writer's words. The reader sees the physical structure of the draft and may comment on that as well. The reader follows all listeners' guidelines as well.	Reader's and listeners' compliments: • I liked the words you used, like.... • I like the way you described.... • This piece made me feel.... • This piece reminded me of....
The listeners: **Take notes and prepare open-ended questions for the writer or make constructive statements.**	The listeners begin with positive statements. The listeners use "I" statements and talk about the writing, not the writer. The listeners make statements and must provide reasons.	Listeners' comments/suggestions: • I really enjoyed the part where.... • What parts are you having trouble with? • What do you plan to do next? • I was confused when....
The writer: **Listens to the draft, takes notes, responds to questions, and asks the writing group questions.**	As his or her work is being read aloud by another, the writer can get an overall impression of the piece. The writer takes notes on what might need to be changed. The writer asks questions to get feedback for effective revision.	Writer's questions: • What do you want to know more about? • What part doesn't make sense? • What section of the text doesn't work?

Communicating in Writing Groups

All members of a writing group need to communicate effectively as speakers and listeners. As a speaker:

- Organize thoughts and speak clearly.
- Ask questions and adapt messages based on listeners' comments.
- Be aware of nonverbal communication such as eye contact, body posture, head nods, hand gestures, and vocal cues.

As a listener:

- Avoid barriers to listening such as daydreaming, looking out the window, fidgeting, or playing with books or papers.
- Ask questions of the speaker to clarify your understanding.
- Be aware of nonverbal communications such as avoiding eye contact, slumping in your chair, or not paying attention.

> **LITERARY TERMS**
> **Speaking** is the process of sharing information, ideas, and emotions using verbal and nonverbal means of communication. **Listening** is the process of receiving a message and making meaning of it from verbal and nonverbal cues.

Revising the Beginning

Leads, Leads, Leads...Revision and Substitution

"The lead is one of the crucial parts of a piece of writing. It's often the point when readers decide if they're going to continue reading. It's where the writer establishes the topic, direction, tone — just about everything."

— Nancie Atwell

Type of Lead	Examples From Published Authors
Action: Some writers choose to open a narrative with the main character doing something; this type of lead puts the reader right in the middle of the action.	**"Thank You M'am," by Langston Hughes** She was a large woman with a large purse that had everything in it but a hammer and nails. It had a long strap and she carried it slung across her shoulder. It was about eleven o'clock at night, and she was walking home alone, when a boy ran up behind her and tried to snatch her purse. The strap broke with the single tug the boy gave it from behind. But the boy's weight and the weight of the purse combined caused him to lose his balance, so instead of taking off full blast as he had hoped, the boy fell on his back on the sidewalk and his legs flew up. The large woman simply turned around and kicked him right square in his blue-jean sitter. Then she reached down, picked up the boy by his shirt front, and shook him until his teeth rattled.
Dialogue: Some writers choose to show the reader a key event, using dialogue between characters	**"Charlotte's Web," by E. B. White** "Where's papa going with that ax?" said Fern to her mother as they were setting the table for breakfast. "Out to the hoghouse," replied Mrs. Arable. "Some pigs were born last night." "I don't see why he needs an ax," continued Fern, who was only eight.
Reaction: Some writers choose to open a narrative with a character thinking or reflecting on the event.	**"The Jacket," by Gary Soto** My clothes have failed me. I remember the green coat that I wore in fifth and sixth grade when you either danced like a champ or pressed yourself against a greasy wall, bitter as a penny toward the happy couples.

1. Revisit the openings from texts you've read in this unit to examine how published authors hook readers with effective leads.

Text	Kind of Lead	Why is this lead effective? How does it "hook" readers and leave them wanting to read more?
Staying Fat for Sarah Byrnes, by Chris Crutcher (Activity 1.6)		
From *Dust Tracks on a Road,* by Zora Neale Hurston (Activity 1. 8)		
"A Hundred Bucks of Happy," by Susan Beth Pfeffer (Activity 1. 9)		
"Ditching," by Alan Lawrence Sitomer (Activity 1.10)		
Your revised lead from your draft using one of the techniques to "hook" your reader *(Complete step 2 and then fill in)*		

2. **Review** a draft from your Working Folder, and **rewrite** your opening using one or more of the lead techniques: action, dialogue, reaction. Your goal is to open with a really strong lead that hooks readers into your personal narrative.

_____

_____

_____

Revising the Middle

ACADEMIC VOCABULARY

Sensory details are words that appeal to the five senses.

Practice with Sensory Images and Details

Your teacher will show you photographs of various scenes. Write your observations for each picture. You might describe images using a sensory detail such as a simile. A *simile* describes sensory details by comparing how one item is like another; for example, his work-roughened hands felt like sandpaper.

Picture	Literal Observation	Revision Adding Sensory Images or Details
A picture of children playing at the park.	A girl is swinging and a boy is playing in the sandbox.	A girl swings happily singing "Pop! Goes the Weasel" loudly enough to entertain a little boy beaming with pride at building a fortress in the sandbox.
Picture 1		
Picture 2		

Revising the Ending

SUGGESTED LEARNING STRATEGIES: Graphic Organizer, Revising,
Think-Pair-Share

1. Revisit the endings of these texts you've read to examine how
   published authors provide effective endings.

Text	Length of Ending	Summarize the Ending	Author's Purpose in Using This Ending
Dust Tracks on a Road, by Zora Neale Hurston (Activity 1. 8)			
"A Hundred Bucks of Happy," by Susan Beth Pfeffer (Activity 1. 9)			
Staying Fat for Sarah Byrnes, by Chris Crutcher (Activity 1.6)			
"Ditching," by Alan Lawrence Sitomer (Activity 1.10)	The length was shorter than the Beggining and Middle	He regreted ditching and ran away from his friend	Ditching is not a good idea.

2. Review your quickwrite from Activity 1.3. Follow your teacher's
   directions for revision, and rewrite your ending to share in your
   writing group.

Revising a Personal Narrative About Choice

SUGGESTED LEARNING STRATEGIES: **Self-Editing, Sharing and Responding, Peer Editing**

Assignment

Your assignment is to revise the personal narrative you created during the timed writing in Activity 1.11. Use the revision techniques you have learned in this unit. You will also write a reflection on the changes you make to improve your first draft and explain the effect of the changes on the final piece.

Steps

Planning

1. Locate your Timed Writing from Activity 1.11, "Choosing a Topic for a Timed Writing." This is your first draft for this Embedded Assessment.

2. Read your first draft and take notes identifying points of revision (that is, narrative structure, clarity of ideas, inclusion of narrative elements, etc.). Be prepared to share these ideas in your writing groups and get feedback on other areas that would benefit from revision.

3. Revisit Activities 1.14, 1.15, and 1.16 for guidance about revising beginnings, middles, and endings. Consider how to apply these revision strategies to your timed-writing draft. Within your writing groups, use the following directions to focus your discussion:

   a. Look closely at the organization of your narrative. Does it contain

   ▶ a clear beginning with an effective lead

   ▶ a detailed, sequenced middle

   ▶ a reflective ending?

   b. Look closely at the narrative elements. Does your narrative contain

   ▶ an event revealing a choice

   ▶ a response that details your feelings and thoughts

   ▶ and reflection on the consequences of that choice?

   c. Look closely at the stylistic elements of your draft. Does your narrative contain

   ▶ sentences of varying lengths and types

   ▶ participles and correct use of verb tenses (including perfect and progressive tenses) that are consistent

   ▶ correct and effective use of punctuation, such as commas in a series or after introductory words?

4. On separate paper, create a plan for revision by responding thoughtfully to the following:

   ▶ What do you like best about your writing at this point? Why?

   ▶ What do you think could be improved? Why?

   ▶ After reading my draft, I realize that in the next draft I should revise _____ because _____.

   ▶ What do you plan to change, and how will those changes improve the draft?

Revising

5. Using your plan for revision and the feedback from your writing group, revise your draft. Consult the Scoring Guide to ensure that you address specific criteria.

Editing for Publication

6. Refer to the Word Wall for correct spelling and use of vocabulary words from this unit.

7. Reread your draft silently, and correct errors in grammar, punctuation, and spelling. Share your edited draft with your writing group to identify additional errors in grammar and usage. Ask them to help you fix the errors in preparation for publication.

8. Next, find a word, phrase, or line in the narrative that captures the major idea. Consider how you could modify it into a title that is original and creative.

9. Rewrite or type your narrative to produce a clean draft. Proofread your text again and make sure it is ready for publication.

Reflection

10. Once you have completed your revision, look back at your first draft and your revision plan. Then write a detailed reflection that explains the following:

    ▶ the most significant changes you made

    ▶ why you made them

    ▶ the intended effect of those changes on your reader.

11. Attach both your first draft and your revised draft to this reflection.

....

⬈TECHNOLOGY TIP If you have access to a computer, you may want to create your narrative using word processing software. You can use the "track changes" feature and save each version of your draft with a different filename so you have all the revisions you make to your text during your revision process. Remember to accept the corrections for the final draft so you deliver a clean paper without revision comments.

SCORING GUIDE

Scoring Criteria	Exemplary	Proficient	Emerging
Ideas	The narrative responds to the prompt skillfully by • effectively describing the choice • clearly explaining the consequences of the decision made • thoroughly reflecting on the lesson learned.	The narrative responds to the prompt by • describing the choice • explaining the consequences of the decision made • reflecting on the lesson learned.	The text does not show an adequate response to the prompt.
Organization	The author effectively revises the organizational structure of the narrative to include: • an engaging beginning that hooks the reader and effectively reveals all aspects of the incident • a middle that vividly describes the series of events leading to the incident as well as the narrator's feelings, thoughts, and actions • a reflective ending that examines the consequences of the choice.	The author revises the organizational structure of the narrative to include: • a beginning that introduces the incident • a middle that adequately describes of the narrator's feelings, thoughts, and actions • an ending that examines the consequences of the choice.	The author's text reflects very little revision to first draft's organizational structure. If present, the draft may or may not include the following: • a beginning with an unfocused hook • a middle that is not descriptive or merely tells the series of events leading to the incident • an ending with minimal reflection and closure
Use of Language	The narrative effectively uses sensory images and details to vividly "show" the incident.	The narrative uses sensory images and details to make the incident clear.	The narrative does not use sensory images and details to make the incident clear.
Conventions	Writing contains few or no errors in spelling, punctuation, or capitalization.	Spelling, punctuation, and capitalization mistakes do not detract from the narrative.	Spelling, punctuation, or capitalization mistakes detract from meaning and/or readability.

SCORING GUIDE

Scoring Criteria	Exemplary	Proficient	Emerging
Revision Plan and Reflection	The author outlines and implements a thorough revision plan. The author revises the text by making significant revisions that improve the meaning, clarity, and the style of the narrative. The reflection includes several thoughtful reasons and explanations for the changes made.	The author outlines and implements an appropriate revision plan. The author revises the text by making revisions that bring clarity to the narrative for the reader. The reflection includes reasons for the changes made.	The author does not outline or implement a plan for revision. The reflection is minimal and/or unclear.
Additional Criteria			

Comments: _____

_____

_____

_____

_____

_____

Learning Focus:

Writing Original Stories

From writing a personal narrative to writing an original story is not as great a leap as you might think. You tell stories every day as you try to recreate an experience as vividly as you can in order to keep the attention of your listeners. When you tell your own personal stories, you try to convey the richness of that experience and sometimes you try to make a point or tell about lessons learned.

Folklore and **myth** began from the oral histories of cultural experiences and often represent attempts to make meaning of the world and to teach important lessons about life. You are probably familiar with many types of folklore such as **fairy tales** or **fables** or **legends**. These stories often have **morals**, or lessons, to teach us about human weaknesses such as greed, pride, recklessness, and thoughtlessness.

Folklore is also a tribute to the human impulse to explain the mysteries of life. The characters of myth and folklore often are ordinary people in extraordinary situations. Inevitably, the actions of the characters in folklore have consequences that affect the lives of an entire culture or help explain the inexplicable.

Human beings have told stories throughout the ages, to entertain, to teach and to explain the mysteries of the world. Maybe you will create a story that will live on long after you.

Folk Literature

A part of a culture's folklore is its folk literature—the stories it tells. Folk literature refers to myths and folk tales, as well as a variety of other kinds of stories.

> **ACADEMIC VOCABULARY**
>
> **Folklore** is a general term that describes the stories, traditions, sayings, and customs of a culture or a society.

1. Fill in the blanks below to match each type of story with its definition.

Fable	Legend	Tall Tale	Myth	Fairy Tale	Folk Tale

1. A _____ is a traditional story believed to be based on actual people and events. These stories, which typically celebrate heroic individuals or significant achievements, tend to express the values of a culture.

2. A _____ is a story that involves fantasy elements such as witches, goblins, and elves. These stories often involve princes and princesses and today are generally told to entertain children.

3. A _____ is a story from the past involving gods or heroes. These stories often explain beliefs, customs, or mysterious natural phenomena or identify acceptable and unacceptable behavior.

4. A _____ is a highly exaggerated and often humorous story about folk heroes in local settings. The characters in these stories might be real, but their actions are greatly exaggerated.

5. A _____ is an anonymous traditional story passed on orally from one generation to another.

6. A _____ is a brief story that teaches a lesson or moral, usually through animal characters that take on human qualities.

2. As a group, you will be assigned one of the above types of literature.

- Make a list of all the stories that you know that fit the definition.
- Choose one story that your group knows well.
- Deliver a brief presentation to the rest of the class in which you tell the story and accompany the story with two or three drawings that illustrate key points of the story.
- Be sure to explain how your selected story fits the criteria of your specific type of folk literature.

WORD CONNECTIONS

The word *fable* comes from the Latin word *fabula*, meaning "tale." Other English words derived from this word are *fabulous*, *affable*, and *confabulate*.

Characters and Choices

Before Reading

Read the following scenarios. Describe what you would do, and why.

1. Imagine that you find $100 in the park. You look around and do not see anyone nearby. What do you do with that $100 bill, and why?

_____

_____

_____

2. Imagine you are in the park, and you find a line of silver dollars about every five feet or so. You pick up the dollars as you go, and you see a man walking ahead of you with a bag that clearly has a hole in it that is leaking silver dollars. What do you do, and why?

_____

_____

_____

3. Imagine scenario 2, except that the man is mean and rude to everyone he passes. As you approach him to tell him about the hole in his bag, he yells at you and calls you a bad name. What do you do, and why?

_____

_____

_____

4. Imagine that the richest man in the United States happens to drop by the park. Before getting into his million-dollar limousine, a $100 bill accidentally slips out of his coat pocket. You pick it up, but he has already driven off. What would you do, and why?

_____

_____

_____

ABOUT THE AUTHOR

Linda Sue Park, the daughter of Korean immigrants, was born in 1960 in Urbana, Illinois, and grew up outside of Chicago. Her first book, *Seesaw Girl*, was published in 1999. Set in twelfth-century Korea, *A Single Shard*, published in 2001, received the Newbery Medal the following year. Park also writes picture books for younger readers, such as *The Firekeeper's Son* and *Mung Mung*.

From

A SINGLE SHARD

CHAPTER 1

by Linda Sue Park

"Eh, Tree-ear! Have you hungered well today?" Crane-man called out as Tree-ear drew near the bridge.

The well-fed of the village greeted each other politely by saying, "Have you eaten well today?" Tree-ear and his friend turned the greeting inside out for their own little joke.

Tree-ear squeezed the bulging pouch that he wore at his waist. He had meant to hold back the good news, but the excitement spilled out of him. "Crane-man! A good thing that you greeted me so just now, for later today we will have to use the proper words!" He held the bag high. Tree-ear was delighted when Crane-man's eyes widened in surprise. He knew that Crane-man would guess at once—only one thing could give a bag that kind of smooth fullness. Not carrot-tops or chicken bones, which protruded in odd lumps. No, the bag was filled with *rice*.

Crane-man raised his walking crutch in a salute. "Come, my young friend! Tell me how you came by such a fortune—a tale worth hearing, no doubt!"

My Notes

Characters and Choices

WORD CONNECTIONS

Many words from other countries have entered the English language. For example, *bok choy* is an Asian vegetable often seen in grocery stores. Among food words borrowed from Spanish are *taco, salsa, enchilada,* and *burrito.*

My Notes

Tree-ear had been trotting along the road on his early-morning perusal of the village rubbish heaps. Ahead of him a man carried a heavy load on a *jiggeh,* an open-framed backpack made of branches. On the *jiggeh* was a large woven-straw container, the kind commonly used to carry rice.

Tree-ear knew that the rice must be from last year's crop; in the fields surrounding the village this season's rice had only just begun to grow. It would be many months before the rice was harvested and the poor allowed to glean the fallen grain from the bare fields. Only then would they taste the pure flavor of rice and feel its solid goodness in their bellies. Just looking at the straw box made water rush into Tree-ear's mouth.

The man had paused in the road and hoisted the wooden *jiggeh* higher on his back, shifting the cumbersome weight. As Tree-ear stared, rice began to trickle out of a hole in the straw box. The trickle thickened and became a stream. Oblivious, the man continued on his way. For a few short moments Tree-ear's thoughts wrestled with one another. *Tell him—quickly! Before he loses too much rice!*

No! Don't say anything—you will be able to pick up the fallen rice after he rounds the bend...

Tree-ear made his decision. He waited until the man had reached the bend in the road, then ran to catch him.

"Honorable sir," Tree-ear said, panting and bowing. "As I walked behind you, I noticed that you are marking your path with rice!"

The farmer turned and saw the trail of rice. A well-built man with a broad suntanned face, he pushed his straw hat back, scratched his head, and laughed ruefully.

"Impatience," said the farmer. "I should have had this container woven with a double wall. But it would have taken more time. Now I pay for not waiting a bit longer." He struggled out of the *jiggeh's* straps and inspected the container. He prodded the straw to close the gap but to no avail, so he threw his arms up in mock despair. Tree-ear grinned. He liked the farmer's easygoing nature.

"Fetch me a few leaves, boy," said the farmer. Tree-ear complied, and the man stuffed them into the container as a temporary patch. The farmer squatted to don the *jiggeh*. As he started walking, he called over his shoulder. "Good deserves good, urchin. The rice on the ground is yours if you can be troubled to gather it."

"Many thanks, kind sir!" Tree-ear bowed, very pleased with himself. He had made a lucky guess, and his waist pouch would soon be filled with rice.

Tree-ear had learned from Crane-man's example. Foraging in the woods and rubbish heaps, gathering fallen grain-heads in the autumn—these were honorable ways to garner a meal, requiring time and work. But stealing and begging, Crane-man said, made a man no better than a dog.

"Work gives a man dignity, stealing takes it away," he often said.

Following Crane-man's advice was not always easy for Tree-ear. Today, for example. Was it stealing, to wait as Tree-ear had for more rice to fall before alerting the man that his rice bag was leaking? Did a good deed balance a bad one? Tree-ear often pondered these kinds of questions, alone or in discussion with Crane-man.

"Such questions serve in two ways," Crane-man had explained. "They keep a man's mind sharp—and his thoughts off his empty stomach."

Now, as always, he seemed to know Tree-ear's thoughts without hearing them spoken. "Tell me about this farmer," he said. "What kind of man was he?"

Tree-ear considered the question for several moments, stirring his memory. At last, he answered, "One who lacks patience—he said it himself. He had not wanted to wait for a sturdier container to be built. And he could not be bothered to pick up the fallen rice." Tree-ear paused. "But he laughed easily, even at himself."

My Notes

GRAMMAR & USAGE

A pronoun takes the place of a noun or another pronoun, called its **antecedent**. Look at the next-to-last paragraph on this page. The pronoun *he* is used twice. Who is *he*? The antecedent, Crane-Man, is not in this paragraph, but it is stated in the previous paragraph, so readers know that *he* refers to Crane-man.

When you use pronouns in your writing, make sure you have clearly stated the nouns to which your pronouns refer.

Characters and Choices

"If he were here now, and heard you tell of waiting a little longer before speaking, what do you think he would say or do?"

"He would laugh," Tree-ear said, surprising himself with the speed of his response. Then, more slowly, "I think. . . he would not have minded."

Crane-man nodded, satisfied. And Tree-ear thought of something his friend often said: *Scholars read the great words of the world. But you and I must learn to read the world itself.*

Tree-ear was so called after the mushroom that grew in wrinkled half-circles on dead or fallen tree trunks, emerging from the rotten wood without benefit of parent seed. A good name for an orphan, Crane-man said. If ever Tree-ear had had another name, he no longer remembered it, nor the family that might have named him so.

Tree-ear shared the space under the bridge with Crane-man—or rather, Crane-man shared it with him. After all, Crane-man had been there first, and would not be leaving anytime soon. The shriveled and twisted calf and foot he had been born with made sure of that.

Tree-ear knew the story of his friend's name. "When they saw my leg at birth, it was thought I would not survive," Crane-man had said. "Then, as I went through life on one leg, it was said that I was like a crane. But besides standing on one leg, cranes are also a symbol of long life." True enough, Crane-man added. He had outlived all his family and, unable to work, had been forced to sell his possessions one by one, including, at last, the roof over his head. Thus it was that he had come to live under the bridge.

After Reading

Complete the following organizer about the three characters in the excerpt from *A Single Shard*.

Character	Qualities that the Character Demonstrates	Action or Dialogue that Illustrates These Qualities (page number)
Tree-ear		
The Farmer		
Crane-Man		

Quickwrite: Respond to one of the following quotations. Be sure to include whether or not you agree or disagree and why. In your response, be aware of the pronouns you use, and make them agree with their antecedents.

- "Was it stealing, to wait as Tree-ear had for more rice to fall before alerting the man that his rice bag was leaking?" (page 47)
- "Did a good deed balance a bad one?" (page 47)
- "Scholars read the great words of the world. But you and I must learn to read the world itself." (page 48)

Introduction to Mythology

Recall the definition of **myth**: "a story from the past involving gods or heroes. Myths often explain beliefs, customs, or mysterious natural phenomena or identify acceptable and unacceptable behavior."

1. You may already be familiar with some of the Greek and Roman gods. Complete the following chart. Conduct research to identify those you don't know, as well as corresponding gods and goddesses of other cultures.

Greek name (Roman name)	Responsibility or Role	Similar God or Goddess in Another Culture (identify the cultures)
Apollo		
Ares (Mars)		
Artemis (Diana)		
Athena (Minerva)		
Demeter (Ceres)		
Aphrodite (Venus)		
Zeus (Jupiter or Jove)		
Hades (Pluto)		
Hermes (Mercury)		
Poseidon (Neptune)		
Hera (Juno)		

2. Select one of the gods or goddesses you identified on the previous page. Conduct further research in order to create a "Missing" or a "Wanted" poster for him or her. Your poster should include all the relevant information identified below and anything else you think would be appropriate. Be prepared to present this poster to a group and display it in the classroom.

Name: _____ Age: _____ Also Known As: _____

Last known location:

_____

Physical description (include a visual; you can sketch what the god or goddess might look like, or provide another visual):

Significant actions/crimes:

_____

_____

Presumed dangerous? Why?

_____

_____

Known Associates:

_____

_____

Additional information/distinguishing features:

_____

_____

_____

Structural Elements of a Narrative Plot

1. In the spaces below, give examples of the advice that various adults give you on a regular basis. Then, in the next column identify how often you either take or ignore this advice. Be sure to offer reasons why you either follow or ignore their advice. If you ignored specific advice, what was the result?

Adults	Specific Advice	Follow? Ignore? Why?	Result
Parents/Guardians			
Teachers			
Other Adults: Coaches, Grandparents, Older Cousins, Etc.			

2. In general, do you think you learn best from other people's advice or from your own experience? On separate paper, explain with an example from your own life. Be sure to analyze the consequences of taking or not taking the advice. Review your writing and check your use of pronouns to make sure they agree with their antecedents.

3. Your teacher may ask you to do an oral reading of "Daedalus and Icarus." **Reading fluency** is an important part of oral reading. When you read aloud, pay attention to the following:

- Accuracy (saying the words correctly)

- Tempo, or rate (reading not too fast or too slow)

- Inflection (reading with expression in your voice)

Daedalus and Icarus

Myth

> **ABOUT THE AUTHOR**
> Geraldine McCaughrean was born in England, where she studied theater and began writing her versions of traditional texts such as *The Canterbury Tales* and Shakespeare's plays. Her goal was to retell these challenging texts in language that young readers could enjoy and understand. She has received numerous awards for her books, and her writing is noted for its strong use of imagery and narrative structure that bring her stories alive for readers.

by Geraldine McCaughrean

The island of Crete was ruled by King Minos, whose reputation for wickedness had spread to every shore. One day he summoned to his country a famous inventor named Daedalus. "Come, Daedalus, and bring your son, Icarus, too. I have a job for you, and I pay well."

King Minos wanted Daedalus to build him a palace, with soaring towers and a high, curving roof. In the cellars there was to be a maze of many corridors—so twisting and dark that any man who once ventured in there would never find his way out again.

"What is it for?" asked Daedalus. "Is it a treasure vault? Is it a prison to hold criminals?"

But Minos only replied, "Build my labyrinth as I told you. I pay you to build, not to ask questions"

So Daedalus held his tongue and set to work. When the palace was finished, he looked at it with pride, for there was nowhere in the world so fine. But when he found out the purpose of the maze in the cellar, he shuddered with horror.

For at the heart of that maze, King Minos put a creature that was half man, half beast—a thing almost too horrible to describe. He called it the Minotaur, and he fed it on men and women!

Then Daedalus wanted to leave Crete at once, and forget both maze and Minotaur. So he went to King Minos to ask for his money.

Structural Elements of a Narrative Plot

My Notes

"I regret," said King Minos, "I cannot let you leave Crete, Daedalus. You are the only man who knows the secret of the maze and how to escape from it. The secret must never leave this island. So I'm afraid I must keep you and Icarus here a while longer."

"How much longer?" gasped Daedalus.

"Oh—just until you die," replied Minos cheerfully. "But never mind. I have plenty of work for a man as clever as you."

Daedalus and Icarus lived in great comfort in King Minos's palace. But they lived the life of prisoners. Their rooms were in the tallest palace tower, with beautiful views across the island. They ate delectable food and wore expensive clothes. But at night the door of their fine apartment was locked, and a guard stood outside. It was a comfortable prison, but it was a prison, even so. Daedalus was deeply unhappy.

Every day he put seed out on the windowsill, for the birds. He liked to study their brilliant colors, the clever overlapping of their feathers, the way they soared on the sea wind. It comforted him to think that they at least were free to come and go. The birds had only to spread their wings and they could leave Crete behind them, whereas Daedalus and Icarus must stay forever in their luxurious cage.

Young Icarus could not understand his father's unhappiness. "But I like it here," he said. "The king gives us gold and this tall tower to live in."

Daedalus groaned. "But to work for such a wicked man, Icarus! And to be prisoners all our days! ... We shan't stay. We shan't!"

"But we can't get away, can we?" said Icarus. "How can anybody escape from an island? Fly?" He snorted with laughter.

Daedalus did not answer. He scratched his head and stared out of the window at the birds pecking seed on the sill.

From that day onward, he got up early each morning and stood at the open window. When a bird came for the seed, Daedalus begged it to spare him one feather. Then each night, when everyone else had gone to bed, Daedalus worked by candlelight on his greatest invention of all.

Early mornings. Late nights. A whole year went by. Then one morning Icarus was awakened by his father shaking his shoulder. "Get up, Icarus, and don't make a sound. We are leaving Crete."

"But how? It's impossible!"

Daedalus pulled out a bundle from under his bed. "I've been making something, Icarus." Inside were four great folded fans of feathers. He stretched them out on the bed. They were wings! "I sewed the feathers together with strands of wool from my blanket. Now hold still."

Daedalus melted down a candle and daubed his son's shoulders with sticky wax. "Yes, I know it's hot, but it will soon cool." While the wax was still soft, he stuck two of the wings to Icarus's shoulder blades.

"Now you must help me put on my wings, Son. When the wax sets hard, you and I will fly away from here, as free as birds!"

"I'm scared!" whispered Icarus as he stood the narrow window ledge, his knees knocking and his huge wings drooping down behind. The lawns and courtyards of the palace lay far below. The royal guards looked as small as ants "This won't work!"

"Courage, Son!" said Daedalus. "Keep your arms out wide and fly close to me. Above all—are you listening, Icarus?"

"Y-y-yes, Father."

"Above all, don't fly too high! Don't fly too close to the sun!"

"Don't fly too close to the sun," Icarus repeated, with his eyes tight shut. Then he gave a cry as his father nudged him off the windowsill. He plunged downward. With a crack, the feathers behind him filled with wind, and Icarus found himself flying. Flying!

"I'm flying!" he crowed.

The guards looked up in astonishment, and wagged their swords, and pointed and shouted, "Tell the king! Daedalus and Icarus are... are ... flying away!"

By dipping first one wing, then the other, Icarus found that he could turn to the left and the right. The wind tugged at his hair. His legs

My Notes

WORD CONNECTIONS

Think about the relationship (analogy) between *feather* and *wing*. Then write a word that has the same relationship with *alphabet*.

Feather : wing ::

_____ : alphabet.

Structural Elements of a Narrative Plot

trailed out behind him. He saw the fields and streams as he had never seen them before!

Then they were out over the sea. The sea gulls pecked at him angrily, so Icarus flew higher, where they could not reach him.

He copied their shrill cry and taunted them: "You can't catch me!"

"Now remember, don't fly too high!" called Daedalus, but his words were drowned by the screaming of the gulls.

I'm the first boy ever to fly! I'm making history! I shall be famous! thought Icarus, as he flew up and up, higher and higher. At last Icarus was looking the sun itself in the face. "Think you're the highest thing in the sky, do you?" he jeered. "I can fly just as high as you! Higher, even!" He did not notice the drops of sweat on his forehead: He was so determined to outfly the sun.

Soon its vast heat beat on his face and on his back and on the great wings stuck on with wax. The wax softened. The wax trickled. The wax dripped. One feather came unstuck. Then a plume of feathers fluttered slowly down.

Icarus stopped flapping his wings. His father's words came back to him clearly now: *"Don't fly too close to the sun!"*

With a great sucking noise, the wax on his shoulders came unstuck. Icarus tried to catch hold of the wings, but they just folded up in his hands. He plunged down, his two fists full of feathers—down and down and down.

The clouds did not stop his fall.

The sea gulls did not catch him in their beaks.

His own father could only watch as Icarus hurtled head first into the glittering sea and sank deep down among the sharks and eels and squid. And all that was left of proud Icarus was a litter of waxy feathers floating on the sea.

Plot

ACADEMIC VOCABULARY

Plot is the sequence of related events that make up a story.

1. Look over the elements of **plot** structure of most stories:

   Exposition: background information or events necessary to understand a story

   Rising Action: the conflicts and complications that develop a story.

   Climax: the turning point; the most intense moment

   Falling Action: the action after the climax

   Resolution: the conclusion; the wrapping up of threads

2. Briefly identify these plot elements in the myth "Daedalus and Icarus":

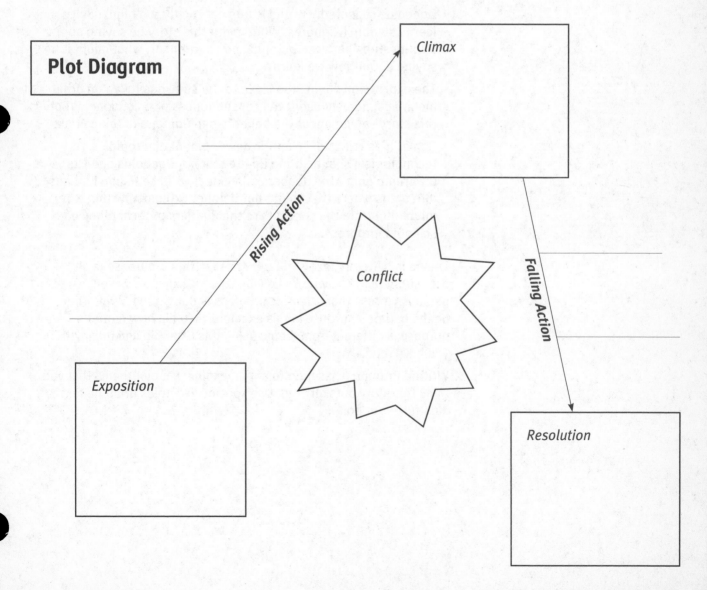

Plot Diagram

Climax

Rising Action

Conflict

Falling Action

Exposition

Resolution

Structural Elements of a Narrative Plot

ACADEMIC VOCABULARY

Theme is the central idea, message, or purpose of a literary work.

Theme

"Daedalus and Icarus," like most myths, teaches us a lesson. Daedalus tells his son, "Don't fly too close to the sun." Since it is not likely that any of us will wear wings made of feathers and wax, the lesson, or theme, of this story is not about how high to fly. The story of Icarus can be read as a metaphor for other, more realistic situations we might face.

1. Discuss the following concepts in pairs or small groups:

   • In the story, Icarus thinks to himself, "I'm the first boy ever to fly! I'm making history!" Icarus also says to the sun, "I can fly just as high as you! Higher, even!" What does this dialogue illustrate about the character of Icarus? How could this relate to the story's theme?

   • Daedalus repeatedly warns Icarus not too fly too high, advice that Icarus obviously ignores. What might this story be saying about relationships between parents and children, or, what might it be saying about how we learn?

   • The expression "flying too close to the sun" has taken on other meanings, namely about the consequences of risk taking. What is this story saying about the benefits and dangers of taking risks?

   • Sometimes critics of scientific development and rapid technological change bring up the story of Daedalus and Icarus as a warning about the dangers of reckless science taking humans into areas where they might not belong. Explain how this story might illustrate the concepts of the dangers of technology and scientific progress.

2. Theme in a literary text is different from author's purpose in an expository text. The writer of a magazine article may present a persuasive case that scientific progress is dangerous. What would be the author's purpose in this example? Explain how author's purpose is different from theme using this example and the myth you have read.

3. **Writing Prompt:** On separate paper, explain a major theme that you think this story puts forward. Use specific examples from the text to illustrate your point.

Know Your Roots: Word Choice

SUGGESTED LEARNING STRATEGIES: **Graphic Organizer, Brainstorming**

1. A word root is a part of the word that conveys its core meaning. If you know the meaning of an unfamiliar word's root, you may be able to determine its meaning. Many English words have roots from Greek, Latin, or Old English words. Working as directed by your teacher, complete the following chart.

Root	Meaning	Example	Example	Example	Example
alt-					
-vert-					
grad-					
therm-					
-phobe					
ge-, geo-					
mania-					
-vid-, -vis-					
bio-					
-graph-, -gram-					
-scope, -scop-					

2. **Writing Prompt:** On separate paper, write a dialogue between Icarus and his father that might have taken place if Icarus had survived the fall. Use 8–10 words from the chart above. Be sure to write dialogue using correct punctuation and capitalization.

GRAMMAR USAGE

When writing dialogue, start a new paragraph each time the speaker changes.

My Notes

As you read "Phaethon," practice reading fluently. You can use the pronunciation guides in the footnotes to say the Greek names accurately. Use a tempo that is not too fast or too slow, and use expression in your voice (inflection).

The dialogue between the two characters is indicated by quotation marks; however, in this section, the speaker is not always named. Decide who is speaking within each set of quotation marks, the yellow-haired boy or the one with black hair. How do you know? Write on your text who is speaking.

Myth

> **ABOUT THE AUTHOR**
> Bernard Evslin wrote many books for young people and is best known for his adaptations of tales from Greek mythology. *Heroes, Gods and Monsters of the Greek Myths* is his best-known work, selling more than 10 million copies worldwide and translated into ten different languages. Evslin's work won a number of awards and his book *The Green Hero* was nominated for a National Book Award.

Phaethon

by Bernard Evslin

1   Long ago, when the world was very new, two boys were racing along the edge of a cliff that hung over a deep blue sea. They were the same size; one boy had black hair, the other had yellow hair. The race was very close. Then the yellow-haired one spurted ahead and won the race. The loser was very angry.

2   "You think you're pretty good," he said. "But you're not so much. My father is Zeus."[1]

3   "My father is Apollo," said the yellow-haired boy, whose name was Phaethon.[2]

4   "My father is the chief god, king of the mountain, lord of the sky."

5   "My father is lord of the sun."

6   "My father is called the thunderer. When he is angry, the sky grows black and the sun hides. His spear is a lightning bolt, and that's what he kills people with. He hurls it a thousand miles and it never misses."

---

[1] **Zeus** [züs]: King of the gods in Greek mythology
[2] **Phaethon** [fā´ə thon]

"Without my father there would be no day. It would always be night. Each morning he hitches up his horses and drives the golden chariot of the sun across the sky. And that is day time. Then he dives into the ocean stream and boards a golden ferryboat and sails back to his eastern palace. That time is called night." 7

"Sometimes I visit my father," said Epaphus,[3] the other boy. "I sit on Olympus[4] with him, and he teaches me things and gives me presents. Know what he gave me last time? A little thunderbolt just like his — and he taught me how to throw it. I killed three vultures, scared a fishing boat, started a forest fire. Next time I go, I'll throw it at more things. Do you visit your father?" 8

Phaethon never had. But he could not bear to tell Epaphus. "Certainly," he said, "very often. I go to the eastern palace, and he teaches me things too." 9

"What kind of things? Has he taught you to drive the horses of the sun?" 10

"Oh, yes. He taught me to handle their reins and how to make them go and how to make them stop. And they're huge horses. Tall as this mountain. They breathe fire." 11

"I think you're making it all up," said Epaphus. "I can tell. I don't even believe there is a sun chariot. There's the sun, look at it. It's not a chariot." 12

---

[3] **Epaphus** [ə pā′ fəs]
[4] **Olympus** [ō lim′ pəs]: A mountain in Greece where ancient gods were said to live

My Notes
This confrontation leads to a choice for Phaethon.

Why do you think Phaethon lies about his relationship with his father?

What choices does Phaethon have at this point?

My Notes

What might be the consequences of each choice you stated?

13   "Oh, what you see is just one of the wheels," said Phaethon. "There's another wheel on the other side. The body of the chariot is slung between them. That is where the driver stands and whips his horses. You cannot see it because your eyes are too small, and the glare is too bright."

14   "Well," said Epaphus, "Maybe it is a chariot, but I still don't believe your father lets you drive it. In fact, I don't believe you've been to the palace of the sun. I doubt that Apollo would know you if he saw you. Maybe he isn't even your father. People like to say they're descended from the gods, of course. But how many of us are there, really?"

15   "I'll prove it to you," cried Phaethon, stamping his foot. "I'll go to the palace of the sun right now and hold my father to his promise. I'll show you."

16   "What promise?"

17   "He said I was getting to be so good a charioteer that next time he would let me drive the sun chariot *alone*. All by myself. From dawn to night. Right across the sky. And this time is next time."

18   "Proof — words are cheap," said Epaphus. "How will I know it's you driving the sun? I won't be able to see you from down here."

19   "You'll know me," said Phaethon. "When I pass the village I will come down close and drive in circles around your roof. You'll see me all right. Farewell."

20   "Are you starting now?"

21   "Now. At once. Just watch the sky tomorrow, son of Zeus."

22   And he went off. He was so stung by the words of his friend, and the boasting and lying he had been forced to do, that he traveled night and day, not stopping for food or rest, guiding himself by the morning star and the evening star, heading always east. Nor did he know the way. For, indeed, he had never once seen his father Apollo. He knew him only through his mother's stories. But he did know that the palace must lie in the east, because that is where he saw the sun start each morning. He walked on and on until finally he lost his way completely, and weakened by hunger and exhaustion, fell swooning in a great meadow by the edge of a wood.

23   Now, while Phaethon was making his journey, Apollo sat in his great throne room on a huge throne made of gold and rubies. This

was the quiet hour before dawn when night left its last coolness upon the Earth. And it was then, at this hour, that Apollo sat on his throne, wearing a purple cloak embroidered with the golden sign of the zodiac.[5] On his head was a crown given him by the dawn goddess, made of silver and pearls. A bird flew in the window and perched on his shoulder and spoke to him. This bird had sky-blue feathers, golden beak, golden claws, and golden eyes. It was one of Apollo's sun hawks. It was this bird's job to fly here and there gathering gossip. Sometimes she was called the spy bird.

Now she said, "Apollo, I have seen your son!"   24

"Which son?"   25

"Phaethon. He's coming to see you. But he has lost his way and lies exhausted at the edge of the wood. The wolves will surely eat him. Do you care?"   26

"I will have to see him before I know whether I care. You had better get back to him before the wolves do. Bring him here in comfort. Round up some of your companions and bring him here as befits the son of a god."   27

The sun hawk seized the softly glowing rug at the foot of the throne and flew away with it. She summoned three of her companions, and they each took a corner of the rug. They flew over a desert and a mountain and a wood and came to the field where Phaethon lay. They flew down among the howling of wolves, among burning eyes set in a circle about the unconscious[6] boy. They pushed him onto the rug, and each took a corner in her beak, and flew away.   28

Phaethon felt himself being lifted into the air. The cold wind of his going revived him, and he sat up. People below saw a boy sitting with folded arms on a carpet rushing through the cold, bright moonlight far above their heads. It was too dark, though, to see the birds, and that is why we hear tales of flying carpets even to this day.   29

Phaethon was not particularly surprised to find himself in the air. The last thing he remembered was lying down on the grass. Now he knew he was dreaming. A good dream — floating and flying — his favorite kind. And when he saw the great cloud castle   30

My Notes

How does Apollo feel about his son, Phaethon?

How does Apollo save Phaethon?

What could have happened if Apollo had not intervened?

---

[5] **zodiac** [zō´ dē ak]: An imaginary belt of the heavens, divided into 12 parts, called signs, and named after 12 constellations

[6] **unconscious** [un kon´ shəs]: Not awake

My Notes

Make a prediction about what Phaethon will ask Apollo.

What promise does Apollo make to Phaethon? Is it wise to make this promise? Why or why not?

on top of the mountain, all made of snow, rise in the early light, he was more sure than ever that he was dreaming. He saw sentries in flashing golden armor, carrying golden spears. In the courtyard he saw enormous woolly dogs with fleece like clouddrift guarding the gate. These were Apollo's great sun hounds.

31   Over the wall flew the carpet, over the courtyard, through the tall portals. And it wasn't until the sun hawks gently let down the carpet in front of the throne that he began to think that this dream might be very real. He raised his eyes shyly and saw a tall figure sitting on the throne. Taller than any man, and appallingly beautiful to the boy — with his golden hair and stormy blue eyes and strong laughing face. Phaethon fell on his knees.

32   "Father," he cried. "I am Phaethon, your son!"

33   "Rise, Phaethon. Let me look at you."

34   He stood up, his legs trembling.

35   "Yes, you may well be my son. I seem to see a resemblance. Which one did you say?"

36   "Phaethon."

37   "Oh, Clymene's[7] boy. I remember your mother well. How is she?"

38   "In health, sire."

39   "And did I not leave some daughters with her as well? Yellow-haired girls — quite pretty?"

40   "My sisters, sire. The Heliads."

41   "Yes, of course. Must get over that way and visit them all one of these seasons. And you, lad — what brings you to me? Do you not know that it is courteous to await an invitation before visiting a god — even if he is in the family?"

42   "I know, Father. But I had no choice. I was taunted by a son of Zeus, Epaphus. And I would have flung him over the cliff and myself after him if I had not resolved to make my lies come true."

43   "Well, you're my son, all right. Proud, rash, accepting no affront,[8] refusing no adventure. I know the breed. Speak up, then. What is it you wish? I will do anything in my power to help you."

---

[7] **Clymene** [klī men ē´]
[8] **affront** [ə frunt´]: Insult

"Anything, Father?" 44

"Anything I can. I swear by the river Styx,[9] an oath sacred to the gods." 45

"I wish to drive the sun across the sky. All by myself. From dawn till night." 46

Apollo's roar of anger shattered every crystal goblet in the great castle. 47

"Impossible!" he cried. "No one drives those horses but me. They are tall as mountains. Their breath is fire. They are stronger than the tides, stronger than the wind. It is all that *I* can do to hold them in check. How can your puny grip restrain them? They will race away with the chariot, scorching the poor Earth to a cinder." 48

"You promised, Father." 49

"Yes, I promised, foolish lad. And that promise is the death warrant. A poor charred cinder floating in space — well, that is what the oracle predicted for the earth — but I did not know it would be so soon . . . so soon." 50

"It is almost dawn, Father. Should we not saddle the horses?" 51

"Will you not withdraw your request—allow me to preserve my honor without destroying the earth? Ask me anything else and I will grant it. Do not ask me this." 52

"I have asked, sire, and you have promised. And the hour for dawn comes, and the horses are unharnessed. The sun will rise late today, confusing the wise." 53

"They will be more than confused when this day is done," said Apollo. "Come." 54

Apollo took Phaethon to the stable of the sun, and there the boy saw the giant fire-white horses being harnessed to the golden chariot. Huge they were. Fire-white with golden manes and golden hooves and hot yellow eyes. When they neighed, the trumpet call of it rolled across the sky — and their breath was flame. They were being harnessed by a Titan, a cousin of the gods, tall as the tree, dressed in asbestos[10] armor with a helmet of tinted crystal against the glare. The sun chariot was an open shell of gold. Each wheel was the flat round disk of the sun as it is seen in the sky. And Phaethon looked very tiny as he stood in the chariot. The reins were thick 55

My Notes

Why does Apollo want Phaethon to change his request?

Predict what might happen if Phaethon drives the horses.

---

[9] **Styx** [stiks]: In Greek myths, a river that led to Hades or Hell
[10] **asbestos** [as bes' təs]: A mineral that does not burn or conduct heat

My Notes

What will happen if Phaethon chooses not to obey Apollo's instructions?

Predict whether or not Phaethon will follow the directions. Give a reason for your prediction.

Mark the text that reveals Phaethon's character.

as bridge cables, much too large for him to hold, so Apollo tied them around his waist. Then Apollo stood at the head of the team gentling the horses speaking softly to them, calling them by name — Pyrocis,[11] Eous,[12] Aethon,[13] Phlegon.[14]

56   "Good lads, good horses, go easy today, my swift ones. Go at a slow trot and do not leave the path. You have a new driver today."

57   The great horses dropped their heads to his shoulder and whinnied softly, for they loved him. Phaethon saw the flame of their breath play about his head, saw Apollo's face shining out of the flame. But he was not harmed, for he was a god and could not be hurt by physical things.

58   He came to Phaethon and said, "Listen to me, son. You are about to start a terrible journey. Now, by the obedience you owe me as a son, by the faith you owe a god, by my oath that cannot be broken, and your pride that will not bend, I put this rule upon you: Keep the middle way. Too high and the earth will freeze, too low and it will burn. Keep the middle way. Give the horses their heads; they know the path, the blue middle course of day. Drive them not too high nor too low, but above all, do not stop. Or you will fire the air about you where you stand, charring the earth and blistering the sky. Do you heed me?"

59   "I do, I do!" cried Phaethon. "Stand away, sire! The dawn grows old and day must begin! Go, horses, go!"

60   And Apollo stood watching as the horses of the sun went into a swinging trot, pulling behind them the golden chariot, climbing the first eastern steep of the sky.

61   At first things went well. The great steeds trotted easily along their path across the high blue meadow of the sky. And Phaethon thought to himself, "I can't understand why my father was making such a fuss. This is easy. For me, anyway. Perhaps I'm a natural-born coachman though . . ."

62   He looked over the edge of the chariot. He saw tiny houses down below and specks of trees. And the dark blue puddle of the sea. The coach was trundling across the sky. The great sun wheels were turning, casting light, warming and brightening the earth, chasing all the shadows of night.

---

[11] **Pyrocis** [pǐ rō´ chis]
[12] **Eous** [e´ us]
[13] **Aethon** [a´ thon]
[14] **Phlegon** [fle´ gon]

"Just imagine," Phaethon thought, "how many people now are looking up at the sky, praising the sun, hoping the weather stays fair. How many people are watching me, me, me . . .?" Then he thought, "But I'm too small to see. They can't even see the coach or the horses — only the great wheel. We are too far and the light is too bright. For all they know, it is Apollo making his usual run. How can they know it's me, me, me? How will my mother know, and my sisters? They would be so proud. And Epaphus — above all, Epaphus — how will he know? I'll come home tomorrow after this glorious journey and tell him what I did and he will laugh at me and tell me I'm lying, as he did before. And how shall I prove it to him? No, this must not be. I must show him that it is I driving the chariot of the sun — I alone. Apollo said not to come too close to earth, but how will he know? And I won't stay too long — just dip down toward our own village and circle his roof three times — which is the signal we agreed upon. After he recognizes me, I'll whip up the horses and resume the path of the day.

63

He jerked on the reins, pulled the horses' heads down. They whinnied angrily and tossed their heads. He jerked the reins again.

64

"Down," he cried. "Down! Down!"

65

The horses plunged through the bright air, golden hooves twinkling, golden manes flying, dragging the great glittering chariot after them in a long flaming swoop. When they reached his village, he was horrified to see the roofs bursting into fire. The trees burned. People rushed about screaming. Their loose clothing caught fire, and they burned like torches as they ran.

66

Was it his village? He could not tell because of the smoke. Had he destroyed his own home? Burned his mother and his sisters?

67

He threw himself backward in the chariot, pulling at the reins with all his might, shouting, "Up! Up!"

68

And the horses, made furious by the smoke, reared on their hind legs in the air. They leaped upward, galloping through the smoke, pulling the chariot up, up.

69

Swiftly the earth fell away beneath them. The village was just a smudge of smoke. Again he saw the pencil-stroke of mountains, the inkblot of seas. "Whoa!" he cried. "Turn now! Forward on your path!" But he could no longer handle them. They were galloping, not trotting. They had taken the bit in their teeth. They did not turn toward the path of the day across the meadow of the sky, but

70

© 2011 College Board. All rights reserved.

GRAMMAR & USAGE

If you were to write a paragraph about Phaethon, you would include a topic sentence. A **topic sentence** states the main idea for a paragraph. A strong topic sentence contains a subject and an opinion that can be proved using textual evidence. Example: **Phaethon** *is a reckless, headstrong boy*. Phaethon is the subject, and the italicized words are the opinion.

My Notes

Why do you think Phaethon chooses to do exactly what Apollo warned him not to do?

My Notes

_____

_____

_____

_____

_____

_____

_____

_____

What are the consequences
of Phaeton's choice?

_____

_____

_____

_____

galloped up, up. And the people on earth saw the sun shooting away until it was no larger than a star.

71   Darkness came. And cold. The earth froze hard. Rivers froze, and oceans. Boats were caught fast in the ice in every sea. It snowed in the jungle. Marble buildings cracked. It was impossible for anyone to speak; breath froze on the speakers' lips. And in village and city, in the field and in the wood, people died of the cold. And the bodies piled up where they fell, like firewood.

72   Still Phaethon could not hold his horses, and still they galloped upward dragging light and warmth away from the earth. Finally they went so high that the air was too thin to breathe. Phaethon saw the flame of their breath, which had been red and yellow, burn blue in the thin air. He himself was gasping for breath; he felt the marrow of his bones freezing.

73   Now the horses, wild with change, maddened by the feeble hand on the reins, swung around and dived toward earth again. Now all the ice melted, making great floods. Villages were swept away by a solid wall of water. Trees were uprooted and whole forests were torn away. The fields were covered by water. Lower swooped the horses, and lower yet. Now the water began to steam — great billowing clouds of steam as the water boiled. Dead fish floated on the surface. Naiads moaned in dry riverbeds.

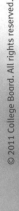

Phaethon could not see; the steam was too thick. He had unbound the reins from his waist, or they would have cut him in two. He had no control over the horses at all. They galloped upward again — out of the steam — taking at last the middle road, but racing wildly, using all their tremendous speed. Circling the earth in a matter of minutes, smashing across the sky from horizon to horizon, making the day flash on and off like a child playing with a lamp. And the people who were left alive were bewildered by the light and darkness following each other so swiftly.

74

Up high on Olympus, the gods in their cool garden heard a clamor of grief from below. Zeus looked upon earth. He saw the runaway horses of the sun and the hurtling chariot. He saw the dead and the dying, the burning forests, the floods, the weird frost. Then he looked again at the chariot and saw that it was not Apollo driving, but someone he did not know. He stood up, drew back his arm, and hurled a thunderbolt.

75

It stabbed through the air, striking Phaethon, killing him instantly, knocking him out of the chariot. His body, flaming, fell like a star. And the horses of the sun, knowing themselves driverless, galloped homeward toward their stables at the eastern edge of the sky.

76

Phaethon's yellow-haired sisters grieved for the beautiful boy. They could not stop weeping. They stood on the bank of the river where he had fallen until Apollo, unable to comfort them, changed them into poplar trees. Here they still stand on the shore of the river, weeping tears of amber sap.

77

And since that day no one has been allowed to drive the chariot of the sun except the sun god himself. But there are still traces of Phaethon's ride. The ends of the earth are still covered with icecaps. Mountains still rumble, trying to spit out the fire started in their bellies by the diving sun.

78

My Notes

Mark the places in the text where Phaethon's character is revealed.

Poor Choices

Indicate whether you agree or disagree with the following statements about Phaethon and Apollo. Then write the textual evidence that supports your position. Go back to the text and highlight your textual evidence.

Agree	Disagree	
		Phaethon is a reckless, headstrong boy. Textual Evidence:
		Phaethon is an adventurous, courageous boy. Textual Evidence:
		Phaethon is _____. (Insert your description) Textual Evidence:
		Apollo is a distant, ineffectual parent. Textual Evidence:
		Apollo is deeply concerned for his son's well-being. Textual Evidence:
		Apollo is _____. (Insert your description) Textual Evidence:

Symbols

Writers commonly use **symbolism** in literary works to add depth of meaning. A *symbol* represents something beyond itself. You might think of a symbol as having two meanings: one meaning is literal, and the other is figurative.

A **literal** meaning of a word or phrase is expected to be understood exactly as it is stated, while a **figurative** meaning is one that suggests some idea beyond the literal level.

> **ACADEMIC VOCABULARY**
>
> A *symbol* is an object, a person, or a place that stands for something else. **Symbolism** is the use of symbols in a literary work.

1. Look over the following expressions that are clearly meant figuratively; identify the intended meaning.

   • I'm so hungry that I could eat a horse.

   _____

   _____

   • It's raining cats and dogs.

   _____

   _____

   • She broke my heart.

   _____

   _____

2. Now, think about objects that appear in well-known fairy tales or stories you have read in this unit and list them below. Then use the graphic organizer on the next page to identify how each object is used literally in the story, and explain its figurative, or symbolic, meaning as well.

   _____

   _____

   _____

   _____

   _____

   _____

Symbols

Story/Object	Literal Usage	Figurative (Symbolic) Meaning
Three Little Pigs: Straw House	Made of straw	Flimsy—not made to last
Three Little Pigs: Brick House	Made of brick	Made to last
Daedalus and Icarus: Wings		
Phaethon: The Chariot		
One of Your Choice: _____		
One of Your Choice: _____		

3. Now, on separate paper, draw a scene from one of the stories above in which the object is shown as a significant symbol. Communicate the figurative, or symbolic, meaning of this object.

Myths and Reality

Myth

My Notes

> **ABOUT THE AUTHOR**
> Olivia Coolidge grew up in England in the early 1900s. She became a teacher of Latin, Greek, and mythology, while also developing her skills as a writer. She wrote numerous histories and biographies for children and young adults. Her work is noted for high interest and vivid descriptions, winning the 1963 Newbery Award for contributions to children's literature.

Arachne

by Olivia Coolidge

Arachne was a maiden who became famous throughout Greece, though she was neither wellborn nor beautiful and came from no great city. She lived in an obscure little village, and her father was a humble dyer of wool. In this he was very skillful, producing many varied shades, while above all he was famous for the clear, bright scarlet which is made from shellfish, and which was the most glorious of all the colors used in ancient Greece. Even more skillful than her father was Arachne. It was her task to spin the fleecy wool into a fine, soft thread and to weave it into cloth on the high, standing loom within the cottage. Arachne was small and pale from much working. Her eyes were light and her hair was a dusty brown, yet she was quick and graceful, and her fingers, roughened as they were, went so fast that it was hard to follow their flickering movements. So soft and even was her thread, so fine her cloth, so gorgeous her embroidery, that soon her products were known all over Greece. No one had ever seen the like of them before.

At last Arachne's fame became so great that people used to come from far and wide to watch her working. Even the graceful nymphs would steal in from stream or forest and peep shyly through the dark doorway, watching in wonder the white arms of Arachne as she stood at the loom and threw the shuttle from hand to hand between the hanging threads, or drew out the long wool, fine as a hair, from the distaff as she sat spinning. "Surely Athene herself must have taught her," people would murmur to one another. "Who else could know the secret of such marvelous skill?"

Myths and Reality

My Notes

GRAMMAR & USAGE

Modifying words should be placed close to the words they modify, to avoid misreading or confusion. However, some modifiers can be placed in different locations for effect.

Notice the adverb *indignantly* in line 6. It could also occur before *turn* or after *say*. How is the meaning of this sentence affected if the adverb is moved to either of those locations?

Notice the adjective phrase *bent and very poor* in the second paragraph. Consider the effect of moving it somewhere else in the sentence. Is it more or less effective in another location?

Predict what will happen in the rest of the myth.

Arachne was used to being wondered at, and she was immensely proud of the skill that had brought so many to look on her. Praise was all she lived for, and it displeased her greatly that people should think anyone, even a goddess, could teach her anything. Therefore when she heard them murmur, she would stop her work and turn round indignantly to say, "With my own ten fingers I gained this skill, and by hard practice from early morning till night. I never had time to stand looking as you people do while another maiden worked. Nor if I had, would I give Athene credit because the girl was more skillful than I. As for Athene's weaving, how could there be finer cloth or more beautiful embroidery than mine? If Athene herself were to come down and compete with me, she could do no better than I."

One day when Arachne turned round with such words, an old woman answered her, a grey old woman, bent and very poor, who stood leaning on a staff and peering at Arachne amid the crowd of onlookers.

"Reckless girl," she said, "how dare you claim to be equal to the immortal gods themselves? I am an old woman and have seen much. Take my advice and ask pardon of Athene for your words. Rest content with your fame of being the best spinner and weaver that mortal eyes have ever beheld."

"Stupid old woman," said Arachne indignantly, "who gave you the right to speak in this way to me? It is easy to see that you were never good for anything in your day, or you would not come here in poverty and rags to gaze at my skill. If Athene resents my words, let her answer them herself. I have challenged her to a contest, but she, of course, will not come. It is easy for the gods to avoid matching their skill with that of men."

At these words the old woman threw down her staff and stood erect. The wondering onlookers saw her grow tall and fair and stand clad in long robes of dazzling white. They were terribly afraid as they realized that they stood in the presence of Athene. Arachne herself flushed red for a moment, for she had never really believed that the goddess would hear her. Before the group that was gathered there she would not give in; so pressing her pale lips together in obstinacy and pride, she led the goddess to one of the great looms and set herself before the other. Without a word both began to thread the long woolen strands that hang from the rollers, and between which the shuttle moves back and forth. Many skeins lay heaped beside them to use, bleached white, and gold, and scarlet, and other shades, varied as the rainbow. Arachne had never thought of giving credit for her success to her father's skill in dyeing, though in actual truth the colors were as remarkable as the cloth itself.

Soon there was no sound in the room but the breathing of the onlookers, the whirring of the shuttles, and the creaking of the wooden frames as each pressed the thread up into place or tightened the pegs by which the whole was held straight. The excited crowd in the doorway began to see that the skill of both in truth was very nearly equal, but that, however the cloth might turn out, the goddess was the quicker of the two. A pattern of many pictures was growing on her loom. There was a border of twined branches of the olive, Athene's favorite tree, while in the middle, figures began to appear. As they looked at the glowing colors, the spectators realized that Athene was weaving into her pattern a last warning to Arachne. The central figure was the goddess herself competing with Poseidon for possession of the city of Athens; but in the four corners were mortals who had tried to strive with gods and pictures of the awful fate that had overtaken them. The goddess ended a little before Arachne and stood back from her marvelous work to see what the maiden was doing.

Never before had Arachne been matched against anyone whose skill was equal, or even nearly equal to her own. As she stole glances from time to time at Athene and saw the goddess working swiftly, calmly, and always a little faster than herself, she became angry instead of frightened, and an evil thought came into her head. Thus as Athene stepped back a pace to watch Arachne finishing her work, she saw that the maiden had taken for her design a pattern of scenes which showed evil or unworthy actions of the gods, how they had deceived fair maidens, resorted to trickery, and appeared on earth from time to time in the form of poor and humble people. When the goddess saw this insult glowing in bright colors on Arachne's loom, she did not wait while the cloth was judged, but stepped forward, her grey eyes blazing with anger, and tore Arachne's work across. Then she struck Arachne across the face. Arachne stood there a moment, struggling with anger, fear, and pride. "I will not live under this insult," she cried, and seizing a rope from the wall, she made a noose and would have hanged herself.

The goddess touched the rope and touched the maiden. "Live on, wicked girl," she said. "Live on and spin, both you and your descendants. When men look at you they may remember that it is not wise to strive with Athene." At that the body of Arachne shriveled up, and her legs grew tiny, spindly, and distorted. There before the eyes of the spectators hung a little dusty brown spider on a slender thread.

All spiders descend from Arachne, and as the Greeks watched them spinning their thread wonderfully fine, they remembered the contest with Athene and thought that it was not right for even the best of men to claim equality with the gods.

My Notes

Creation Stories

1. Look over the following elements of nature. Explain how people in the distant past might have explained the origins of these natural phenomena.

	Explanation
The Sun	
The Stars	
The Earth	
The Moon	
Rainbows	
Thunder	
Snow	

2. Compare your prediction of they way someone in the distant past might have explained these aspects of nature with the way they are explained in this creation story.

_____

_____

_____

Raven and the Sources of Light

Raven goes through a series of transformations in this story. Keep track of his significant actions, and provide an illustration that might accompany one of main actions.

	Significant Actions	Illustration
Before Transformation		
After Transformation into Child		
After Transformation Back to Raven		

My Notes

Myth

> **ABOUT THE AUTHOR**
> Donna Rosenberg has written several books on world mythology. She specializes in retelling myths and other stories in vivid prose that appeals to readers. Her writing is known for excellent translations that preserve the character and style of the original.

RAVEN AND THE SOURCES OF LIGHT

by Donna Rosenberg

Long ago when the world was young, the earth and all living creatures were shrouded in the darkness of an eternal night, for neither the sun nor the moon shone in the sky. It was said that a great chief who lived at the headwaters of the Nass River was keeping all this light for himself, but no one was certain, for the light was so carefully hidden that no one had ever actually seen it. The chief knew that his people were suffering, but he was a selfish man and did not care.

Raven was sad for his people, for he knew that without the sun the earth would not bring forth the food the Haida needed to survive, and without the moon his people could not see to catch fish at night. Raven decided to rescue the light. He knew that the way from the Queen Charlotte Islands to the source of the Nass River was very long, so he collected a group of pebbles. As he flew, whenever he became tired he dropped a pebble into the sea. It immediately formed an island where Raven could alight on solid land and rest for a while.

When Raven arrived at the chief's village, he said to himself, "I must find a way to live in the chief's house and capture the light." Raven thought and thought. Finally he exclaimed, "I know just the way! I will change myself into something very small and wait in the stream to be caught."

So Raven transformed himself into a seed and floated on the surface of the nearby stream. When the chief's daughter came to draw water, Raven was ready. No matter how she tried to drink some of the water, the seed was always in her way. Finally she tired of trying to remove it, and she drank it along with the water.

The woman became pregnant, and in time she gave birth to a son, who was Raven in disguise. The chief loved his grandson, and whatever the child wanted, his grandfather gave him.

As the boy crawled, he noticed many bags hanging on the walls of the lodge. One by one he pointed to them, and one by one his grandfather gave them to him. Finally his grandfather gave him the bag that was filled with stars. The child rolled the bag around on the floor of the lodge, then suddenly let go of it. The bag immediately rose to the ceiling, drifted through the smoke hole, and flew up into the heavens. There it burst open, spilling the stars into the sky.

As the days passed, the boy still wanted to play with toys. He pointed to this bag and that box, stored here and there in grandfather's lodge. His grandfather gave him whatever he chose.

Finally the child cried, "Mae! Mae!" His grandfather took down a bag containing the moon and gave it to his grandson as a toy. The boy chuckled with delight as he rolled it around and around upon the floor of the lodge. Suddenly he let go of that bag just as he had let go of the bag of stars. The bag immediately rose to the ceiling, drifted through the smoke hole, and flew up into the heavens. There it burst open, spilling the moon into the sky.

The boy continued to play with bag after bag and box after box until one day he pointed to the last box left in the lodge. His grandfather took him upon his lap and said, "When I open this box, I am giving you the last and dearest of my possessions, the sun. Please take care of it!"

My Notes

My Notes

Then the chief closed the smoke hole and picked up the large wooden box he had kept hidden among other boxes in the shadows of one corner of the lodge. Inside the large box a second wooden box nestled in the wrappings of a spider's web, and inside that box, a third wooden box nestled. The chief opened box after box until he came to the eighth and smallest of the wooden boxes. As soon as the chief removed the sun from this box, his lodging was flooded with a brilliant light.

The child laughed with delight as his grandfather gave him the fiery ball to play with. He rolled the sun around the floor of the lodging until he tired of the game and pushed it aside. His grandfather then replaced the sun in its box and replaced the box inside the other seven boxes.

Day after day Raven and his grandfather repeated this process. Raven would point to the sun's box, play with it until he tired of it, and then watch as his grandfather put the fiery ball away into its series of boxes.

Finally the day came when the chief was not as careful as usual. He forgot to close the smoke hole, and he no longer watched Raven play with the fiery ball. The child resumed his Raven shape, grasped the ball of light in his claws, and flew up through the smoke hole into the sky, traveling in the direction of the river.

When he spied people fishing in the dark, he alighted on a tree and said to them, "If you will give me some fish, I will give you some light."

At first they did not believe him. They knew that the light was well hidden and that Raven was often a lazy trickster. However, when Raven raised his wing and showed enough light for them to fish with ease, they gave him part of their catch. Day after day they repeated this procedure, until Raven tired of eating fish.

Finally he lifted his wing, grabbed the sun with both claws and tossed it high into the sky. "Now my people will have light both day and night!" he exclaimed. And from that day until this, the sun, moon, and stars have remained in the sky.

Creating an Illustrated Myth

SUGGESTED LEARNING STRATEGIES: **Brainstorming, Graphic Organizer, Prewriting, Drafting, Revising, Self-Editing, Sharing and Responding, Peer-Editing**

Assignment

Working with a partner, create an original myth that explains a natural phenomenon and also teaches a lesson or a moral. Include illustrations that complement the myth as it unfolds.

Steps

Prewriting

1. Review the myths that you have read in this unit. Identify the purpose of each myth and its theme. What does it explain? What moral or lesson does it teach?

2. Complete the brainstorming chart below. In the left column, identify natural phenomena; then fill in the other columns to develop ideas for possible myths. Think about illustrations that might accompany your ideas for myths.

Natural Phenomenon	Describe character(s) that are associated with the phenomenon	Ideas for Story: What choices will character(s) face?	Lesson It Teaches
Volcano			

3. Now, select the one idea that seems most promising for you to write. On separate paper, identify at least three illustrations that you can imagine for your myth.

4. Create an outline for your myth by working out the plot structure on the plot diagram. Answer the following questions as you prepare your outline:

▶ How will your myth begin? Why?

▶ What will be the main action in your myth?

▶ How will your myth conclude?

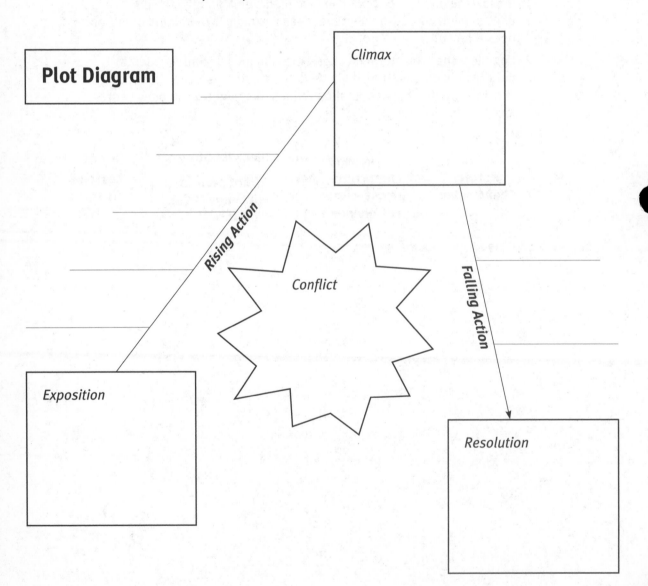

Plot Diagram

Climax

Rising Action

Falling Action

Conflict

Exposition

Resolution

Drafting

5. Draft your myth, taking care to include the elements of an effective narrative that you have examined earlier in this unit:

   ▶ An opening or lead that hooks the reader

   ▶ An event retold vividly

   ▶ Details and thorough descriptions of characters and settings

   ▶ The characters' response to the event, including their feelings and thoughts

   ▶ Effective and purposeful dialogue

   ▶ A reflection on the lesson learned or significance of the experience.

6. Provide illustrations to accompany your myth. You can draw pictures yourself, or you can locate appropriate images online or in magazines. Be sure that the illustrations capture the key parts of your myth and that they add a visual layer to your story.

⊼TECHNOLOGY TIP Be aware of using copyrighted images in ways that violate copyright law. You may download or copy an image for personal use and give the source of the image. You may not broadcast the image or use it in another product without obtaining permission from the owner.

Revising Through Self-Assessment

7. What is the strongest aspect of your myth at this point? Why?

8. What are the TWO areas that need the most work at this point? Why?

9. What revision strategies can you use to improve your draft?

Revising Through Sharing and Responding

10. Share your draft in your writing group. Use the Peer Response Form on the next page to provide feedback. Then, using responses to your draft, revise it for narrative structure and elements, vivid details, and complementary illustrations.

11. Review the grammar and usage tips in this unit as you revise. Be sure to use a variety of sentences and adjectival phrases. Look for and address correct use of pronouns and their antecedents. Also consult the Scoring Guide to aid your revision.

Editing for Publication

12. Edit your draft to correct errors in grammar, punctuation, capitalization, and spelling.

13. Create a title, and assemble your myth and illustrations for publication.

Peer Response Form

Read your myth in your **writing group,** and ask for one member to complete the following.

1. What natural phenomenon is being explained?

2. What lesson or moral does this myth put forward?

3. a. Describe one of the main characters in the myth.

   b. Where should the writers add more details about any of the characters so that readers can understand them better?

4. a. Describe one of the main settings of this myth.

    b. What other details can be added to give readers a more vivid picture
of the setting?

5. Does the story have dialogue? _____Is it in proper format? _____
Where could the writer add more dialogue in order to make the writing
come alive?

6. Does the draft follow the rules of dialogue with correct punctuation and
capitalization?

7. What specific revision strategies in this unit do you recommend the writer
review? Why these?

SCORING GUIDE

Scoring Criteria	Exemplary	Proficient	Emerging
Ideas	The myth explains a natural phenomenon and includes the idea of choice while cleverly teaching a lesson. The myth skillfully uses narrative elements to engage the reader and lead him/her to a satisfying conclusion by • clearly describing the setting • revealing key attributes of character in relation to the choices made • establishing realistic dialogue that moves the action of the plot.	The myth explains a natural phenomenon and teaches a lesson. The myth uses narrative elements to engage the reader by • describing the setting • revealing aspects of character • creating dialogue that advances the plot.	The myth lacks an explanation of the natural phenomenon or may fail to teach a lesson. The myth is hard to follow and does not include sufficient use of narrative elements to assist the reader.
Organization	The myth is well organized and contains the following: • a clear exposition • detailed rising action leading to a suspenseful climax • engaging falling action that cleverly resolves itself, revealing a lesson about life.	The myth is organized and contains the following: • exposition • rising action • conflict • climax • falling action • resolution • lesson about life.	The myth is unorganized and is missing key elements of plot structure and a lesson about life.
Presentation	The myth includes many vivid illustrations that enhance the ideas using effective symbolism.	The myth includes illustrations that connect with the ideas presented in the myth.	The myth does not include illustrations that demonstrate the ideas presented.

SCORING GUIDE

Scoring Criteria	Exemplary	Proficient	Emerging
Use of Language	Vivid details are used to enhance the description.	Details are attempted to enhance the description.	Inappropriate details are used and/or the description is inadequate.
Conventions	Writing has few or no errors in spelling, punctuation, or capitalization.	Spelling, punctuation, and capitalization mistakes do not detract from the myth.	Spelling, punctuation, and capitalization mistakes detract from meaning and/ or readability.
Evidence of Writing Process	The myth demonstrates extensive evidence of the various stages of the writing process.	The myth demonstrates evidence of the various stages of the writing process.	The myth demonstrates little or no evidence of the stages of the writing process.
Additional Criteria			

Comments: _____

_____

_____

_____

_____

_____

Reflection

An important aspect of growing as a learner is to reflect on where you have been, what you have accomplished, what helped you to learn, and how you will apply your new knowledge in the future. Use the following questions to guide your thinking and to identify evidence of your learning. Use separate notebook paper.

Thinking about Concepts

1. Using specific examples from this unit, respond to the Essential Questions:

   • How do authors use narrative elements to create a story?

   • Why is storytelling an important aspect of a culture or society?

2. Consider the academic vocabulary from this unit (**Personal Narrative, Sensory Details, Characterization, Folklore, Plot, Theme,** and **Symbolism**) and select 3–4 terms of which your understanding has grown. For each term, answer the following questions:

   • What was your understanding of the word prior to the unit?

   • How has your understanding of the word evolved throughout the unit?

   • How will you apply your understanding in the future?

Thinking about Connections

3. Review the activities and products (artifacts) you created. Choose those that most reflect your growth or increase in understanding.

4. For each artifact that you choose, record, respond, and reflect on your thinking and understanding, using the following questions as a guide:

   a. What skill/knowledge does this artifact reflect, and how did you learn this skill/knowledge?

   b. How did your understanding of the power of language expand through your engagement with this artifact?

   c. How will you apply this skill or knowledge in the future?

5. Create this reflection as Portfolio pages—one for each artifact you choose. Use the following model for your headings and commentary on questions.

Thinking About Thinking

Portfolio Entry

Concept:

Description of Artifact:

Commentary on Questions:

What Influences
My Choices?

Essential Questions

? How do advertisers attempt to influence consumers?

? How do purpose and audience shape the content in a persuasive text?

Unit Overview

There are many reasons why people choose to do something, buy something, or think a certain way. In this unit, you will investigate how persuasion influences people's choices. First, you will look at the art of persuasion in nonprint texts, then move on to print texts. By the end of the unit, you will become a skilled reader and writer of persuasive texts and be able to recognize the techniques writers use to influence the choices you make.

What Influences My Choices?
Contents

Goals

▶ To understand how our lives are affected by persuasion

▶ To identify and analyze persuasive techniques, appeals, language, and images in print and nonprint texts

▶ To create persuasive advertisements and to write persuasive letters to the editor

ACADEMIC VOCABULARY

Consumerism

Media

Advertising

Persuasion

Audience

Purpose

Editorial

Learning Focus:

Persuasive Advertising

In previous activities, you have worked extensively to investigate personal choices and to read about choices found in fictional stories. Have you thought about how your personal choices are influenced by the outside world, especially the media?

You may be thinking to yourself that you're independent and like to go your own way. Or you may like to fit in with others and follow their lead. Advertisers use the media to try to appeal to different viewpoints and to sway opinions. The various types of **media** are a powerful and persuasive force in all of our lives. Media includes broadcast, electronic, and print. Examples of broadcast or electronic media are the Internet, television, radio, movies, electronic billboards, and video games. Print media includes billboards, newspapers, magazines, newsletters, and direct mail advertising.

Whether surfing the Web, viewing television, reading a magazine, or walking through a mall, you are constantly bombarded by advertisements trying to influence you to buy something. In order to help you buy what you need (versus impulse purchases of items you later regret buying), you must become active, critical **consumers** of media messages.

So why are **media** so successful? What do they do that affects us and influences our choices? Advertisers use persuasive words, phrases, techniques, and **advertising** claims to convince specific audiences to buy their products. With an understanding of these features, you will be able to interpret, analyze, and evaluate the media messages you encounter daily, as well as create media that express a point of view and influence others.

Independent Reading: In this unit, you will read several informational texts about advertising. To learn more about media and how the various media channels present information, you may want to choose nonfiction articles, either print or online, related to current events.

SUGGESTED LEARNING STRATEGIES: **Marking the Text, Think-Pair-Share, Skimming/Scanning, Summarizing/Paraphrasing, Graphic Organizer, Close Reading**

Essential Questions

1. How do advertisers attempt to influence consumers?

    They make appealing images and famous people sponser it so every wants to copy them.

2. How do purpose and audience shape the content in a persuasive text?

    It tells you the advantages of buying the product

Unit Overview and Learning Focus

Predict what you think this unit is about. Use the words or phrases that stood out to you when you read the Unit Overview and the Learning Focus.

Persuasive Essays,

Embedded Assessment 1

What knowledge must you have (what do you need to know) to succeed on the Embedded Assessment? What skills must you have (what must you be able to do)?

Looking at My Choices

Every single day we make choices. Sometimes these are important choices, and sometimes they are not: What will I eat? What clothes will I wear? Will I do my homework now or later? Should I go to that movie? When you answer these questions, you have made a choice.

1. List some choices you have made in the last day or two.

1.	**2.**	**3.**
4.	**5.**	**6.**

2. Select three choices from your list above, and explain why you made each choice. A sample has been done for you.

Identify Choice	Explain Why You Made That Choice
I ate a salad today.	A salad is healthier than french fries.

3. Often people close to you directly influence your choices. Identify a few of your choices that were at least somewhat influenced by the people listed below.

Person	Choices Made Because of That Person and the Person's Influence Over You
A friend	
A parent or guardian	
A teacher	

Today's Youth Look to Advertising as Much as Their Friends When Making Purchase Decisions

from Harris Interactive

Today's youth have an income of $233 billion and influence many household purchases—and not only youth products. Today's "wired" kids are receiving many advertisers' messages directly and some are particularly attuned to advertising to guide their purchase decision-making. Youth, particularly tweens, agree that they often pay close attention to advertisements to make sure they buy the right products (36% of tweens ages 8-12 and 22% of teens ages 13-18). The influence of advertising is similar to the influence of friends on young people's purchase decisions, with 36 percent of tweens and 23 percent of teens saying that they often look to see what their friends use and buy when making purchase decisions.

These are the results of a nationwide survey of 1,306 U.S. children and teenagers (ages 8 to 18) surveyed online by Harris Interactive® between May 18 to 23, 2006. Harris Interactive collaborated with the University of Delaware's Lerner College of Business and Economics on development of the questionnaire for this study.

Advertising likes and dislikes

When it comes to advertising tactics employed by companies, the top three liked by both tweens and teens relate to celebrity and notoriety, including having a famous person use a product (tweens 39% and teens 21%), having a person in a movie use a product (tweens 33% and teens 20%), and getting the company name included in the name of a sporting event or stadium (tweens 33% and teens 22%). Newer advertising tactics are viewed more negatively by young people. For example, only five percent of youth like it when companies advertise their product on cell phones (compared to 50% who dislike it), and four percent like it when companies get someone to mention a product in online chat sessions (with 41% disliking this tactic).

Truth in advertising

Youth seem to consider themselves to be discerning when it comes to advertising, and they can even be skeptical about what companies tell them. Fewer than one in ten (6%) 8-18 year olds agree with the statement "advertisements tell the truth", and more than half (57%) say they often notice tricks companies use to get them to buy something. About three-quarters (73%) agree that companies try to get people to buy things they do not really need. And, regarding mention of a product in an online chatroom, very few (only 1% of teens and 6% of tweens) feel that they can trust the discussion.

My Notes

TABLE 1
PURCHASE DECISION-MAKING
"How much do you agree with the following?"

Base: All youth ages 8-18 years	Summary of Strongly / Somewhat Agree		
	Teens age 8-12	Teens age 13-18	Total age 8-18
	%	%	%
I like to buy things my friends have.	62	32	44
To make sure that I buy the right products, I often look to see what my friends use and buy.	36	23	29
To make sure I buy the right products I often pay close attention to advertisements.	36	22	29
If I do not have much experience with a product, I often ask my friends to tell me what to buy.	29	33	31
If I do not have much experience with a product, I often ask someone who works in a store to tell me what to buy.	22	28	26
I try to buy products that I've seen before on television or in the movies	53	29	40
I often use the Internet to get information about products before I buy them	30	51	40

TABLE 2
TELLING THE TRUTH ABOUT PRODUCTS
"How much do you agree with the following?"

Base: All youth ages 8-18 years	Summary of Strongly / Somewhat Agree		
	Teens age 8-12	Teens age 13-18	Total age 8-18
	%	%	%
What famous people say about a product is true	17	5	11
When companies say their product is the best, they are always telling the truth	10	3	6
Companies can say anything about their product, even if it isn't true	54	42	47
When someone in an online chatroom tells you about a product, you can trust what they say	6	1	3
Advertisements tell the truth	9	4	6
Products are used in movies just to make the movies more realistic	42	26	33
Companies want you to buy their product only if it is the best one for you	15	8	11
I often notice tricks that companies use to get me to buy something	51	61	57
Companies try to get people to buy things that they don't really need	76	71	73
Companies tell you only the good things about their products; they don't tell you the bad things	77	70	72

FROM RAMP TO RICHES

by Lea Goldman

Tony Hawk has been falling off skateboards for three decades, but in November he took the scariest tumble of his high-flying career. Inverted 11.5 feet in the air on a fullloop, Hawk, 36, stalled and crashed, plummeting headfirst. The botched stunt left him with a concussion, a fractured pelvis, 15 stitches above his left eye, the bull's-eye for one beauty of a shiner. It was so violent that even MTV, which was filming, kept it off the air.

Broken bones are a cost of doing business for the world's most famous skateboarder. "The Birdman," a beanpole at 6 foot 3, has endured a dozen concussions, broken his elbow, and cracked his skull and several ribs. He has two screws in one elbow, has knocked out his two front teeth three times and has ripped up his legs so often that his shins bear more scars than skin. He jokes that his ankles sound like a tin drum roll when he climbs the stairs.

But look at the feats for fans to savor — the 80 air-bending tricks he created, the 73 first-place titles. Hawk earns upwards of $9 million a year, all for defying gravity on a toy that once was the domain of 12-year-old boys. Last year Tony Hawk's brand generated $300 million in retail sales: clothes, skateboards, arena tours and, above all, videogames. Now he must pull off a daunting new stunt: phasing out his bone-crunching performances while keeping the money rolling in for years to come.

In a decade skateboarding has swerved from the fringe into the mainstream, rolling up $5.7 billion a year in equipment and apparel sales. Eleven million kids use skateboards in the U.S., more than the number in organized baseball. Tony Hawk drives the sport harder than anyone else, having transformed himself from cult hero into a richly compensated pitchman for McDonald's and other brands looking to buy attention from youngsters. "Used to be a successful skateboarder had his picture in a magazine and then got some free stuff," he says.

Skateboarding's big rise began in 1995, when ESPN aired its first X Games, a faux Olympics for "alternative" sports. Hawk, who started skateboarding at age 8 in San Diego, Calif., was already a legend among skateboarders. He signed on and enlisted cool skateboarders who might otherwise have rejected the event as crass commercialism. Hawk took first place in the "vert" category for aerial tricks and gained a national following. "From the get-go, Tony realized the value of the exposure," says Christopher Stiepock, general manager of the X Games.

My Notes

GRAMMAR & USAGE

A **preposition** links the noun or pronoun following it (its object) to another word in a sentence. **Prepositional phrases** add specific or necessary detail in sentences. They function as adjectives or adverbs.

Adverb phrase modifying the verb *has swerved*: ...skateboarding has swerved *from the fringe* ...

Adjective phrase modifying the noun *cost*: cost *of doing business*

You can use prepositional phrases to add specific details when you write. Take care to use correct subject-verb agreement. When a prepositional phrase separates the subject and verb, the verb agrees with the subject, not with the object of the prepositional phrase.

My Notes

Three years later Hawk struck a deal with Activision for his own skateboarding videogame. An avid gamer, Hawk insisted on creative input and met with the developers weekly, tweaking the combinations of aerial stunts while ruling out outlandish moves and rejecting some backdrops as too cornball, like one of an Egyptian pyramid. Released in 1999, Tony Hawk's Pro Skater was an instant success, selling 5 million copies. Activision has since churned out five Tony Hawk games (another is on its way) and sold 20 million copies.

Two years ago Hawk got Activision to give him a $20 million advance, a royalty as high as $1.50 per game and use of a private plane. The deal expires in 2015, when Hawk will be 47. Only John Madden, the NFL-coach-turned-announcer-turned-videogame-star, surpasses Hawk in sport videogames. Hawk, semiretired, hasn't seriously competed since 1999, when he became the first-ever to land a "900" — two-and-a-half rotations — high above the steel lips of the half-pipe; few daredevils perform it.

"When we signed him, he was basically retired, like Madden," says Activision's chief executive, Robert Kotick. "But that's what you want— there's no risk of him losing. It's a franchise that doesn't end when his activities end."

To ensure his staying power, Hawk is judicious about licensing deals, rejecting some sponsors the way he rejected the pyramid scene. He refused permission to a pasta company that wanted to manufacture Hawk-shaped pasta pieces. He keeps his $50 million-a-year clothing line (T shirts and cargo shorts) out of Kmart and Wal-Mart, limiting them to department stores, his own three stores (in Paramus, N.J., Los Angeles and Salt Lake City) and skateboard shops. "You won't ever find a Hawk T shirt for $5 in the discount bin. It ain't gonna happen," says Hawk's manager — and older sister — Patricia Hawk.

These days Tony Hawk spends less time suspended in midair and more time on-air, doing analysis for ESPN and appearing on MTV. Two years ago he launched the Boom Boom HuckJam, a raucous 30-city tour featuring stunts using skates, BMX bikes and motorcycles, set to live music. Hawk, the majority owner, fronted $2 million to mount the arena show. Last fall HuckJam brought in $14 million in merchandise, ticket sales and sponsorships.

4. Working with a partner or a small group, discuss how the following influences affect your choices. You do not need to list actual choices that you have made, but rather you can discuss choices in general.

Influence	Effect on Choices
Friends/peers	
Advertisements	
Politicians or government	
Movies/TV/Music	
Other	

> **GRAMMAR & USAGE**
> Learn to use affect and effect correctly. *Affect* is generally used as a verb and means "to influence." *Effect* is generally used as a noun and means "a result."

5. Rate each of the following categories in terms of their influence on your choices. Use the scale below.

4	3	2	1	X
A lot of influence	Some influence	A little influence	No influence	I do not know

1. _____	My parents or guardian	2. _____	My friends
3. _____	My teachers	4. _____	Myself
5. _____	Peer pressure	6. _____	Advertisements
7. _____	Politicians or government	8. _____	Society
9. _____	Other _____	10. _____	Other _____

6. Create a bar graph to represent the influences that others have on your choices. Then explain your graph to a partner.

Looking at My Choices

WORD CONNECTIONS

An analogy may show a part-to-whole relationship in which the first word is part of the second word. In a whole-to-part relationship, the opposite occurs. Which of the following has a part-to-whole relationship like that in *topic sentence : paragraph*?

a. exclamation point : period

b. chapter : book

c. book : movie

As your teacher provides a lesson on the structure and components of an **expository paragraph**, pay attention to the following elements. Take additional notes as necessary.

Topic Sentence: a statement of opinion; the main idea of a paragraph

Details: evidence (facts, statistics, examples) that supports the topic sentence

Commentary: explanation of the importance of the detail and the way it supports the topic sentence; elaboration reflects voice and style

Concluding Sentence: universal idea; reflects voice and style; answers the question "So what?"

Your teacher will guide you through the process of writing a sample expository paragraph in response to the writing prompt below. Copy the sample in the space below.

Sample Topic Sentence: I am most influenced by my parents, especially when I have to choose between right and wrong.

Writing Prompt: On your own paper, write a well-developed expository paragraph about what and who most influence the choices you make. Provide support by describing actual choices you have made because of those influences, and explain the effect of those choices on your life. Be sure to use a variety of sentence structures with prepositional, adjectival, and adverbial phrases in your draft. Edit for correct use of punctuation and subject-verb agreement.

Consumeropoly

Consumeropoly: Rules of the Game

1. In your group of four, select one person to be the banker. This person will be in charge of managing and distributing the money ($1200, or $300 per student).

2. Your teacher will give each group a game board, a die, and four game pieces. Put each game piece on START.

3. The banker will give $100 to each player.

4. The person whose birthday is the nearest to today's date goes first. The person to the right will go next, and so on.

5. Players roll the die and move the number of spaces showing on the die. Players always move in the direction of the arrow, unless instructed to move differently.

6. If a player lands on a space and buys something, the player gives the stated amount to the banker. If a player lands on a space with directions to move to another space, the player moves to that space.

7. A player's turn ends when he or she has rolled, moved, and paid the amount owed. Some spaces earn players money from the bank, and some are Free Zones. Each player rolls only once per turn.

8. When a player lands on or passes START, he or she will receive $100 from the bank.

9. A player who is unable to pay for an item in any round is out of the game. A player is not allowed to receive a "loan" from any other player or from the bank.

10. The game ends when only one person has money remaining, or when your teacher calls time.

During Play

Keep track of all the money that you earn and spend during each round you play. A "round" ends every time you reach or pass START.

Round	Amount Earned	Amount Spent	Round	Amount Earned	Amount Spent
1	$100		7	$100	
2	$100		8	$100	
3	$100		9	$100	
4	$100		10	$100	
5	$100		11	$100	
6	$100		Total		

Consumeropoly

After Playing

1. Overall, how much money did you spend? _____

   How much did you earn? _____

2. Did anyone in your game go bankrupt? _____

3. Look back at the game board. Some spaces sent you to a store, where you then had to spend money. What were some of the stores and directions? Are these anything like real life? How?

   _____

   _____

4. You did not have any choice about what you spent during the game. How did this make you feel? Is this at all like real life? How?

   _____

5. The game is called "Consumeropoly," a combination of the words *consumer* and *monopoly*. What do you think the word *consumer* means?

   _____

6. Read the following sentence and define the highlighted word: "America is a society based on consumerism."

   Definition:

   _____

   Do you agree or disagree with the statement made in the sentence above? Explain.

   _____

7. If you could add a new space to the board or a new rule to the game, what would you add?

   What effect might your new space or rule have on the game?

   _____

8. What do you think was the point in playing the game?

   _____

9. What do you think this unit will be about?

   _____

Media, Advertising, and Consumer Choices

SUGGESTED LEARNING STRATEGIES: Discussion Groups, Graphic Organizer, Visualizing, Word Map

Part One: Anticipation Guide for "Facts About Marketing to Children"

Before Reading

1. Before you read the article on the next page, read the statements below and mark each statement as either true or false. After you read the article, return to this chart and check your responses.

Before Reading	After Reading	
		1. The average American child is exposed to almost 22,000 television commercials a year.
		2. American youth typically spend more time with various media (TV, iPods, cell phones, and instant messaging) than they do in the classroom.
		3. Twenty-five percent of kids say that buying a certain product makes them feel better about themselves.
		4. American children aged 12 to 17 will ask their parents for products they have seen advertised an average of three times until the parents finally give in.
		5. Over half of American kids say that nagging their parents for products almost always works.
		6. Advertising aimed at children is estimated at $5 billion.

After Reading

2. In "Facts About Marketing to Children," which facts were most surprising or interesting to you? Why?

_____

_____

_____

_____

_____

_____

My Notes

Informational Text

FACTS About Marketing to CHILDREN

From The Center for a New American Dream

Children as Targets

- Advertising directed at children is estimated at over $15 billion annually – about 2.5 times more than what it was in 1992.[1]

- Over the past two decades, the degree to which marketers have scaled up efforts to reach children is staggering. In 1983, they spent $100 million on television advertising to kids. Today, they pour roughly 150 times that amount into a variety of mediums that seek to infiltrate every corner of children's worlds.[2]

- According to a leading expert on branding, 80 percent of all global brands now deploy a "tween strategy."[3]

Commercial Television

- The average American child today is exposed to an estimated 40,000 television commercials a year — over 100 a day.[4]

- A task force of the American Psychological Association (APA) has recommended restrictions on advertising that targets children under the age of eight, based on research showing that children under this age are unable to critically comprehend televised advertising messages and are prone to accept advertiser messages as truthful, accurate and unbiased.[5]

Beyond the Tube

- According to the Kaiser Family Foundation, youth are multitasking their way through a wide variety of electronic media daily, juggling iPods and instant messaging with TV and cell phones. In fact, they pack 8.5 hours of media exposure into 6.5 hours each day, seven days a week — which means that they spend more time plugged in than they do in the classroom.[6]

WORD CONNECTIONS

Advertisements sometimes include foreign words that have entered the English language. For example, advertising about holidays may include *piñata, fiesta, Kwanzaa,* or *Mardi Gras.*

- By the mid 1990s, direct marketing, promotions, and sponsorships actually accounted for 80 percent of marketing dollars.[7]

New Dream Poll, "Nag Factor"

According to a national survey commissioned by the Center for a New American Dream:

- American children aged 12 to 17 will ask their parents for products they have seen advertised an average of nine times until the parents finally give in.

- More than 10 percent of 12- to 13-year-olds admitted to asking their parents more than 50 times for products they have seen advertised.

- More than half of the children surveyed (53%) said that buying certain products makes them feel better about themselves. The number is even higher among 12- to 13-year-olds: 62% say that buying certain products makes them feel better about themselves.

- Nearly a third of those surveyed (32%) admitted to feeling pressure to buy certain products such as clothes and CDs because their friends have them. Over half of 12- to 13-year-olds (54%) admitted to feeling such pressure.

- The nagging strategy is paying dividends for kids and marketers alike: 55% of kids surveyed said they are usually successful in getting their parents to give in.[8]

What Kids Really Want

- According to a 2003 New American Dream poll, 57 percent of children age 9-14 would rather do something fun with their mom or dad than go to the mall to go shopping.[9]

In Schools

- The American Beverage Association (formerly National Soft Drink Association) at one point estimated that nearly two thirds of schools nationwide had exclusive "pouring rights" contracts with soda companies.[10]

Harming Children's Well-Being

- Obesity: Rising levels of childhood obesity track an explosion of junk food ads in recent years[13].

- Emotional well-being: Author and Boston College sociology professor Juliet Schor finds links between immersion in consumer culture and depression, anxiety, low self esteem, and conflicts with parents[14].

My Notes

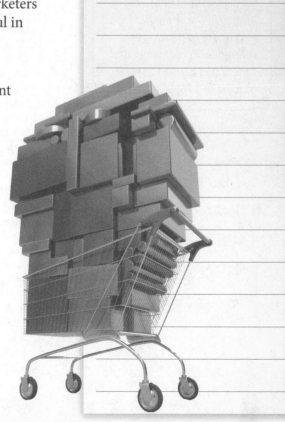

My Notes

- Financial self-control: National surveys reveal that kids are leaving high school without a basic understanding of issues relating to savings and credit card debt. No surprise, then, that over the past decade, credit card debt among 18-24 year olds more than doubled[16].

End notes

1. Susan Linn, *Consuming Kids: The Hostile Takeover of Childhood* (New York: The New Press, 2004), 1.
2. Juliet Schor, *Born to Buy: The Commercialized Child and the New Consumer Culture* (New York: Scribner, 2004), 21.
3. Ann Hulbert, "Tweens 'R' Us," *The New York Times*, November 28, 2004, www.nytimes.com/2004/11/28/magazine/28WWLN.html?ex=1259384400&%2338;en=056ae35fb63f65eb&%2338;ei=5088& (accessed March 8, 2006).
4. American Psychological Association, "Television Advertising Leads to Unhealthy Habits in Children; Says APA Task Force," February 23, 2004,www.apa.org/releases/childrenads.html (accessed March 8, 2006).
5. Ibid.
6. Donald F. Roberts, Ulla G. Foehr, Victoria Rideout, *Generation M: Media in the Lives of 8-18 Year-Olds*, The Henry J. Kaiser Family Foundation, March 9, 2005, www.kff.org/entmedia/7251.cfm (accessed March 9, 2006).
7. Schor, 85.
8. "Thanks to Ads, Kids Won't Take No, No, No, No, No, No, No, No, No for an Answer," Center for a New American Dream, 2002, www.newdream.org/kids/poll.php (accessed March 5, 2006).
9. "What Do Kids Really Want That Money Can't Buy?" Center for a New American Dream, 2003, www.newdream.org/publications/bookrelease.php (accessed March 8, 2006).
10. Katherine Battle Horgen, "Big Food, Big Money, Big Children," in *Childhood Lost: How American Culture is Failing Our Kids*, Sharna Olfman, ed, 128. (Westport, Connecticut: Praeger Publishers, 2005).
11. "Fat Profits From Channel One's Junk Food Advertising: 1 Out Of 4 Ads is for Junk Food / Soft Drinks," Obligation, Inc., December 9, 2002, www.obligation.org/channelone/2003/fatprofits.html (accessed March 8, 2006).
12. "Channel One," Commercial Alert, www.commercialalert.org/issues-landing.php?subcategory_id 32& category=2 (accessed March 8, 2006).
13. American Psychological Association 2004.
14. Schor, 167-172.
15. Diane Levin, as quoted in Michelle Stockwell, *Childhood for Sale: Consumer Culture's Bid for Our Kids* (Washington, DC: Progressive Policy Institute, July 2005), 2, www.ppionline.org/documents/MARKETING_0804.pdf (accessed March 8, 2006).
16. "Young People Taking on More Debt," www.pbs.org/newshour/extra/features/jan-june05/debt_5-25.html (accessed March 8, 2006).

WORD CONNECTIONS

Endnotes and footnotes sometimes contain foreign words such as *ibid* and *et al.* (short for et alia). *Ibid* means *in the same place* and refers to a previous reference. *Et al.* means *and others* and is used to refer to a list of people.

Part Two: Media Choices

The term *media* refers to specific sources of information and entertainment. Media channels may be print, such as newspapers and magazines, or electronic, like television and the Internet.

ACADEMIC VOCABULARY

Media refers to the various means, or channels, of mass communication, such as radio, television, newspapers, magazines, and the Internet.

1. Place a check mark next to the media channels that you access at least three hours a week.

	Television		Video Games
	Magazines		Music (CDs or MP3s)
	Newspapers		Radio
	Movies		Internet

2. Which type of media do you access most often? _____

   About how many hours a week? _____

   Why do you think you enjoy this media channel more than the others?

   _____

   _____

3. Which type of media do you access least often? _____

   About how many hours a week? _____

   Why do you think you spend so little time with this media channel?

   _____

   _____

4. Just about every type of media is supported by **advertisements**. Commercials appear throughout TV shows, and ads fill many pages of a magazine. We are saturated with advertisements, yet we rarely take time to really notice them. Based on your experience, which type of media has the most ads? How many do you think you would see if you were watching or listening for one hour?

   _____

   _____

   _____

ACADEMIC VOCABULARY

Advertising refers to any form of communication— print, video, sound— that businesses and organizations use to try to convince people to buy their products or services.

Media, Advertising, and Consumer Choices

5. Where else do you see ads? _____

Do you ever see ads in your school? _____ If so, where and when?

_____

_____

6. Spend ONE HOUR with **one** of the media channels below. As you listen, read, or watch, count the number of advertisements. Then, describe and evaluate one specific advertisement.

Media Channel	Number of Ads Per Hour	Specific Advertisement	Would you buy this product? Why or why not?
Television Title of show:		Product: Persuasive Words: Persuasive Images:	
Newspaper or Magazine Name:		Product: Persuasive Words: Persuasive Images:	
Internet Site(s):		Product: Persuasive Words: Persuasive Images:	

7. After you complete the chart, write about your impressions, feelings, and reactions to the advertisements: Are they necessary, annoying, interesting, or funny? Are they effective?

_____

_____

8. Share your responses with a peer or small group. Fill in the rest of the chart above with information from students who accessed different types of media.

Part Three: Consumer Choices

1. Think about some of your most recent consumer choices. Next to each category in the chart below, list at least one specific item that you purchased or spent money on within the past year. If you have not purchased an item from the category, leave that category blank. In the last box, note whether or not you saw an advertisement for the product before you made the purchase.

Category	Brand, Name, or Title of Product	Ad?
Clothing/Shoes		
Movies		
Music		
Food or Soft Drinks		
Another Category: _____		

2. In your opinion, what effect does advertising have on creating popular brands?

• Shoes: _____

• Clothes: _____

3. Does a particular brand affect whether you buy a product? Explain.

_____

_____

4. Are you influenced by advertisements? Explain.

_____

_____

Part Four: Peers' Consumer Choices

1. Survey your classmates about the products they tend to buy. Ask them, "Which brand of _____ do you purchase most often?"

Type of Product	Specific Brands / Tally Marks
Beverage	
Fast Food	
Athletic Shoe	
Clothing	

2. What did you learn about your peers' consumer choices?

_____

_____

_____

_____

3. Do you think peer pressure influences consumer choices? Explain.

_____

_____

_____

_____

Part Five: Celebrities and Consumer Choices

1. With a partner or a small group, identify famous singers, musicians, actors, or sports figures who have influenced how people dress or behave.

Celebrity	Influence

2. Many celebrities earn millions of dollars promoting products to consumers. Working again in pairs or groups, identify two celebrities (athletes or actors) who regularly promote particular products.

Celebrity	Product	Have you bought this product?

3. Write a paragraph responding to the prompt below. Answer the question in your topic sentence, and support your topic sentence with detail (evidence) and commentary (analysis) in the rest of your paragraph.

   Quickwrite: Why do celebrities have a significant influence on consumer choices?

   _____

   _____

   _____

   _____

   _____

4. Working in discussion groups, share your responses. Then paraphrase each writer's viewpoint. Ask questions as needed to help clarify each writer's ideas.

Persuasive Techniques

WORD CONNECTIONS

Persuade comes from a Latin word meaning "to advise or urge." The root *-suad-* is also related to "sweet." To *persuade* is to present in a pleasing manner.

1. Advertisers use many techniques of persuasion to make us want to purchase their products. Read the descriptions of advertising techniques that follow. Then, paraphrase and create a visual representation of each technique. Your visualization may include both words and symbols.

As you read about the techniques, think about **cause and effect**. For example, with bandwagon the persuasion may be that "Everyone is buying this product (cause) so you should buy this product, too (effect)." With the avant-garde appeal, it might be "This product is the newest on the market (cause) and you should be one of the first to have it (effect)."

Technique	Paraphrase	Visualize
Bandwagon: Advertisers make it seem that everyone is buying this product, so you feel you should buy it too. For example, the Consumeropoly game states: "The best, most exciting board game is sweeping the nation. All your friends and neighbors are playing." This statement is intended to make you feel left out if you are not playing.	This makes you feel that it is the most popular game.	Toy →
Avant-Garde: This technique is the opposite of Bandwagon. Advertisers make it seem that the product is so new that you will be the first on the block to have it. The idea is that only super-cool people like you will even know about this product.	Makes you feel the coolest thing and you have to buy it.	

Technique	Paraphrase	Visualize
Testimonials: Advertisers use celebrities and regular people to endorse products. For example, a famous actor urges consumers to buy a product. Pay close attention: sometimes the celebrity does not actually say that he or she uses the product.	Using regular or famous people to show off products	✗
Facts and Figures: Statistics, percentages, and numbers are used to convince you that this product is better or more effective than another product. However, be aware of what the numbers are actually saying. What does "30 percent more effective than the leading brand" really mean?	It is a very vague numbers	✗
Transfer: This technique may be hard to spot. To recognize it, you need to pay attention to the background of the ad or to the story of the commercial. The transfer technique wants you to associate the good feelings created in the ad with the product. For example, a commercial that shows a happy family gathered around a bowl of soup may want you to associate a feeling of comfort and security with their product.	Theres an event going on and the coffee is kind of focused on in the scene	✗

Persuasive Techniques

2. As you look at print and television advertisements your teacher
shows you, analyze the use of persuasive techniques. Circle
the technique(s) used in the ads, and provide evidence for each
technique.

Ad	Persuasive Techniques + Evidence from Ad
Source: *Zoo Safari* Product:	Bandwagon: Avant-Garde: Testimonials: Facts and Figures: Transfer: *Because it because there is a lion in the program*
Source: Product:	Bandwagon: Avant-Garde: Testimonials: Facts and Figures: Transfer:
Source: Product:	Bandwagon: Avant-Garde: Testimonials: Facts and Figures: Transfer:

Which advertisement was the most persuasive? Why? Would you buy
this product based on the advertisement? Why or why not?

_____

_____

Advertising Claims

1. Advertisers portray their products in the most favorable way possible. In some cases, they may stretch the boundaries to make a more persuasive claim. Read the information below, paraphrase it, and give an example of each technique.

> **LITERARY TERMS**
> A **rhetorical question** is asked to emphasize a point or create an effect. No answer is expected.

Technique	Paraphrase	Example
Weasel Words: Advertisers sometimes use words or phrases that seem significant, but on closer inspection are actually meaningless. For example, what does it really mean when a toothpaste ad claims to "help the prevention of cavities"? It does not claim to prevent, only to *help* prevent cavities. Anything that does not hurt can be said to help. Other weasel words or phrases are *virtually*, *looks like*, *fights*, and *best*. You have to look closely to determine whether the word or the claim has merit.		
The Unfinished Claim: Normally, when you make a comparison, you state the two things that are being compared (for example, "I am taller than you"). Advertisers may intentionally not finish the comparison: "This battery has more power to get the job done right." More power than what?		
The Unique Claim: Many products on the market are nearly identical, so advertisers try to make their product stand out. Legally they cannot make false claims, so they focus on a single element that is found only in their product, hoping that consumers will think this means that the product is better. For example: "You'll find that only our cars have the Deluxe Air-flow system." Or, "Hypoglicia can only be found in our product." Do these features make the products better?		
The Rhetorical Claim: Advertisers ask rhetorical questions or make statements so that consumers associate certain ideas and emotions with their product. For example: "Shouldn't you buy the best?" Advertisers try to convince consumers to buy based on their emotional response to the questions; they have made no real claims that their products will deliver on these promises.		

Advertising Claims

2. As you look at various print and television advertisements your teacher shows you, record examples of each type of claim.

Weasel Words	Unfinished Claims
Unique Claims	**Rhetorical Claims**

3. Which advertisement do you think gives the most outrageous claim? Would you buy this product? Why or why not?

_____

_____

_____

_____

4. Look at just the headlines of a few print advertisements. Do you find most of these types of claims in the headlines, or are the claims in the small print text? Why do you think that is?

_____

_____

_____

_____

Audience in Advertisements: Part One

SUGGESTED LEARNING STRATEGIES: Graphic Organizer,
Think-Pair-Share, Word Map

1. List your associations with the word *target*.

goals, you want to achieve

2. Define *target audience*.

audience that you want to reach.

3. List three TV shows, and identify the target audience for each.

TV Show	Intended Audience/Characteristics
Barney	Toddlers
Orange is the new Black	Young adults +11
Dora	Young Kids

4. Your teacher will give you magazine ads intended for the different
audiences below. Study the ads and complete the graphic organizer.

Audience	Persuasive Techniques and Examples from Ads	Advertising Claims and Examples from Ads	Intended Effect
Young Children	Avant a Garde	Unique!	You can only have this store
Teenage Boys	Transference	Un Finished	Feel Special
Teenage Girls	Avant Garde	Weasal Words	Makes you feel that if you got it
Adult Males	Facts and Figures	Unique Claims	Makes you feel
Adult Females	Transfer	Rhetorical	Background there is a panda

5. Choose one advertisement. What is the relationship between **purpose**,
audience, and content in the advertisement?

Common Persuasive Words and Phrases

Janal

1. As you skim through ads, keep a running tally of the following words commonly found in advertising. Use the blank spaces to write other words that you see or hear more than once.

Word: Adjectives	Tally	Word: Verbs	Tally
new		make	
good		get	
better/best		give	
free		have	
delicious		see	
full		look	
clean		need	
special		love	
easy		feel	
extra		choose	

2. In a book called *Confessions of an Advertising Man*, David Ogilvy identified words and phrases that he used most frequently to persuade his audience. Look through newspaper ads and cross off a word or phrase below when you see it. When you cross off five words in a row (across, up, or diagonally), yell "Bingo!"

Bingo Card

suddenly	now	announcing	introducing	improvement (or improved)
amazing	remarkable	miracle	offer	quick
easy	bargain	hurry	free	new
revolutionary	challenge	last chance	it's here	just arrived
important	makes you feel	truth	sensational	compare

3. Why do you think the words listed in the Bingo game are so commonly found in advertising?

_____

_____

4. Working with a partner, choose a common object to sell. Identify your target audience, and create an advertisement for the product. Use a persuasive technique and persuasive words you have learned.

_____

_____

Audience in Advertisements: Part Two

1. List specific ads that you notice in the following types of magazines.

Sports	News	Teen
Music/Entertainment	**Fashion**	**Other:** _____

What do the ads in each type of magazine reveal about their target audience(s)?

_____

_____

Look back through the lists of persuasive words in Activity 2.8. Write the words below that you think are most appropriate for the audiences listed. Why? What other words might appeal to each of these audiences?

Males	Females
Adults	**Teenagers**

Elements of Advertisements

The following text defines five common elements of print advertisements. The first three directly relate to ads, while the last two are associated with the company itself and usually appear in multiple ads. As you read through the text below, identify examples of each element.

Elements of Print Advertisements	Examples
Headline: A short piece of text, usually in larger type, designed to be the first words the audience reads. The headline is usually not the slogan (see below) but is unique to one particular product.	
Image: Any drawing, photograph, illustration, chart, or other graphic that is designed to affect the audience in some purposeful way. For example, an image of an SUV perched high up on a rugged mountain cliff may appeal to one's sense of adventure.	
Copy: The actual text of the ad. The copy is where particular claims are usually made and specific persuasive words are used. For example: "Four out of five dentists . . . ." The amount of copy varies from ad to ad.	
Slogan: A catchphrase that evokes some kind of feeling about the company and the product. Companies look for slogans that are motivating and empowering. A company's slogan rarely changes, especially during a particular ad campaign.	
Logo: A unique design symbol that helps identify the company visually. Nike's swoosh, McDonald's golden arches, and Apple's partially bitten apple are examples of widely recognized company logos. Not all companies have logos like these; sometimes the company's name is written in a distinctive style or font that acts as a logo.	

Elements of Advertisements

Create a new advertisement using all five elements of advertisements.

Product: _____   **Company Name:** _____

Purpose:

Target Audience:

Headline:

Image:

Copy:

Slogan:

Logo:

Analysis of an Advertisement

1. **Prewriting:** Select a print advertisement that stands out to you. In the chart below, analyze the ad to determine how the advertiser is trying to influence a particular audience.

Company: _Armtrong_   **Product:** _Watch_

Persuasive Techniques: *Transte in backround colors*	**Persuasive Claims:** *Weasal Words*
Persuasive Language: *Quality Value, Innovated.*	**Persuasive Images: (layout/design/color)** *Colorful background*
Purpose: *To make you feel magical*	**Target Audience:** **Evidence:** *Adults*

2. **Guided Writing:** Your teacher will guide the class in creating a model analytical paragraph in response to the following writing prompt. Copy the model in the space provided.

Writing Prompt: How does the advertisement attempt to influence the targeted audience? Is the ad effective? Provide specific detail from the ad to support your analysis.

_____

_____

_____

_____

_____

_____

> **LITERARY TERMS**
>
> To **analyze** is to study details of a work to identify essential features or meaning. An analysis may also look at the parts of a work and how they relate to the whole work.

3. Drafting: Write your own response to the writing prompt below, using the ad that you selected and analyzed in Step 1.

Writing Prompt: How does the advertisement attempt to influence the targeted audience? Is the ad effective? Provide specific detail from the ad to support your analysis.

_____

_____

_____

_____

_____

_____

_____

_____

_____

_____

4. Revising: Use feedback from your peers to revise your draft.

_____

_____

_____

_____

_____

_____

_____

_____

_____

_____

Analyzing an Advertisement and Creating a New One

SUGGESTED LEARNING STRATEGIES: **Graphic Organizer, Marking the Text, Drafting, Self-Editing, Peer Editing**

Assignment

Your assignment has three parts. First, select a print advertisement, and write a well-developed analytical paragraph that identifies specific techniques, claims, language, and images in the ad and analyzes the effect of these elements on the intended audience. Next, create a new advertisement for the same product that is targeted to a different audience. Finally, write a reflection to explain the relationship between the content of an ad and the intended audience. Support your explanation by pointing out differences between the original and new ads.

Steps

Analytical Paragraph: Prewriting/Planning

1. Look through magazines and newspapers to locate effective print advertisements. Select two that you think might work well for this project. Be sure your teacher approves the advertisements you select.

2. Complete the following graphic organizers to examine the persuasive techniques, claims, language, images, and the targeted audience for each advertisement.

Product One:_____

Persuasive Techniques	Claims

Persuasive Language	Images

Intended Audience + Evidence:

Product Two:_____

Persuasive Techniques	Claims
Persuasive Language	**Images**

Intended Audience + Evidence:

Analytical Paragraph: Drafting

3. Choose one of the advertisements and draft an analytical paragraph. Briefly describe the product and tell where the advertisement was placed (for example, type of magazine). Then identify and analyze the advertisement's purpose, target audience, techniques, claims, language, images, and effect on the audience. You will share your paragraph with others, so make your draft as legible as possible.

Analytical Paragraph: Revising and Editing for Publication

4. Share your draft with your writing group to get feedback about the clarity of your ideas, the accuracy and depth of your analysis, and the organization of your paragraph. Incorporate appropriate suggestions into the final draft of your paragraph. Revisit the Scoring Guide to ensure that you are meeting specific criteria.

5. Next, brainstorm ideas for a new advertisement for the product: What other audiences may be interested in this product? Which persuasive techniques would be most effective for each audience?

	New Audiences	Persuasive Techniques
Product:		

New Advertisement: Prewriting/Planning

6. Select a new audience, and use the graphic organizer to begin designing your new advertisement.

New Audience: _____

Persuasive Elements	New Advertisement	Why would this be effective for the new audience?
Techniques		
Claims		
Language: • **Words** • **Phrases** • **Slogan**		
Images: • **Layout/Design** • **Colors** • **Logo**		

New Advertisement: Drafting/Revising

7. Create a draft of your new advertisement. You may sketch your images at this stage, but use the colors you plan to use in your final visuals. Show your sketches to several people in your targeted audience who are willing to give you honest feedback. Ask each person if your advertisement appeals to him or her and whether or not it is persuasive. Incorporate appropriate suggestions for revision into your draft. Take detailed notes on separate paper; you may want to refer to these responses in your analysis. Revisit the Scoring Guide to ensure that you are meeting specific criteria.

New Advertisement: Editing for Publication

8. Following your teacher's instructions, edit your advertisement and create a final copy. You can draw the final images or use photographs, online images, or pictures from magazines.

↗ **TECHNOLOGY TIP** You may use digital photography, but obtain permission before you take photographs of people. If you use copyrighted images, remember that you must obtain permission before using them for anything other than this class assignment.

Reflection: Prewriting/Planning

9. Use the Venn diagram below to contrast specific elements of the original and new advertisements.

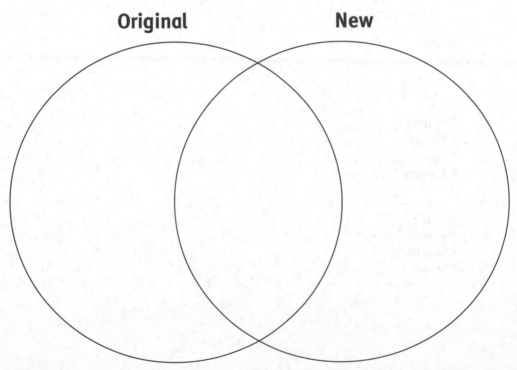

Original   New

Reflection: Drafting/Revising

10. Write a reflection that explains the relationship between the content of an advertisement and the intended audience. Support your explanation by citing and analyzing differences between the original and new advertisements. After you have created a draft, revise your ideas and organization. Revisit the Scoring Guide to ensure you are meeting specific criteria.

Reflection: Editing for Publication

11. Create a final copy of your reflection on separate paper. Remember to check your work for spelling, punctuation, grammar, and correct sentence structure.

Analyzing an Advertisement and Creating a New One

SCORING GUIDE

Scoring Criteria	Exemplary	Proficient	Emerging
Ideas	The analysis of the original advertisement is well written and demonstrates a thorough understanding of persuasive elements including purpose, target audience, persuasive techniques, and effect.	The analysis of the original advertisement demonstrates an understanding of persuasive elements including purpose, target audience, persuasive techniques, and effect.	The analysis of the original advertisement does not show a clear understanding of persuasive elements including purpose, target audience, persuasive techniques, and/or effect.
Presentation	The new advertisement is skillfully designed and visually appealing. It contains persuasive techniques, claims, language, and images that powerfully entice the new target audience to purchase the product.	The new advertisement is designed with persuasive techniques, claims, language, and images that encourage the new target audience to purchase the product.	The new advertisement does not contain relevant and/or accurate persuasive techniques, claims, language, and/or images. It does not appeal to the new target audience or encourage the purchase of the product.
Reflection	The reflection demonstrates a sophisticated understanding of the relationship between advertising content and the intended audience. An insightful comparison between old and new ads demonstrates the writer's understanding of this relationship.	The reflection demonstrates an understanding of the relationship between advertising content and the intended audience. A comparison between the old and new ads demonstrates the writer's understanding of this relationship.	The reflection does not adequately demonstrate an understanding of the relationship between advertising content and the intended audience. A comparison between the old and new ads is vague or irrelevant.
Conventions	The writing has few or no errors in spelling, punctuation, or capitalization.	Spelling, punctuation, and capitalization mistakes do not detract from the text.	Spelling, punctuation, and capitalization mistakes detract from meaning and/or readability.
Evidence of Writing Process	There is extensive evidence of each stage in the writing process.	There is evidence of each stage in the writing process.	The texts demonstrate little or no evidence of the stages of the writing process.
Additional Criteria			

Comments: _____

Learning Focus:

Persuasive Writing

In the first part of this unit, you learned how to analyze and create a persuasive advertisement, which requires an understanding of how **purpose** and **audience** shape content (use of persuasive words, phrases, and techniques). Now you will extend your knowledge of *persuasion* by learning how to write a persuasive text in the form of a letter to the editor.

How do you persuade others? You may influence, or persuade, friends because you have a long-standing relationship with them. When you are communicating with friends and classmates, it may seem easy to persuade or influence because you can react to their comments and continue to add your own.

This skill may come naturally to you when you are making an oral appeal. Think about the times you have wanted something from a parent, teacher, or friend: you had to state your position and offer different types of arguments to support your position, depending on your audience. An **argument** is a statement, a reason, or a fact for or against a point. Its purpose is to convince or persuade. As part of your argument, you might explain the causes of a situation and their effects. Or you might make a comparison or an analogy to argue your case. You could also quote an authority to give your case credibility. Developing an informal oral argument for a familiar audience is often easier than crafting a formal written argument for a large and diverse audience.

In writing, you do not have the opportunity for such back-and-forth discussion. You must make your position on an issue clear for your reader and use persuasive appeals to develop a convincing argument. Analyzing a variety of published texts is an effective way to become familiar with this process. You will have the opportunity to do so before you craft your own persuasive text.

Fighting Back

1. **Quickwrite:** Sometimes people are dissatisfied with a product they have purchased. Select an item that disappointed you, and describe the experience below. Consider the following:

   • Why did you buy the product in the first place?

   • Why were you disappointed?

   • Do you recall seeing an advertisement for that product?

   • What kinds of claims or persuasive techniques do you recall from that advertisement?

GRAMMAR & USAGE

When writing a letter, use commas in the following manner:

1. In a date, place the comma after the day, prior to the year.

2. In an address, place the comma after the city, prior to the state abbreviation.

3. In a friendly letter, place a comma after the salutation; in both friendly and business letters, place a comma after the closing.

2. On a separate paper, write a letter to the company that makes the product you described in the previous step. Explain why you were not satisfied; focus on claims and persuasive techniques the company used in its advertising. Be sure to state a position: What do you want the company to do? Use the proper business letter format, shown on the next page, and take your letter through the writing process: draft, revise, edit, and publish.

Standard Business Letter Block Format

1122 Maple Lane
Seattle, WA 98105   **Heading**
May 12, 20XX

    3 blank lines

Customer Service Department   **Inside Address**
Rainbow Gum Company
P.O. Box 228
Dallas, TX 75201

> *Consider addressing the letter to a person with some real authority -- someone who can fix the problem. This is usually the head of customer service, or a top officer such as the president of the company.*

    1 blank line
Dear _____: **Salutation**
    1 blank line

Paragraph 1: *Start out with data. State (a) the name and model of the product, (b) when you bought the product, (c) where you bought it. Explain the problem clearly. Address the claims and persuasive techniques used. Be businesslike and objective.*   **Body of letter**

    1 blank line
Paragraph 2: *State what you want. Do you want a refund? Do you want to exchange the product? If so, for what? Do you just want an apology?*

    1 blank line
Sincerely, **Closing**
    3 blank lines

Sam Stone

> **WORD CONNECTIONS**
>
> Sometimes a business letter, a personal letter, or an invitation will ask the recipient for a response. *RSVP* is a common abbreviation in a personal letter or invitation asking for a response. The letters stand for "répondez s'il vous plaît," which is a French phrase meaning *please respond.*

What We Choose to Believe

SUGGESTED LEARNING STRATEGIES: Metacognitive Markers,
Predicting, Rereading, Think-Pair-Share

Anticipation Guide

Review the statements below, and decide whether you agree or
disagree with them. Circle the word *Agree* or *Disagree*. Provide an
explanation for your opinion.

Statement	Explanation
America is a wasteful society. Agree or Disagree	
Everyone should be forced to recycle his or her used goods. Agree or Disagree	
Excessive trash is destroying our planet. Agree or Disagree	
There should be a law that mandates the number of items people can buy and throw away annually. Agree or Disagree	
People should be allowed to create as much trash as they want as long as they dispose of it properly. Agree or Disagree	

Next, share your responses with a partner. Remember to use
appropriate speaking and listening skills, including nonverbal cues,
to gain understanding of your partner's positions.

AMERICA

The NOT-SO-BEAUTIFUL

> **ABOUT THE AUTHOR**
> Since 1978, Andrew A. Rooney has been a TV commentator on the program *60 Minutes*. He has written more than 800 essays, which he presents on television or in a national newspaper column. His essays, which are sometimes humorous and sometimes controversial, have earned him three Emmy awards.

From Not That You Asked
by Andrew A. Rooney

Next to saving stuff I don't need, the thing I like to do best is throw it away. My idea of a good time is to load up the back of the car with junk on a Saturday morning and take it to the dump. There's something satisfying about discarding almost anything.

Throwing things out is the American way. We don't know how to fix anything, and anyone who does know how is too busy to come, so we throw it away and buy a new one. Our economy depends on us doing that. The trouble with throwing things away is, there is no "away" left.

Sometime around the year 500 B.C., the Greeks in Athens passed a law prohibiting people from throwing their garbage in the street. This Greek law was the first recognition by civilized people that throwing things away was a problem. Now, as the population explodes and people take up more room on Earth, there's less room for everything else.

The more civilized a country is, the worse the trash problem is. Poor countries don't have the same problem because they don't have much to discard. Prosperity in the United States is based on using things up as fast as we can, throwing away what's left, and buying new ones.

We've been doing that for so many years that (1) we've run out of places to throw things because houses have been built where the dump was and (2) some of the things we're throwing away are poisoning the Earth and will eventually poison all of us and all living things.

Ten years ago most people thought nothing of dumping an old bottle of weed or insect killer in a pile of dirt in the back yard or down the drain in the street, just to get rid of it. The big companies in America had the same feeling, on a bigger scale. For years the chemical companies dumped their poisonous wastes in the rivers behind the

My Notes

Prediction about content, based on the title:

Connotation of *America*:

📖 **WORD CONNECTIONS**

Prosperity comes from the Latin word meaning "to cause to succeed" or "fortunate." The root *-sper-*, meaning "hope," is also found in *desperate*.

The suffix *-ity* forms a noun.

What We Choose to Believe

mills, or they put it in fifty-gallon drums in the vacant lots, with all the old, rusting machinery in it, up behind the plants. The drums rusted out in ten years and dumped their poison into the ground. It rained, the poisons seeped into the underground streams and poisoned everything for miles around. Some of the manufacturers who did this weren't even evil. They were dumb and irresponsible. Others were evil because they knew how dangerous it was but didn't want to spend the money to do it right.

The problem is staggering. I often think of it when I go in the hardware store or a Sears Roebuck and see shelves full of poison. You know that, one way or another, it's all going to end up in the Earth or in our rivers and lakes.

I have two pint bottles of insecticide with 3 percent DDT in them in my own garage that I don't know what to do with. I bought them years ago when I didn't realize how bad they were. Now I'm stuck with them.

The people of the city of New York throw away nine times their weight in garbage and junk every year. Assuming other cities come close to that, how long will it be before we trash the whole Earth?

Of all household waste, 30 percent of the weight and 50 percent of the volume is the packaging that stuff comes in.

Not only that, but Americans spend more for the packaging of food than all our farmers together make in income growing it. That's some statistic.

Trash collectors are a lot more independent than they used to be because we've got more trash than they've got places to put it. They have their own schedules and their own holidays. Some cities try to get in good with their trash collectors or garbage men by calling them "sanitation engineers." Anything just so long as they pick it up and take it away.

We often call the dump "the landfill" now, too. I never understood why land has to be filled, but that's what it's called. If you're a little valley just outside town, you have to be careful or first thing you know you'll be getting "filled."

If 5 billion people had been living on Earth for the past thousand years as they have been in the past year, the planet would be nothing but one giant landfill, and we'd have turned America the beautiful into one huge landfill.

The best solution may be for all of us to pack up, board a spaceship, and move out. If Mars is habitable, everyone on Earth can abandon this planet we've trashed, move to Mars, and start trashing that. It'll buy us some time.

GRAMMAR & USAGE

Notice that when Rooney uses a series in the final paragraph, he puts all of the elements in the same grammatical form:

...for all of us to *pack up, board a spaceship,* and *move out.*

Rooney is using **parallel structure,** or similar grammatical forms to express similar ideas. Use parallelism in your writing to express your ideas smoothly and effectively.

Post-Reading: What We Choose to Believe

SUGGESTED LEARNING STRATEGIES: Graphic Organizer, Prewriting, Skimming/Scanning, SOAPSTone, Think Aloud, Word Map

SOAPSTone: "America the Not-So-Beautiful"

SOAPSTone	Analysis	Textual Support
Subject: What is the topic?	about how the earth is getting polluted with trash	
Occasion: What are the circumstances surrounding this text?		
Audience: Who is the target audience?		
Purpose: Why did the author write this text?		
Speaker: What does the reader know about the writer?		

Post-Reading: What We Choose to Believe

SOAPSTone	Analysis	Textual Support
Tone: What is the writer's attitude toward the subject?		

GRAMMAR & USAGE

Like a topic sentence, a thesis statement consists of a **subject** and an **opinion** that can be supported with evidence. A thesis statement:

- Is an assertion, not a statement of fact.
- Takes a stand rather than announces a subject.
- Is the main idea, not the title.
- Is a complete sentence that explains in some detail what you intend to write about.

Exploring a Thesis

A **thesis** in a persuasive text is the writer's position or point of view on an issue. When you write a **thesis statement** describing a persuasive text, you tell the writer's position, purpose, and audience. Read the example below. Then use information from your SOAPSTone analysis to practice writing two additional thesis statements that capture Rooney's purpose for writing "America the Not-So-Beautiful."

Example:

Rooney wrote "America the Not-So-Beautiful" to convince Americans that their wastefulness is destroying the planet.

Practice:

Rooney wrote "America the Not-So-Beautiful" to convince

_____ that _____

_____

_____

Practice:

Rooney wrote "America the Not-So-Beautiful" to convince

_____ that _____

_____

_____

Fact or Opinion?

SUGGESTED LEARNING STRATEGIES: Marking the Text, Skimming/
Scanning, SOAPSTone, Summarizing/Paraphrasing

Anticipation Guide

Review the statements listed below and decide whether you agree or
disagree with them. Circle *Agree* or *Disagree*. Provide an explanation for
your opinion.

Statement	Explanation
Everyone should contribute to the Green Movement in order to save our planet. Agree or Disagree	
Purchasing "earth-friendly" products is a great way to contribute to the Green Movement. Agree or Disagree	
The Green Movement is currently just a stylish fad that will not last. Agree or Disagree	

My Notes

WORD CONNECTIONS

Bio- comes from the Greek word meaning "life" or "living." This word part appears in many English words, such as *biography* and *biology*.

Degrade contains the Latin root *-grade-*, meaning "step" or "grade" and the prefix *de-*, meaning "down."

Something that is biodegradable will eventually break down from the action of bacteria or other living organisms.

WORD CONNECTIONS

Eco-, from the Greek word meaning "house," is used in many English words related to the environment, such as *ecology* and *ecosystem*. *Eco-* is also found in *economy*, which originally referred to household management.

Feature Article

BUYING INTO THE
GREEN
movement

by Alex Williams

Correction Appended

HERE'S one popular vision for saving the planet: Roll out from under the sumptuous hemp-fiber sheets on your bed in the morning and pull on a pair of $245 organic cotton Levi's and an Armani biodegradable knit shirt.

Stroll from the bedroom in your eco-McMansion, with its photovoltaic solar panels, into the kitchen remodeled with reclaimed lumber. Enter the three-car garage lighted by energy-sipping fluorescent bulbs and slip behind the wheel of your $104,000 Lexus hybrid.

Drive to the airport, where you settle in for an 8,000-mile flight—careful to buy carbon offsets beforehand — and spend a week driving golf balls made from compacted fish food at an eco-resort in the Maldives.

That vision of an eco-sensitive life as a series of choices about what to buy appeals to millions of consumers and arguably defines the current environmental movement as equal parts concern for the earth and for making a stylish statement.

Some 35 million Americans regularly buy products that claim to be earth-friendly, according to one report, everything from organic beeswax lipstick from the west Zambian rain forest to Toyota Priuses. With baby steps, more and more shoppers browse among the 60,000 products available under Home Depot's new Eco Options program.

Such choices are rendered fashionable as celebrities worried about global warming appear on the cover of Vanity Fair's "green issue," and pop stars like Kelly Clarkson and Lenny Kravitz prepare to be headline acts on July 7 at the Live Earth concerts at sites around the world.

Consumers have embraced living green, and for the most part the mainstream green movement has embraced green consumerism. But even at this moment of high visibility and impact for environmental activists, a splinter wing of the movement has begun to critique what it sometimes calls "light greens."

Critics question the notion that we can avert global warming by buying so-called earth-friendly products, from clothing and cars to homes and vacations, when the cumulative effect of our consumption remains enormous and hazardous.

"There is a very common mind-set right now which holds that all that we're going to need to do to avert the large-scale planetary catastrophes upon us is make slightly different shopping decisions," said Alex Steffen, the executive editor of Worldchanging.com, a Web site devoted to sustainability issues.

The genuine solution, he and other critics say, is to significantly reduce one's consumption of goods and resources. It's not enough to build a vacation home of recycled lumber; the real way to reduce one's carbon footprint is to only own one home.

Buying a hybrid car won't help if it's the aforementioned Lexus, the luxury LS 600h L model, which gets 22 miles to the gallon on the highway; the Toyota Yaris ($11,000) gets 40 highway miles a gallon with a standard gasoline engine.

It's as though the millions of people whom environmentalists have successfully prodded to be concerned about climate change are experiencing a SnackWell's moment: confronted with a box of fat-free devil's food chocolate cookies, which seem deliciously guilt-free, they consume the entire box, avoiding any fats but loading up on calories.

My Notes

Fact or Opinion?

GRAMMAR & USAGE

Hyphens connect the parts of compound words. Notice the hyphen between two words used as a single phrase to modify a noun: *fat-free* cookies, *old-school* environmentalism, *high-style...* items, *earth-friendly* products.

The writer also uses hyphens to separate certain prefixes and nouns, such as *self-abnegation* and *eco-narcissism*.

Using correct hyphenation in your writing helps to make your meaning clear.

My Notes

LITERARY TERMS

An **oxymoron** is a figure of speech in which the words seem to contradict each other; for example, "jumbo shrimp."

The issue of green shopping is highlighting a division in the environmental movement: "the old-school environmentalism of self-abnegation versus this camp of buying your way into heaven," said Chip Giller, the founder of Grist.org, an online environmental blog that claims a monthly readership of 800,000.

"Over even the last couple of months, there is more concern growing within the traditional camp about the Cosmo-izing of the green movement—'55 great ways to look eco-sexy,'" he said. "Among traditional greens, there is concern that too much of the population thinks there's an easy way out."

The criticisms have appeared quietly in some environmental publications and on the Web.

George Black, an editor and a columnist at OnEarth, a quarterly journal of the Natural Resources Defense Council, recently summed up the explosion of high-style green consumer items and articles of the sort that proclaim "green is the new black," that is, a fashion trend, as "eco-narcissism."

Paul Hawken, an author and longtime environmental activist, said the current boom in earth-friendly products offers a false promise. "Green consumerism is an oxymoronic phrase," he said. He blamed the news media and marketers for turning environmentalism into fashion and distracting from serious issues.

"We turn toward the consumption part because that's where the money is," Mr. Hawken said. "We tend not to look at the 'less' part. So you get these anomalies like 10,000-foot 'green' homes being built by a hedge fund manager in Aspen. Or 'green' fashion shows. Fashion is the deliberate inculcation of obsolescence."

He added: "The fruit at Whole Foods in winter, flown in from Chile on a 747 — it's a complete joke. The idea that we should have raspberries in January, it doesn't matter if they're organic. It's diabolically stupid."

Environmentalists say some products marketed as green may pump more carbon into the atmosphere than choosing something more modest, or simply nothing at all. Along those lines,

a company called PlayEngine sells a 19-inch widescreen L.C.D. set whose "sustainable bamboo" case is represented as an earth-friendly alternative to plastic.

But it may be better to keep your old cathode-tube set instead, according to "The Live Earth Global Warming Survival Handbook," because older sets use less power than plasma or L.C.D. screens. (Televisions account for about 4 percent of energy consumption in the United States, the handbook says.)

"The assumption that by buying anything, whether green or not, we're solving the problem is a misperception," said Michael Ableman, an environmental author and long-time organic farmer. "Consuming is a significant part of the problem to begin with. Maybe the solution is instead of buying five pairs of organic cotton jeans, buy one pair of regular jeans instead."

For the most part, the critiques of green consumption have come from individual activists, not from mainstream environmental groups like the Sierra Club, Greenpeace, and the Rainforest Action Network. The latest issue of Sierra, the magazine of the Sierra Club, has articles hailing an "ecofriendly mall" featuring sustainable clothing (under development in Chicago) and credit cards that rack up carbon offsets for every purchase, as well as sustainably-harvested caviar and the celebrity-friendly Tango electric sports car (a top-of-the-line model is $108,000).

One reason mainstream groups may be wary of criticizing Americans' consumption is that before the latest era of green chic, these large organizations endured years in which their warnings about climate change were scarcely heard.

Much of the public had turned away from the Carter-era environmental message of sacrifice, which included turning down the thermostat, driving smaller cars, and carrying a cloth "Save-a-Tree" tote to the supermarket.

Now that environmentalism is high profile, thanks in part to the success of "An Inconvenient Truth," the 2006 documentary featuring Al Gore, mainstream greens, for the most part, say that buying products promoted as eco-friendly is a good first step.

"After you buy the compact fluorescent bulbs," said Michael Brune, the executive director of the Rainforest Action Network, "you can move on to greater goals like banding together politically to shut down coal-fired power plants."

My Notes

Fact or Opinion?

My Notes

John Passacantando, the executive director of Greenpeace USA, argued that green consumerism has been a way for Wal-Mart shoppers to get over the old stereotypes of environmentalists as "tree-hugging hippies" and contribute in their own way.

This is crucial, he said, given the widespread nature of the global warming challenge. "You need Wal-Mart and Joe Six-Pack and mayors and taxi drivers," he said. "You need participation on a wide front."

It is not just ecology activists with one foot in the 1970s, though, who have taken issue with the consumerist personality of the "light green" movement. Anti-consumerist fervor burns hotly among some activists who came of age under the influence of noisy, disruptive anti-globalization protests.

Last year, a San Francisco group called the Compact made headlines with a vow to live the entire year without buying anything but bare essentials like medicine and food. A year in, the original 10 "mostly" made it, said Rachel Kesel, 26, a founder. The movement claims some 8,300 adherents throughout the country and in places as distant as Singapore and Iceland.

"The more that I'm engaged in this, the more annoyed I get with things like 'shop against climate change' and these kind of attitudes," said Ms. Kesel, who continues her shopping strike and counts a new pair of running shoes — she's a dog-walker by trade — as among her limited purchases in 18 months.

"It's hysterical," she said. "You're telling people to consume more in order to reduce impact."

For some, the very debate over how much difference they should try to make in their own lives is a distraction. They despair of individual consumers being responsible for saving the earth from climate change and want to see action from political leaders around the world.

Individual consumers may choose more fuel-efficient cars, but a far greater effect may be felt when fuel-efficiency standards are raised for all of the industry, as the Senate voted to do on June 21, the first significant rise in mileage standards in more than two decades.

"A legitimate beef that people have with green consumerism is, at end of the day, the things causing climate change are more caused by politics and the economy than individual behavior," said Michel Gelobter, a former professor of environmental policy at Rutgers who is now president of Redefining Progress, a nonprofit policy group that promotes sustainable living.

"A lot of what we need to do doesn't have to do with what you put in your shopping basket," he said. "It has to do with mass transit, housing density. It has to do with the war and subsidies for the coal and fossil fuel industry."

In fact, those light-green environmentalists who chose not to lecture about sacrifice and promote the trendiness of eco-sensitive products may be on to something.

Michael Shellenberger, a partner at American Environics, a market research firm in Oakland, Calif., said that his company ran a series of focus groups in April for the environmental group Earthjustice, and was surprised by the results.

People considered their trip down the Eco Options aisles at Home Depot a beginning, not an end point.

"We didn't find that people felt that their consumption gave them a pass, so to speak," Mr. Shellenberger said. "They knew what they were doing wasn't going to deal with the problems, and these little consumer things won't add up. But they do it as a practice of mindfulness. They didn't see it as antithetical to political action. Folks who were engaged in these green practices were actually becoming more committed to more transformative political action on global warming."

Correction: July 8, 2007

An article last Sunday about eco-friendly consumerism misstated the number of products sold through the Home Depot Eco Options program. It is 2,500 — not 60,000, which was the number originally submitted by the store's suppliers for inclusion in the program.

My Notes

GRAMMAR & USAGE

An **appositive** is a noun or phrase that explains or renames the noun or pronoun next to it in a sentence. If the appositive adds meaning to the sentence but is not necessary for the sentence to make sense, it should be placed inside commas.

Example: "Paul Hawken, **an author and longtime environmental activist,** said the current boom in earth-friendly products offers a false promise.

Fact or Opinion?

SOAPSTone: "Buying into the Green Movement"

SOAPSTone	Analysis	Textual Support
Subject: What is the topic?		
Occasion: What are the circumstances surrounding this text?		
Audience: Who is the target audience?		
Purpose: Why did the author write this text?		
Speaker: What does the reader know about the writer?		
Tone: What is the writer's attitude toward the subject?		

Writing Prompt: Write a thesis statement responding to the author's opinion about the Green Movement.

_____

_____

_____

Article

City Schools Cut Parents' Lifeline (the Cellphone)

by Elissa Gootman

My Notes

> **LITERARY TERMS**
> To **debate** is to present the sides of an argument by discussing opposing points.

During the final stretch of David Ritter's hourlong trip to middle school, he pulls a cellphone from his jeans and calls his mother in Washington Heights to say he is out of the subway and moments from the Salk School of Science on East 20th Street.

"It's one thing I can cross off my list of things to worry about," his mother, Elizabeth Lorris Ritter, said. "It's a required part of our everyday life. We have a refrigerator, we have running water, we have cellphones."

Cellphones are the urban parent's umbilical cord, the lifeline connecting them to children on buses, emerging from subways, crisscrossing boroughs and traipsing through unknown neighborhoods.

Though the phones have been banned in New York City schools for years, parents say that many schools without metal detectors have operated under a kind of "don't ask, don't tell" policy, with the cellphones ignored as long as they do not ring in the middle of class.

But as the city began random security scanning at middle and high schools yesterday in its latest effort to seize weapons, the gap between school rules and parents' expectations has set off a furor. Some principals recently sent home letters reminding parents that cellphones are not allowed, and at the one school searched yesterday, 129 cellphones were confiscated.

News or Views?

Anxious parents say that cellphones are not a frill but the mortar holding New York City's families together in these times of demanding schedules, mounting extracurricular activities, tutoring sessions and long treks to school.

Some of these parents, also fearful of child predators and terrorist attacks, say that sending their children to school without cellphones is unimaginable. "I have her call me when she gets out of school, and she's supposed to get on the bus right away," Lindsay Walt, an artist, said of her daughter, Eve Thomson, 11, a sixth grader at Salk. "Then I have her call me when she gets off the bus, and I have her call me when she gets in the house. The chancellor will have civil disobedience on his hands. No one in New York is going to let their child go to school without a cellphone."

Dr. Moira Kennedy, a psychiatrist with daughters at the New York City Lab School for Collaborative Studies and at Stuyvesant High School, said the policy indicated "a disregard for the concerns of parents," adding, "I think it shows a big lack of awareness of the essential nature of having a way to communicate with your child during the day."

Police officers set up a random scanning operation at the Acorn High School for Social Justice in Brooklyn yesterday, Department of Education officials said. Along with the 129 cellphones, 10 CD players and two iPods were confiscated, along with a box cutter and a knife that was left in a trash can. A student carrying marijuana ran away after seeing the scanning operation, Schools Chancellor Joel I. Klein said. The electronic items will be returned.

Chancellor Klein defended the scanning and the cellphone ban yesterday, telling reporters that students had used cellphones to take pictures in locker rooms, cheat on exams and summon friends to start fights.

"We all understand the concerns that parents are talking about, but I think they have to see it from our point of view," he said. "There is always an enforcement issue, but the enforcement issue doesn't mean the policy is wrong. And obviously through the work we're doing now, I think that will improve enforcement."

Dumbfounded students said cellphones were essential, so familiar they were like an extra limb. But they had different reasons from their parents'. "I feel so empty," said May Chom, 14, speaking wistfully after hearing of the policy and leaving her phone at home in Queens. With no cellphone, May said, there was also no way to listen to music on the way to the Lab School, on West 17th Street, making for a "really, really boring" trip.

Another Lab student, Noah Benezra, 18, carried his phone yesterday despite the new scanning program, saying it was "pretty much vital" to his social life.

Blocks away, Ayoni Warburton, 17, made no effort to conceal her cellphone, arriving at the High School of Fashion Industries with it prominently affixed to her hip.

"Electronics are part of the fashion statement," she said, adding, "My mother calls me a lot."

A fellow student, who identified himself as Jose but was whisked inside the school by safety agents before he could give his last name, said he needed his phone for emergencies.

"Don't lie — girls," corrected his friend.

At the Acorn school, Lisa Miller, an English teacher, said the phones were a distraction, adding, "If it's really an emergency, the parents can call the school."

Parents say they are not satisfied with that answer, or even with efforts by some principals to distance themselves from the cellphone ban by assuring parents that phones taken during random security checks will be returned.

"We sit here and we tell our parents, 'Care about your kids, do this, do that,' and then you say, 'You've just lost that safety net that you rely on,' " said Jane Reiff, a Queens parent whose daughter Nikki, 12, uses her cellphone to call for a ride if the friends she usually walks home with are out sick. "It's just not safe out there."

Kate Hammer contributed reporting for this article.

My Notes

Editorial

by OP-ED CONTRIBUTOR Jesse Scaccia

You're a teacher in the New York City public school system. It's September, and you're lecturing the class on the structure of an essay. Your students need to know this information to pass your class and the Regents exam, and you, of course, hope that one day your talented students will dazzle and amaze English professors all over the country.

You turn your back to write the definition of "thesis" on the chalk board. It takes about 15 seconds. You turn around to the class expecting to see 25 students scribbling the concept in their notebook. Instead, you see a group of students who have sprung appendages of technology.

Jose has grown an earphone. Maria's thumbs have sprouted a two-way. Man Keung, recently arrived from China, is texting away on a cellphone connected to his wrist. And Christina appears to be playing Mine Sweeper on a Pocket PC on her lap.

Come the end of the term, a handful will fail the class. A number will never pass the Regents. As we all know, far too many will drop out of school. And I can tell you with no hint of pride that it isn't the teacher's fault. As much as any other problem plaguing our schools, the onus for failure should be placed on distractions in the classroom, specifically the cellphone.

Though electronic devices have been banned in public schools for years, the issue came to the forefront last month when Chancellor Joel Klein announced the random placement of metal detectors in schools. The result: more than 800 cellphones have been confiscated.

Students and their parents, who say they rely on cellphones for safety reasons, are outraged. There's even talk of a lawsuit arguing that the rule should be struck down.

My Notes

But as a former New York City public school teacher, I can tell you that cellphones don't belong in the classroom. A student with a cellphone is an uninterested student, one with a short attention span who cares more about his social life than education.

Parents think of cellphones as a connection to their children in an emergency. I have a few questions for those parents: First, when was the last situation that genuinely called for immediate interaction with your child? In most cases, the hospital or the police would seem more urgent. Second, is phoning the main office and having it patch you through to your child not quick enough? And third, do you know why your children really want to take cellphones to school?

Because just like the new Jordans and Rocawear they desire, cellphones are status symbols. Because when their cellphone rings while the teacher is talking, everyone laughs. Because playing video games on their cell makes them look cool. Because text messaging their friend in the next room is more fun than learning about the topic sentence. So is listening to the new Three 6 Mafia song they just downloaded onto their cell.

And saying students can store their phones in the locker is a joke. If they have cellphones, they're going to bring them into class.

There are legitimate causes that parents should be taking on. Rally against crowding in the classroom. Fight against the oppressive and culturally biased Regents tests. But you're wrong on this cellphone issue. In this case, you are part of the problem, not the solution.

Jesse Scaccia, a film producer, taught at Franklin D. Roosevelt High School in Brooklyn.

News or Views?

News Article: "City Schools Cut Parents' Lifeline (the Cellphone)"

1. Look at the opening paragraphs (often called the "lead" in a news story), and note the who, what, when, where, why, and how of the story.

   _____

   _____

2. List the people and organizations that are **against** having cell phones in schools. In the article, highlight their main objections. In the My Notes space on the article pages, make notes about the arguments and whether they are using cause and effect, analogy, or authority as their basis.

   _____

   _____

3. List the people and organizations that are **in favor** of having cell phones in schools. Highlight their main reasons for support with a different color. In the My Notes space, identify whether the arguments use cause and effect, analogy, or authority to support cell phones in school.

   _____

   _____

Editorial: "Hang It Up"

1. Look at the opening paragraphs. How does the author choose to open the piece?

   _____

   _____

2. State the author's position on the issue. Highlight text that reveals this position.

   _____

   _____

   _____

3. Mark the section(s) of the text where the **editorial** addresses the opposition. Make a comment about whether the author addresses the opposition fairly, and explain why you think so.

_____

_____

ACADEMIC VOCABULARY

An **editorial** is the opinion of an editor or writer who works for the publisher. An editorial can also be a television or radio piece representing the network or radio station.

Compare and Contrast News Articles and Editorials

Use the Venn diagram below to organize the differences and similarities between news articles and editorials.

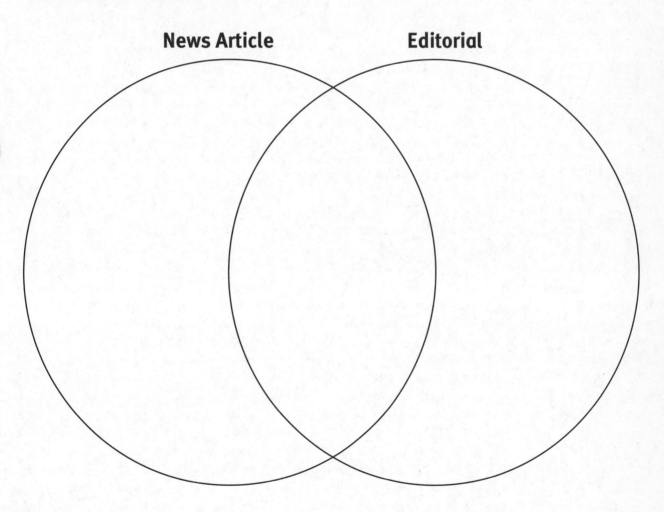

News Article   **Editorial**

News or Views?

Editorial Scavenger Hunt

Find three editorials on issues that are interesting to you and that you know a lot about. Then, complete the graphic organizer below, and attach the editorials to this page.

Author and Title	Date and Source	Topic Addressed: Decisions or Choices	Personal Opinion
1.			
2.			
3.			

Exploring My Opinions

SUGGESTED LEARNING STRATEGIES: Discussion Groups, Graphic
Organizer, Quickwrite

Quickwrite: Should schools require students to wear uniforms? Explain.

_____

_____

_____

_____

Prereading Group Discussion:

Position:

Reasons to Support this Opinion:

  1.

  2.

  3.

Exploring My Opinions

My Notes

Article

IRONING OUT POLICIES
on school uniforms

by Carol Motsinger

As the new school year approaches, more schools are requiring students to wear uniforms or otherwise restricting what they may wear — and parents are objecting.

Their complaint: The policies trample students' right of expression and parents' right to raise children without government interference, says Vickie Crager, founder of Asserting Parental Rights — It's Our Duty, a parents rights group that opposes school uniforms.

Parents Laura and Scott Bell filed suit over an Anderson, Ind., uniform plan that will begin when students return to school Aug. 20. A hearing was scheduled today in federal court in Indianapolis.

The Anderson policy requires black, navy, or khaki pants or skirts and a solid-color shirt with a collar.

"As a parent, we felt our rights were being violated," says Laura Bell. They have five children, ages 5 to 17.

The Bells' suit makes two claims: that the uniform requirement violates their children's constitutional right of free expression and that it violates the guarantee of a free public education. The Bells would have to pay $641 for five sets of pants and shirts required by the policy, Laura Bell says.

About one in four public elementary schools and one in eight public middle and high schools in the USA have policies dictating what a student wears to school, says David Brunsma, a sociologist who wrote *Uniforms in Public Schools: A Decade of Research and Debate* in 2005.

Private schools first imported the British tradition of student uniforms to mark a student's social status, Brunsma says. Urban public schools began to adopt uniforms in the late 1980s to reduce social pressure from fashion-savvy students.

The idea spread to suburban and rural schools when President Clinton said uniforms make schools more orderly. As the trend grew, so did the opposition, Brunsma says.

Charles Rubright, lawyer for the Anderson school district, says the board expects uniforms to improve academic performance by eliminating distracting clothing and creating an orderly atmosphere.

Cyndi Regis of Congress, Ariz., says her son, Story Stringfellow, 9, doesn't wear anything inappropriate to Congress Elementary School. He wants to wear his Phoenix Suns T-shirts and jeans, she says, but he'll be required to wear a polo shirt and khaki or navy shorts or pants starting today.

"We teach him to be himself and we encourage it," Regis says. "He's not out of line with what he wants to wear."

Toni Wayas, principal and superintendent of the Congress school and district, says parents suggested the policy and most families support it.

Most lawsuits against school uniforms fail, says David Hudson, a First Amendment scholar at the First Amendment Center in Nashville. Judges usually decide that uniform policies are meant to improve schools and not to suppress student speech, he says.

The Supreme Court has not ruled on school uniforms, Hudson says.

Other lawsuits are pending:

- **Bayonne, N.J.** A group of parents have appealed a dismissal of their challenge to a uniform requirement of khaki bottoms and navy tops. Their lawyer plans to file a case brief Aug. 13. A judge ruled last year that the suit was not filed in time. School officials have said the uniforms foster school spirit, self-respect, and self-discipline.

- **Napa County, Calif.** On July 2, a judge temporarily banned the enforcement of a middle school dress code while a suit challenging its constitutionality heads to trial. Under the code, students may wear only solid-color clothing with no logos or stripes. The code was designed to eliminate gang insignia, says Mike Pearson, principal of Redwood Middle School.

Others who object to uniforms and strict dress codes make their case outside the courtroom. Nashville parents created Metro Parents Against Standard School Attire after the school board announced plans for uniforms this spring.

"We perceive it as an educational fad," says Ashley Crownover, the group's spokeswoman. She says research does not support claims that uniforms increase safety or improve academic performance.

Some members of the group are considering suing or encouraging their children not to wear uniforms when school starts Aug. 13, Crownover says.

"We expect our school systems to do a lot, but this is taking it too far," she says. "That's my job — to help my children learn what is and isn't appropriate clothing."

My Notes

GRAMMAR & USAGE

Use a colon to formally introduce the material that follows, such as a list or an explanatory statement that completes the sentence. Notice the colon after the word *pending*. The bulleted list that follows describes the pending lawsuits.

Do not use a colon between a preposition or a verb and the rest of the sentence.

Exploring My Opinions

1. After you have read the article "Ironing Out Policies On School Uniforms," complete the graphic organizer.

Arguments for School Uniforms	Your Opinion	Arguments Against School Uniforms	Your Opinion

2. **Writing Prompt:** Work collaboratively with your group to write a response to the article. Include the following in your response:

- Your position statement.
- Direct reference to the article and a point that you agree or disagree with.
- Support for your position.

Developing an Argument

SUGGESTED LEARNING STRATEGIES: Graphic Organizer, Marking the Text, Oral Reading, Rereading, Skimming/Scanning, Word Map

Examining and Evaluating Arguments

In news articles, writers objectively present both sides of an issue. Writers of opinion pieces or editorials use one or more appeals to convince readers to support their positions:

Logos: Appeals to logic, through statistics, facts, and examples.

Pathos: Appeals to emotion through connotative language and imagery.

Ethos: Appeals to ethics by making the audience believe that the writer is credible and trustworthy.

Revisit the article your teacher assigns and identify two or more persuasive arguments and appeals. Record your analysis of the persuasive appeals.

Title and Author	Persuasive Arguments	Appeal(s)	Intended Effect
"America the Not-So-Beautiful," by Andrew Rooney			
"Buying into the Green Movement," by Alex Williams			
"City Schools Cut Parents' Lifeline (the Cellphone)," by Elissa Gootman			
"Hang It Up," by Jesse Scaccia			

Developing an Argument

My Notes

Letter to the Editor

Cellphones in School

To the Editor:

Re: "Hang It Up," by Jesse Scaccia (Op-Ed, May 23):

Schools should not be confiscating student cellphones. Using metal detectors to alert school administrators to student possession of cellphones does not seem to reflect the original intent of using metal detectors. Walking into a school with a phone should not raise the same alarms as carrying concealed weapons.

Administrators and teachers know that most students have cellphones. Parents agree that cellphones should not be used during the time students are in school. The actual issue in the cellphone debate is about parents being able to contact their children before and after school.

A blanket policy that bans all cellphones from the school grounds does not allow parents the basic right to monitor the safety of their children. I have provided my 15-year-old daughter with a cellphone so that I can keep track of her whereabouts before and after school. Part of my responsibility as a parent is to know where my child is. In addition, if she needs help I want to be readily available to give this help.

There needs to be some flexibility in this policy. Parents' concerns about safety must be balanced against educators' concerns about students being off-task in class. A more logical approach must be discussed and agreed upon by parents, students, and educators.

Sincerely,

Jill Reiss
New York

Reading an Editorial

SUGGESTED LEARNING STRATEGIES: Graphic Organizer, Marking the Text, Notetaking, Predicting, Quickwrite, Summarizing/Paraphrasing, Word Map

The main purpose of an editorial is to persuade the audience to support the writer's position on an issue. When you read an editorial, follow these steps:

1. Examine the headline, sub-headline, and related cartoon (if it exists). **Predict** what the editorial will be about.

2. **Identify** the writer's position on the issue.

3. Stop reading for a moment and **reflect** on the other side of the issue. Who might think differently? Which arguments might support the other side?

4. Continue reading the editorial. Identify the strongest pieces of **evidence** that the writer uses to support his or her position.

5. Determine whether the writer addresses the main objections of the other side with **counter-arguments**. If so, give an example. What does he or she not address? Do you feel that the writer is fair to the other side? Why or why not?

6. Reread the text, and highlight **appeals** (logos, pathos, ethos) as well as **persuasive techniques** (bandwagon, avante garde, testimonial, facts/figures, transfer). Label this information using the My Notes space beside the editorial. Look at the arguments and identify the use of cause and effect, analogy, and authority. How do these appeals and techniques affect your attitude toward the issue?

After Reading

Write a **response** to the editorial: Explain whether you agree or disagree with the writer's views, and why.

> **LITERARY TERMS**
> A **counter-argument** is given in opposition to an argument. It provides reasoning or facts to oppose the argument.

Use this graphic organizer to take notes as you read the editorial with the class.

Title _____ Author _____ Issue _____

Process	Notes
1 **Predict**	
2 **Identify**	
3 **Reflect**	
4 **Evidence**	
5 **Counter-Arguments**	
6 **Appeals and Techniques**	
7 **Response**	

Balancing Act on Cell Phones

My Notes

MEMPHIS COMMERCIAL APPEAL

Schools should have rational policies that keep students safe and classrooms orderly.

Most parents and public education officials ultimately want the same things for children – a good education, discipline, a safe environment.

It's not easy to find the right balance for those needs, though—a difficulty that has been brought into sharp focus as public school districts in Memphis and Shelby County clamp down on students who misuse cell phones in the schools.

Families of the 21st Century have incorporated cell phone communication in their daily routines to accommodate busy schedules and to enhance the safety of children in an increasingly violent world.

The child walking home from school needs to be able to call 911 when she's being harassed by a dirty old man in a car. The soccer goalie needs to tell a parent to pick him or her up early because practice has been cancelled.

Misused, however, the cell phones are a menace.

At Shelby County Schools, a crackdown is under way because parents have been sending children text messages in class and students have been using them to cheat on tests and snap inappropriate pictures at school. But students are still allowed to take cell phones to school, as long as they're kept in the locker.

At Memphis City Schools, two years ago the Board of Education voted 7-1 against a policy that would have allowed students to use cell phones before and after school, retaining a policy that outlaws cell phones in school altogether.

Supt. Kriner Cash made it clear at the beginning of the school year in a recorded message to students' homes that the policy would be enforced to the letter.

This is clearly an issue, however, on which a search for middle ground should be under way.

My Notes

Schools are able to enforce strict rules against fighting. They can lay down the law on the school dress code. They can make it clear that plagiarism on English papers is a serious violation of academic standards.

Surely they can make the punishment for turning on a cell phone in class harsh enough to serve as a deterrent. Anyone taking inappropriate snaps in a locker room should have the book thrown at him or her.

Students wouldn't dream of leaving their phones on during a Jonas Brothers concert. We suspect that most students understand the disruption that's caused by cell phone use in the classroom just as well.

Perhaps a policy allowing three strikes before a student's phone is confiscated for the semester would make sense for students (or parents) who just don't get it. In-school suspensions could also send a strong message to anyone who misuses a cell phone.

For most families, that should be enough to prevent cell phone misuse. A Draconian[1] ban on calling anyone before and after school should not be necessary.

WORD CONNECTIONS

The word *Draconian* is an analogy for extreme measures. The word comes from the Greek statesman, Draco, who put the laws of Athens in writing. The laws were thought to be too severe because even minor offenses could result in death.

---

[1] **Draconian:** harsh, severe

Writing a Letter to the Editor

SUGGESTED LEARNING STRATEGIES: Drafting, Manipulatives, Peer Response, Revising, Self-Editing, Word Map

Choose a timely editorial or use one your teacher gives you, and write a letter to the editor expressing your thoughts. Make sure you review the newspaper's requirements for letters to the editor before you begin (for example, length, format, and contact information). Follow the guidelines below, and carefully revise and edit your letter.

Guidelines for Writing a Letter to the Editor

1. Indicate the specific editorial you are responding to by stating the editorial title and date of publication. This reference should occur at the beginning of your letter to set the context for the reader.

   Example: It is unfair to punish students for bringing cell phones to class ("Balancing Act on Cell Phones," September 3, 2008).

2. State your position on the issue within the first two sentences.

3. Refute or support one or two specific arguments from the editorial. Support your position with a variety of appeals and incorporate persuasive techniques.

4. Offer a solution to the problem, if appropriate.

5. Maintain a civil tone.

Prewriting

1. Think through your position on the issue:

   I am writing this letter to convince _____ that they should _____
                                   (Audience)   **(Position)**

   _____.

2. What does your audience currently believe about this issue? Why?

   _____

   _____

3. How can you get your audience to accept your position?
   Appeals:

   _____

   Techniques:

   _____

Writing a Letter to the Editor

SUGGESTED LEARNING STRATEGIES: Graphic Organizer, Prewriting, Drafting, Self-Editing, Peer Editing, SOAPSTone, Sharing and Responding

Assignment

Your assignment is to choose an editorial, analyze the persuasive arguments, and write a letter to the editor, agreeing or disagreeing with the writer of the editorial.

Steps

Prewriting/Planning

1. Choose a timely and relevant newspaper editorial about an issue that you are interested in and feel strongly about. You may use one of the editorials you found in your Editorial Scavenger Hunt (Activity 2.16) or one your teacher gives you.

2. Read through the editorial slowly and carefully. As you read, highlight the persuasive appeals and techniques, and identify points or comments that you would like to respond to.

3. Use the "Guidelines for Reading an Editorial" (page 167) and/or SOAPSTone (page 168) graphic organizer to develop a thorough understanding of the editorial.

4. Review the "Guidelines for Writing a Letter to the Editor" in Activity 2.20. Then use a prewriting strategy to generate ideas.

Drafting

5. Draft your letter in business-letter format.

....

⌐TECHNOLOGY TIP Word processing programs offer templates for several types of business documents, such as business letters, reports, and memorandums. Compare the format of the various business letters and choose one for your draft.

Revising Through Sharing and Responding

6. Share your draft in your writing group to gather suggestions for revision (format, organization, ideas, and language); revise accordingly. Consult the Scoring Guide to aid revisions. Also, refer to the Grammar Handbook and the grammar and usage tips in this unit to revise for sentence structure and variety (for example, prepositional, adverbial, and adjectival clauses; appositives; and parallel structures).

Editing for Publication

7. Edit your draft: Check for spelling, capitalization, grammar, and usage errors. Also edit your draft for correct usage of punctuation, such as dashes, hyphens, colons, semicolons, and commas. Prepare to publish your letter. If you are writing your letter by hand, use your best penmanship to make your letter readable.

8. Write a reflection on how you have incorporated your knowledge of persuasive appeals and techniques into your letter to the editor. Be sure to identify the particular appeals and techniques you used, and explain why you think these are effective choices.

Guidelines for Reading an Editorial

Title _____ Author _____ Topic _____

Process	Notes
Examine the headline, sub-headline and related cartoon (if it exists). **Predict** what the editorial will be about.	
Once you have determined the author's position, stop reading for a moment or two. **Reflect** on the other side of the issue. Who might think differently? Which arguments might support the other side?	
Continue reading the editorial. Identify the strongest pieces of **evidence** that the writer uses to support his or her position.	
Determine whether the writer addresses the main objections of the other side. If so, give an example. What does he or she not address? Do you feel that the author is fair to the other side? Why or why not?	
Reread the text and highlight **appeals** (logos, pathos, ethos) as well as **persuasive techniques** (bandwagon, avant garde, facts/figures, transfer). How do these appeals and techniques affect your attitude toward the issue?	

SOAPSTone

SOAPSTone	Analysis	Textual Support
Subject: What is the topic?		
Occasion: What are the circumstances surrounding this text?		
Audience: Who is the target audience?		
Purpose: Why did the author write this text?		
Speaker: What does the reader know about the writer?		
Tone: What is the writer's attitude toward the subject?		

SCORING GUIDE

Scoring Criteria	Exemplary	Proficient	Emerging
Ideas	The writer asserts a sophisticated position that agrees or disagrees with a specific point made by the author of the editorial; the writer uses a variety of appeals and techniques to convince a particular audience to support his or her position; and the writer proposes a strong solution (if applicable).	The writer states a position that agrees or disagrees with the author of the editorial; the writer uses at least two types of appeals and one technique to convince an audience to support his or her position; and the writer proposes a solution (if applicable).	The writer shows a limited understanding of the author's ideas in the editorial. The position is unfocused or missing, persuasive appeals and techniques are not used to persuade the audience, and the writer does not offer a solution (if applicable).
Organization	The letter is written in business letter format, and the writer skillfully organizes the letter to suit the purpose and audience.	The letter is written in business letter format, and the writer organizes the letter to suit the purpose and audience	The letter is not properly formatted and/or the organization is difficult to follow. The writer shows a limited understanding of the purpose and/or audience.
Use of Language	The writer's word choice skillfully supports the opinion.	The writer's word choice effectively supports the opinion.	The writer's word choice ineffectively supports the opinion.
Conventions	Writing contains few or no errors in spelling, punctuation, or capitalization.	Spelling, punctuation, and capitalization mistakes do not detract from the letter.	Spelling, punctuation, or capitalization mistakes detract from meaning and/ or readability.
Evidence of Writing Process	The texts demonstrate extensive evidence of the various stages of the writing process.	The texts demonstrate evidence of the various stages of the writing process.	The texts demonstrate little or no evidence of the stages of the writing process.
Additional Criteria			

Comments: _____

_____

_____

Reflection

An important aspect of growing as a learner is to reflect on where you have been, what you have accomplished, what helped you to learn, and how you will apply your new knowledge in the future. Use the following questions to guide your thinking and to identify evidence of your learning. Use separate notebook paper.

Thinking about Concepts

1. Using specific examples from this unit, respond to the Essential Questions:
   - How do advertisers attempt to influence consumers?
   - How do purpose and audience shape the content in a persuasive text?

2. Consider the new academic vocabulary from this unit (**Consumerism, Media, Advertising, Persuasion, Audience, Purpose, Editorial**) as well as academic vocabulary from previous units, and select 3-4 terms of which your understanding has grown. For each term, answer the following questions:
   - What was your understanding of the word prior to the unit?
   - How has your understanding of the word evolved throughout the unit?
   - How will you apply your understanding in the future?

Thinking about Connections

3. Review the activities and products (artifacts) you created. Choose those that most reflect your growth or increase in understanding.

4. For each artifact that you choose, record, respond to, and reflect on your thinking and understanding, using the following questions as a guide:

   a. What skill/knowledge does this artifact reflect, and how did you learn this skill/knowledge?

   b. How did your understanding of the power of language expand through your engagement with this artifact?

   c. How will you apply this skill or knowledge in the future?

5. Create this reflection as Portfolio pages—one for each artifact you choose. Use the model in the box for your headings and commentary on questions.

Thinking About Thinking
Portfolio Entry

Concept:

Description of Artifact:

Commentary on Questions:

Our Choices and
Life's Lessons

Essential Questions

? What is the relationship between choices and consequences?

? How does research contribute to the discovery of solutions?

Unit Overview

This unit will engage you with a text closely connected to your own life as a middle school student, as a member of a family, and as a member of society. You will explore a text that focuses on one young man's emerging realizations about himself, his family, and the society he lives in. You will interpret, analyze, and evaluate a novel in terms of point of view, characterization, plot, structure, and other elements that create a unique text. Finally, you will analyze the choices made by the characters in the novel and relate the concept of choices and consequences to your own life.

Unit 3

Our Choices and Life's Lessons

Contents

Goals

▶ To make connections between texts and your own life

▶ To analyze, interpret, and evaluate a novel on a variety of levels and for a variety of purposes

▶ To read with fluency and apply appropriate language conventions (sentence structure, usage, punctuation) in oral reading, discussion, and writing

▶ To conduct research and present a convincing argument

ACADEMIC VOCABULARY

Imagery

Point of View

Literary Analysis

Problem/Solution Essay

Research

Texts not included in these materials.

Learning Focus:

Understanding Literary Analysis

If you have ever "lost" yourself in a book, you know what it feels like to become so immersed in another world that you can vividly visualize the scene and action as well as feel the emotions of the characters. If you read a book more than once, you have a sense of anticipation about the story and you pay closer attention to the language of the writer and the **foreshadowing** of the action. The written word is a powerful tool of the imagination, and the human mind responds to words as powerfully as it responds to other sensory stimuli.

Do you watch a favorite movie many times over? You probably see something new every time you watch it. Perhaps a character's **motivation** becomes clearer, or some event in the plot seems more significant. Or maybe you see how scenes foreshadow later events, or you notice that the film uses certain images, colors, or characters **symbolically**.

In each of these cases, you are beginning to **analyze and evaluate the effects of literary elements,** and your understanding grows as a result of that knowledge. Part of the pleasure of reading as well as viewing is being able to appreciate how all the parts work together to create a powerful imaginary experience. This is what **literary analysis** can provide. Studying literary works and applying the language of literary analysis is a way of giving you the vocabulary to describe your appreciation for and understanding of how writers use the tools of their trade – words – to create a realistic effect emotionally and intellectually. To know why you respond to a certain character or **imagery** or plot event is to be able to discuss it in a more meaningful way.

To pay careful attention to the words and imagery of an author through a close reading is to anticipate the time when you will consciously craft language and manipulate words to create a certain effect. As your writing becomes more deliberate, you will think more consciously about how to use **transitions** and specific **organizational patterns** and **sentence structures** to effectively communicate your ideas.

Previewing the Unit

SUGGESTED LEARNING STRATEGIES: Marking the Text, Think-Pair-Share, Skimming/Scanning, Summarizing/Paraphrasing, Graphic Organizer

Essential Questions

1. What is the relationship between choices and consequences?

_____

_____

_____

_____

2. How does research contribute to the discovery of solutions?

_____

_____

_____

_____

Unit Overview and Learning Focus

Predict what you think this unit is about. Use the words or phrases that stood out to you when you read the Unit Overview and the Learning Focus.

_____

_____

_____

_____

_____

Embedded Assessment 1

What knowledge must you have (what do you need to know) to succeed on the Embedded Assessment? What skills must you have (what must you be able to do)?

_____

_____

_____

Peeling a Tangerine

LITERARY TERMS

A **simile** is a comparison between two unlike things, using *like* or *as*, to make a vivid and emphatic description.

A **metaphor** is a comparison between two unlike things, in which one thing is said to be another.

1. How are similes and metaphors similar?

_____

_____

2. How are similes and metaphors different?

_____

_____

3. Examine the tangerine your teacher has given you. Take notes about it on the following characteristics.

Appearance:

Smell:

Feel:

4. Using your notes, create a descriptive statement about a tangerine. Include a simile or a metaphor in your statement.

_____

_____

_____

5. Revise your statement by adding additional details about the texture and perhaps the taste of the tangerine.

Texture (touch):

Taste:

ACADEMIC VOCABULARY

Imagery is the use of descriptive or figurative language to create word pictures.

6. Add the concept of **imagery** to your Vocabulary Notebook. What is the function of imagery in descriptive writing? How does it strengthen your voice as a writer?

_____

_____

Selling the Novel

SUGGESTED LEARNING STRATEGIES: **Close Reading, Graphic Organizer, KWHL Chart, Predicting, Think-Pair-Share**

1. Examine carefully the design, color, images, and text on the front cover. Take notes on the organizer below.

Background: List all the details.

Inferences and predictions about the setting of the novel:

Character depicted: Describe in detail.

Inferences and predictions about the main character of the novel:

Lettering: Describe in detail.

Inferences and predictions drawn from the words on the cover:

Selling the Novel

2. Read the back cover of the novel. Copy words or phrases from the plot summary that you find intriguing, interesting, or confusing.

_____

_____

3. Why do you think the author chose to title this novel *Tangerine*?

_____

_____

4. Complete the KWHL chart as your teacher directs.

K: What I Know	W: What I Want to Know	H: How I Will Learn It	L: What I Learned

5. Quickwrite: What are some insights you have and predictions you can make about the novel *Tangerine*?

_____

_____

_____

Previewing the Novel

1 Set up a double-entry journal as your teacher instructs (use the format below). Copy the following questions onto the left-hand side of your double-entry journal.

- Can human beings choose not to remember? When and why might a person make a choice to forget?

- What is the relationship between forgiving and forgetting? Explain.

- Think of an example from your own life, a television show or movie you have seen, a short story or novel you have read, or a story you have heard, of someone who chose not to remember. Briefly describe the situation, and consider the consequences of choosing not to remember.

2. Think about the questions above. Then choose one and write a response on the right-hand side of your double-entry journal. Be sure to include a lead that makes it clear which prompt you have chosen.

> **GRAMMAR & USAGE**
>
> When analyzing literature, do not use the first-person perspective of "I." Instead, use the characters' names or third-person pronouns such as "he" or "she."
>
> In addition, when discussing or writing about literature, use the present tense because the characters and events of a story are described in the present tense.

Double-Entry Journal

Date:	Title of Entry:
Quotes from or questions related to the novel *Tangerine*. *(This section may also include instructions or concepts presented by your teacher.)*	Personal Responses: Answers to the questions, reflections, connections to the text, and so on.

Getting into the Text: A Close Reading of the Prologue

1. You will read and discuss the prologue together as a class. Write the following questions or points on the left side of your double-entry journal. On the right side, write answers or descriptions as your class reads the text.

   - Who are the characters and their relationships?
   - What happens in the plot?
   - What is the setting?
   - Flashback (a sudden and vivid memory of an event in the past)
   - From what point of view is the novel written?

2. In the last paragraph on page 4, Paul says, "The zombie was locked out." In your double-entry journal make some predictions about who or what the zombie might be.

3. In your double-entry journal, summarize what you know about the novel based on your reading and discussion of the prologue.

ABOUT THE AUTHOR

Growing up in New Jersey, Edward Bloor loved playing soccer. His love for soccer found its way into *Tangerine*, his first novel, which has won several awards. He has since written three other novels. A former English teacher, Bloor writes about teenage characters and the issues they face.

Beginning the Novel

SUGGESTED LEARNING STRATEGIES: Double-Entry Journals, Oral Reading, Questioning the Text, Summarizing/Paraphrasing

Levels of Questioning

An effective way to think actively and interpretively about your reading is to ask questions on different levels. As you read this novel, you will be expected to question it on three levels:

- **Literal Level**: You can answer questions on the literal level by looking to the text directly.

  Example: What kind of car does Mrs. Fisher drive?

- **Interpretive Level**: You cannot find answers to interpretive questions directly in the text; however, textual evidence points to and supports your answers.

  Example: What emotions does Paul feel as he remembers the incident with the mailbox?

- **Universal Level**: These questions go beyond the text. They require you to think of the larger issues or ideas raised by the novel.

  Example: Is it possible that people who are visually impaired can see some things more clearly than people whose vision is 20/20?

Mood and Atmosphere

What details and inferences do you have so far about Paul's new neighborhood? List as many as you can. Then, draw a map of the neighborhood in Lake Windsor Downs. Give attention to color, structures, and other details that create this setting. These details of setting help create the **mood** and **atmosphere** of a novel. What specfic details establish the atmosphere of Lake Windsor Downs?

WORD CONNECTIONS

Literal contains the root *-liter-* from the Latin word *littera*, meaning "letter." This root also appears in *literacy, literature,* and *alliteration*.

Universal contains the Latin prefix *uni-*, meaning "one," and the root *-ver-*, meaning "turn." The root *-ver-* appears in *reverse, adversary, introvert, vertigo,* and *conversation*. The suffix *-al* indicates an adjective.

LITERARY TERMS

Atmosphere is the feeling created by a literary work or passage. Details of setting often create atmosphere, which contributes to the **mood**, or the overall emotional quality of a work. Mood is created by the author's language and tone and the subject matter.

Choices and Consequences One

SUGGESTED LEARNING STRATEGIES: Double-Entry Journal, Graphic
Organizer, Predicting

In *Tangerine*, as in real life, people make decisions that carry
consequences. Some consequences are obvious right away, while
others are not apparent until some time has passed. As you read the
novel, keep a record of the choices made by Paul, his parents, and
other characters. For some of the choices, you will be able to fill in the
consequences and the impact on Paul right away. For other choices, you
may not know a consequence or its impact on Paul until you have read
more of the novel.

Friday, August 18–Wednesday, August 23

Choice (include page number)	Who made the choice	Consequence(s)	Impact on Paul
Dad and Erik go to Florida first. (1)	It's not stated; probably Paul's parents.	• Paul gets to spend some time alone with his mother. • Erik spends time alone with his father.	

Friday, August 18–Wednesday, August 23

Choice (include page number)	Who made the choice	Consequence(s)	Impact on Paul

Writing Prompt: Identify which of the choices above is the most significant, and explain why.

_____

_____

A Memo

GRAMMAR & USAGE

A **subordinate clause** is a group of words with a subject and a verb, but it cannot stand alone as a sentence because it does not contain a complete thought. **Subordinating conjunctions** introduce subordinate (or dependent) clauses. When you write a sentence that includes at least one subordinate clause, you are writing a **complex sentence**.

WORD CONNECTIONS

The word *subordinate* is made up of the Latin prefix *sub-*, meaning "under" or "below," and the Latin root *-ord-*, meaning "order" or "rank."

A subordinate clause is lower in rank than an independent clause.

After reading the entries for Monday, August 21, pretend that you are Mrs. Gates, the principal of Lake Windsor Middle School. Think for a minute about the voice of a principal and the voice of Mrs. Gates in the novel.

1. Write a memo from Mrs. Gates to the head counselor at Lake Windsor Middle School summarizing her meeting with the new student, Paul Fisher. In the memo, include Mrs. Gates's perceptions of Paul and his mother and her predictions for Paul's success at her school. Remember that the content of the memo should be text-based, meaning that it should rely on details included in the text.

2. Revise your memo to include subordinating conjunctions and subordinate clauses.

Revising with Subordinate Clauses

Subordinate clauses and the **subordinating conjunctions** that introduce them enable you to show a relationship between ideas in a sentence.

Common subordinating conjunctions:

after	although	if	when
as	because	unless	whenever
as if	before	until	while

Sentences with subordinate clauses:

- **Although** Mr. Fisher seems like a concerned father, he is inattentive to Paul.
- **After** she talked to the principal, Mrs. Fisher worried about the lack of a disaster plan.
- **Because** Paul is serious about soccer, the Seagulls accept him as a teammate.
- **When** anyone touches Paul's glasses or eyes, he goes berserk.

The subordinate clauses in these sentences are **adverbial clauses**. Each modifies the verb in the sentence.

Notice that when a subordinate clause begins a sentence, it is followed by a comma.

Notice, also, that you can sometimes place adverbial clauses in different locations in a sentence:

- The Seagulls accept Paul as a teammate because he is serious about soccer.

When you use subordinate clauses, try putting them in different locations to see which is most effective.

First Day of School Experiences

Respond to the following in your double-entry journal.

1. Reread Paul's entry for Monday, August 28. Write the following four topics on the left side of your journal. Then, using complete sentences, write what you believe to be the five most important pieces of information on the right side of the double-entry journal, focusing on these topics:

   • The main events of the entry

   • Joey

   • Erik's nature

   • Whether the sibling relationships depicted in the novel correspond to what you know about such relationships.

2. In Activity 3.7, you made predictions about the visually-impaired label placed on Paul. Have your predictions matched the events in the novel? Explain.

Using Appositives

Your teacher may ask you to work on specific usage and mechanics issues as you review your sentences.

You may also want to practice using **appositives** in your writing. Here are some examples of sentences with appositives:

   • Edward Bloor's first novel, *Tangerine*, takes place in Florida.

   • Paul, *the main character of the novel*, is a soccer player.

   • Erik, *Paul's brother*, is a senior in high school.

If the appositive adds meaning to the sentence but is not necessary for the sentence to make sense, set it off with commas.

Go back to the sentences you wrote in your journal indicating the most important pieces of information you learned. Insert appositives in several of your sentences. Share your revised sentences with a partner.

GRAMMAR & USAGE

An **appositive** is a noun or phrase placed near another noun to explain or identify it.

Film Connections

LITERARY TERMS

A **flashback** is an interruption in the sequence of events to relate events that occurred in the past.

Flashback

As you viewed the film clip from *Sandlot*, you were aware of the use of **flashback**. How does the filmmaker let you know that what you are about to see is a flashback? Make notes in the left side of the diagram below.

Tangerine is also a text that uses flashbacks. Look back at the prologue and Paul's entry for Monday, August 28. How does the author let you know that what you are about to read is a flashback? Make notes in the right side of the diagram to complete this comparison.

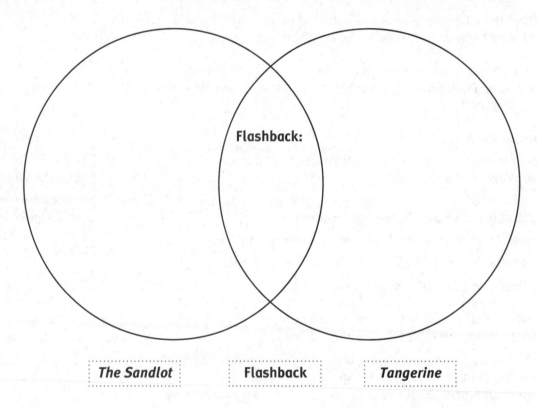

The Sandlot   **Flashback**   **Tangerine**

Writing Prompt: Write an interpretative response about the use of flashback. Use sentence structures you have learned in this unit, such as a subordinate clause with a subordinating conjunction. If appropriate, use an appositive in your response.

Foreshadowing

Both film and novels use **foreshadowing** to prepare the audience for action that is to come. Foreshadowing creates an atmosphere of suspense and keeps the audience wondering about what will happen. Both *The Sandlot* and *Tangerine* use foreshadowing. Document those examples and what they hint at in the chart below.

LITERARY TERMS
Foreshadowing is the use of clues to hint at events that will occur later in the plot.

Evidence of foreshadowing in *The Sandlot*	Inference about what is being foreshadowed in *The Sandlot*	Evidence of foreshadowing in *Tangerine*	Inference about what is being foreshadowed in *Tangerine*

Film Connections

Characterization

As you watch the film, note how the character, Scott Smalls, is revealed through various techniques of characterization. Next, note details from *Tangerine* that reveal the character of Paul Fisher. Then write a sentence in your double-entry journal that answers this question: How are Paul and Scott alike and different?

Elements of Characterization	Scott Smalls	Paul Fisher
His Actions		
His Appearance		
His Thoughts		
What He Says		
What Others Say About Him		

Lightning Strikes

SUGGESTED LEARNING STRATEGIES: Double-Entry Journal, Graphic
Organizer, Questioning the Text, Think-Pair-Share, Word Map

Before Reading

1. Before reading the entries from Tuesday, September 5, through
   Saturday, September 9, think about what you know about lightning.
   Take a few minutes to record in your journals any facts you know.

During Reading

2. Your teacher will instruct you to use the levels of questioning
   strategy. Write the questions in your journal and identify the level of
   each question.

After Reading

3. Record and discuss information on the Sibling Relationships
   organizer. Then create one sentence comparing the Costello brothers'
   relationship to the Fisher brothers' relationship. This will become a
   topic sentence or a thesis statement for a comparison.

Writing a Comparison

4. Begin your literary analysis paragraph or essay with your sentence of
   comparison. You will explain and support this sentence in the rest of
   your essay.

5. Organize your ideas by discussing each of the relationships
   separately. Then compare them in concluding remarks.

6. Use transition words to help your reader follow your ideas.

   Transitions to use when comparing: *also, alike, both, in the same
   way, likewise, similarly*

   Transitions to use when contrasting: *but, different,however, in
   contrast, instead,on the other hand, unlike, yet*

Lightning Strikes

Sibling Relationships

Using the graphic organizer below, compare the ways the Costello brothers relate to each other with the ways the Fisher brothers relate to each other. Then, write one sentence describing the relationship of the Costello brothers and one sentence describing the relationship of the Fisher brothers.

Joey's Relationship with Mike	Mike's Relationship with Joey
Paul's Relationship with Erik	Erik's Relationship with Paul

Relationship of the Costello brothers:

_____

_____

Relationship of the Fisher brothers:

_____

_____

SUGGESTED LEARNING STRATEGIES: Drafting, Double-Entry Journal, Peer Editing, Word Map

1. Think about how you would feel on September 9 if you were Paul. Then, on the left side in your double-entry journal, write one sentence stating how Paul feels about himself on September 9.

2. On the right side of your double-entry journal, list the reasons why you think Paul feels this way about himself. Then, number the reasons you included, from most to least significant.

3. On separate paper, draft a paragraph about Paul's self-concept at this point in the novel. Use your first sentence as the topic sentence and the numbered list of reasons as support. Include a comment about how realistic it is for Paul to feel this way.

4. Read, revise, and edit your paragraph with a partner. During the editing process, consider where your paragraph could benefit from the use of a transition word. Insert transitions in your next draft.

>
> GRAMMAR & USAGE
> When you use a **transition** at the beginning of a sentence, follow it with a comma. When you use a transition to connect two complete thoughts, precede the transition with a semicolon and follow it with a comma.

Following is a list of transition words and phrases to use as you write and revise. These transitions are adverbs. When you use one of these transitions to connect two complete thoughts (independent clauses), they are called **conjunctive adverbs**.

Transition	When to Use It /What It Means
Additionally	To introduce a new fact or argument in support of your thesis or topic sentence.
Nevertheless	Means "in spite of that"; use when making a counter argument to a previous statement.
In addition	To introduce a new fact or argument in support of your thesis or topic sentence.
Consequently	Means "because of the reason given"; use when making a statement from the evidence previously provided.
However	Use to introduce a statement that contrasts with or contradicts something that has previously been stated.
Finally	Use to introduce a final point or reason.
Moreover	Means "as a further reason"; use to introduce a similar fact or argument to support your thesis or topic sentence.

The Sinkhole

Reviewing Point of View

Tangerine is all told in **first-person point of view**. Using the T-chart below, record the benefits and limits of first-person point of view in this novel.

Benefits	Limits

GRAMMAR & USAGE

A writer's **verbs** and verb forms determine the intensity and the precision of the content. Intense, strong action words make a story come alive for the reader. Notice the action words in this sentence: "The kids came **diving** out, **jamming** in the doorways, **pushing** into the backs of other kids, **knocking** each other flat."

Weak, vague words can often make what was originally an exciting story seem dull and boring.

Understanding Paul's Perspective

Respond to the following prompts in your double-entry journal.

1. Copy quotations that convey how others judge Paul's actions on September 11, and how Paul judges himself after the sinkhole episode. On the right side of the journal, reflect on Paul's new sense of himself.

2. Explain why the geographical setting of the novel is important to the plot in these chapters.

3. Part 1 ends with Paul mentioning a "miracle." In the last sentence, he says, "The heavens had opened up for me." Copy that statement onto the left side of your journal; then use the right side to reflect on what the miracle is and what Paul means by his last statement in the entry for Friday, September 15.

Amazing Rescues

SUGGESTED LEARNING STRATEGIES: Double-Entry Journal, Role Playing

1. Read a true report of an amazing rescue. Fill in the information below using complete sentences.

Title of report: _____

Author: _____

Who:

_____

_____

What:

_____

_____

_____

When:

_____

_____

_____

Where:

_____

Why:

_____

_____

_____

How:

_____

_____

_____

Amazing Rescues

2. Review the description of the sinkhole disaster and rescue in Paul's entry for Monday, September 11. In news reporting, you will find answers to the 5 Ws and an H: Who, What, When, Where, Why, and How. Can you identify these in the novel?

Who:

_____

_____

What:

_____

_____

_____

When:

_____

_____

Where:

_____

Why:

_____

_____

How:

_____

_____

_____

Revising with Coordinating Conjunctions

Review the sentences you wrote about the rescue article. If they are short and choppy, you may want to combine them. One way to combine **simple sentences** (independent clauses) is to use a **coordinating conjunction** to create a **compound sentence**. Following is a list of coordinating conjunctions:

> *and, but, or, for, so, yet, nor*

Here are examples of sentences combined with coordinating conjunctions:

> Old Charley Burns did not inspect construction sites.
>
> Buildings were constructed in unsafe places.
>
> **Combined:** Old Charley Burns did not inspect construction sites, **so** buildings were constructed in unsafe places.

> The sinkhole was extremely dangerous.
>
> Paul and Joey rescued many students.
>
> **Combined:** The sinkhole was extremely dangerous, **yet** Paul and Joey rescued many students.

> Paul expected school to be closed for a month.
>
> Mrs. Gates announced that the relocation plan would begin Monday.
>
> **Combined:** Paul expected school to be closed for a month, **but** Mrs. Gates announced that the relocation plan would begin Monday.

When you join two sentences with a coordinating conjunction, use a comma before the coordinating conjunction. Be careful *not* to begin sentences with these coordinating conjunctions; they often lead to sentence fragments.

3. Revise the sentences you wrote about the rescue article in Question 1, using coordinating conjunctions to combine sentences.

GRAMMAR&USAGE

Coordinating conjunctions join words or groups of words that perform the same function in a sentence.

Choices and Consequences Two

As you read to the end of Part 1 of *Tangerine*, keep a record of the
choices made by Paul, his parents, and the other characters. For some
of the choices, you will be able to fill in the consequence right away.
For other choices, you may not know a consequence until you have read
more of the novel.

Through Friday, September 15
End of Part 1

Choice (include page number)	Who Made the Choice	Consequence(s)	Impact on Paul

Through Friday, September 15
End of Part 1

Choice (include page number)	Who Made the Choice	Consequence(s)	Impact on Paul

Writing Prompt: Using information from your double-entry journal above, identify which of the choices is the most significant, and explain why.

_____

_____

_____

_____

_____

The Choices We Make

Who or What Influences Your Choices?

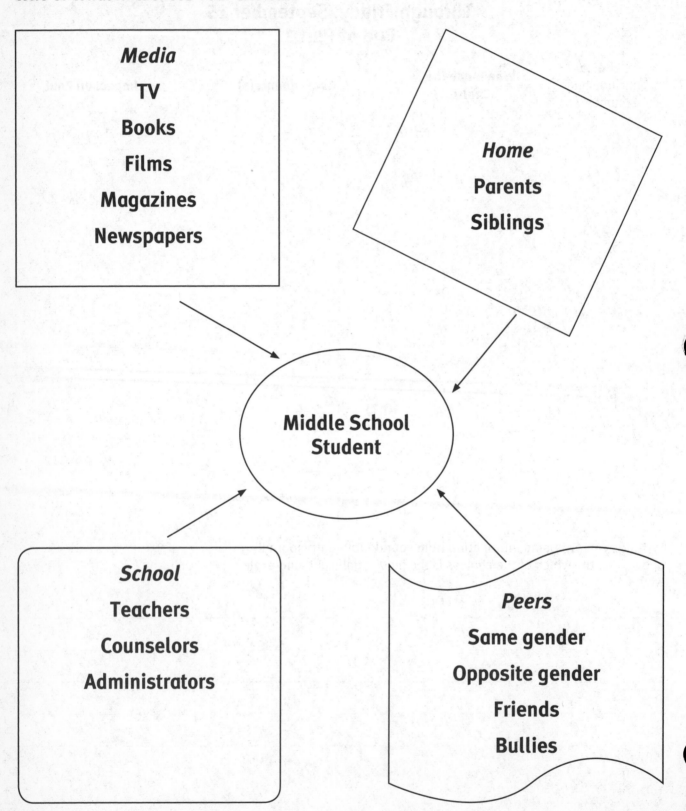

Media

TV

Books

Films

Magazines

Newspapers

Home

Parents

Siblings

Middle School
Student

School

Teachers

Counselors

Administrators

Peers

Same gender

Opposite gender

Friends

Bullies

Who or What Influences Paul's Choices?

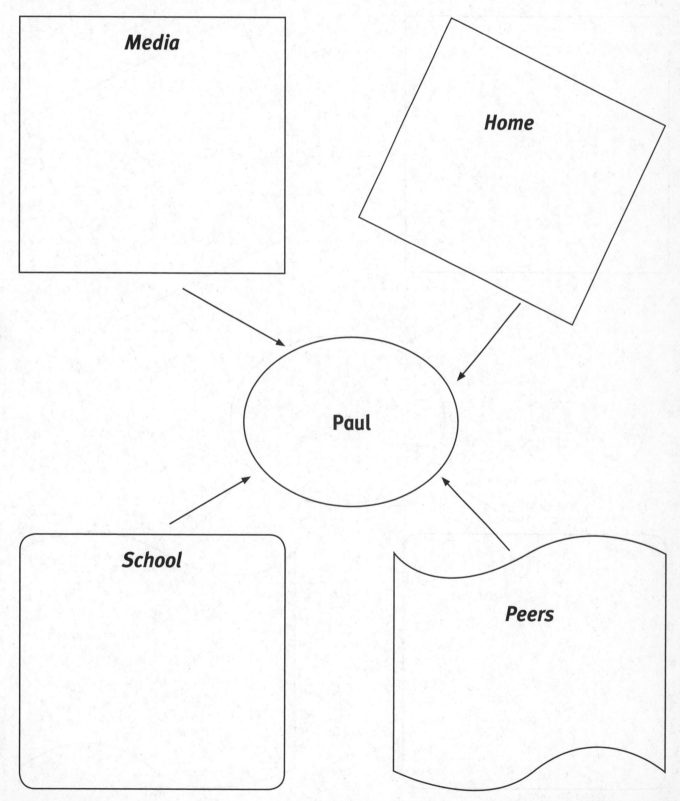

The Choices We Make

Who or What Influences My Choices?

Me

Another New School

SUGGESTED LEARNING STRATEGIES: Graphic Organizer, Close Reading, Metacognitive Markers, Revising, Self-Editing

1. As you read Paul's entry for Friday, September 22, use the following text-marking procedure:

   • Place a checkmark (√) by passages you understand.

   • Place a question mark (?) by sections you do not understand.

   • Place an exclamation point (!) by passages you find interesting.

2. Reread closely Paul's entry for Wednesday, September 20. Add new information to the Sibling Relationships graphic organizer you started in Activity 3.11, "Lightning Strikes."

Revising with Correlative Conjunctions

Correlative conjunctions are useful when you compare or contrast. You can use **correlative conjunctions** to connect details or combine sentences as you are writing or revising. Following is a list of correlative conjunctions:

both…and	not only…but (also)
either…or	just as…so (too)
neither…nor	whether…or

GRAMMAR & USAGE

Correlative conjunctions are a pair of conjunctions that work together to connect words used in the same way.

Here are examples of sentences using correlative conjunctions:

Paul is afraid of **both** Erik **and** Arthur.

The Lake Windsor Downs students have to choose **either** to stay at their school **or** to transfer to Tangerine Middle School.

At first, **neither** Tino **nor** Victor seems happy to have Paul on their soccer team.

Not only does Paul love soccer, **but** he is **also** a great goalie.

The War Eagles love to play soccer, **whether** the day is sunny **or** rainy.

3. Revise the comparison paragraphs you wrote about sibling relationships in Activity 3.11. Include the new details you recorded on your chart, and use correlative conjunctions.

Comparing Schools

SUGGESTED LEARNING STRATEGIES: Drafting, Graphic Organizer, Revising

1. Using the Venn diagram, compare and contrast Lake Windsor Middle School and Tangerine Middle School. Write details shared by both schools in the middle space, details specific to Lake Windsor in the left space, and details specific to Tangerine in the right space.

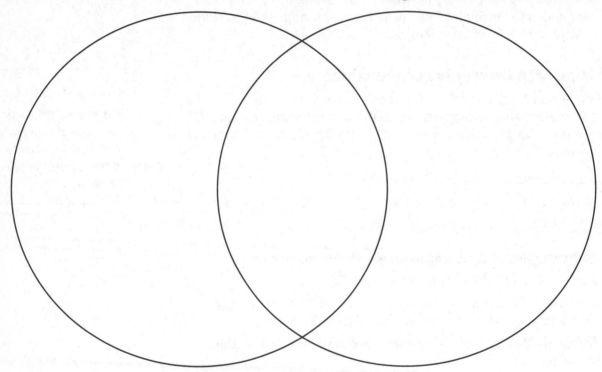

Lake Windsor Middle School   **Both**   **Tangerine Middle School**

2. **Writing Prompt:** Write a paragraph that focuses on the differences between the two schools. Include a strong topic sentence that makes a point about the differences. Use transition words and conjunctions from previous activities as you draft and revise your paragraph.

_____

_____

_____

_____

_____

The New Team

ACTIVITY
3.19

1. **Quickwrite:** Think about a time when you were a new member of a sports team, club, school, or other group. Compose a quickwrite describing some of the feelings you experienced as "the new kid."

_____
_____
_____
_____
_____
_____
_____

> **WORD CONNECTIONS**
>
> Analogies can be written as part-to-whole or as whole-to-part. Rewrite the following analogy as whole-to-part.
>
> Athlete : team ::
> flower : garden

2. Reread Paul's entry for Tuesday, October 3, and write three to five interpretive questions in the space below.

_____
_____
_____
_____
_____
_____
_____
_____
_____
_____
_____

3. In your double-entry journal, analyze the situation. Explain why Paul feels the need to write about something now that he did not feel the need to write about when it happened.

Seeing and Understanding

LITERARY TERMS

A **motif** is a repeated element such as an image, symbol, or theme.

Who Sees? Who Doesn't See?

1. After reading and discussing the entries for November, think about the word *see* and its meanings, both literal and figurative. Select one of the characters listed below. In one lens of the glasses, list the things the character sees or understands; in the other lens, list the things the character does not see or understand (or refuses to see).

   Characters: Paul, Paul's father, Paul's mother, Joey, Erik, or another character.

   Write the name of the character you have chosen:

   _____

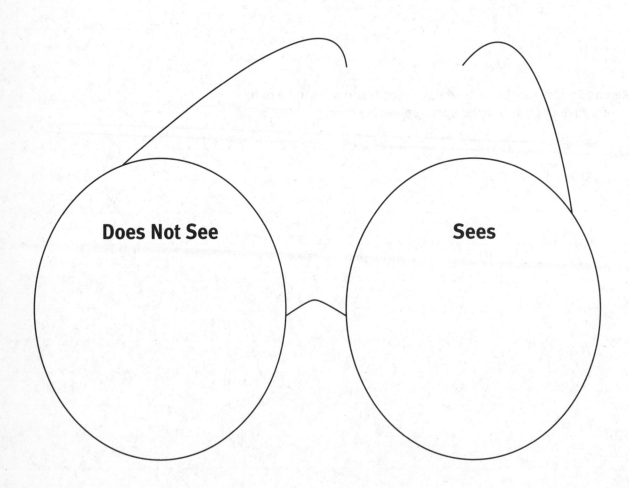

2. After you have worked on the graphic organizer, meet with others who chose the same character. Compare and discuss what your character sees and doesn't see, and add details to your graphic organizer.

3. Draft a paragraph about your character based on the details in your graphic organizer. As a topic sentence, make a judgment statement about whether or not the character does or does not "see."

It's Just a Game

LITERARY TERMS

Hyperbole is exaggeration used for effect. An example is "He's taller than most trees."

1. Read and discuss Paul's entry for Thursday, November 2. Look especially at the final paragraph of the entry. Find and copy into your journal an example of *hyperbole* in this paragraph. On the right side of your journal, explain why the example is hyperbolic.

2. Look closely at this sentence: "They are beaten by their own fear before the game even begins." In your journals write a response to this question: What does this statement mean to Paul in a sports situation and in his life?

3. After you have read through Friday, November 10, work with a group to create a newspaper article for the sports page of the *Tangerine Times* about either the soccer or football teams. In your article, include information on Erik's progress in football or Paul's progress in soccer. Write in the style of a sports story.

GRAMMAR & USAGE

A verb is in the **active voice** when the subject of the sentence performs the action. It is in the **passive voice** when the subject receives the action—that is, has something done to it.

Active versus Passive Voice

Verbs change form to show **active voice** or **passive voice.** The active voice is generally more lively, concise, and easier to understand.

Active voice: The goalie **deflected** the ball.

In this example, the subject (the goalie) is performing the action of deflecting.

Passive voice: The ball **was deflected** by the goalie.

In this example, the subject (the ball) is receiving the action of deflecting.

You can recognize passive voice because the verb phrase includes a form of *to be,* such as *am, is, was, were, are,* or *been.* Another way to recognize sentences with verbs in the passive voice is that they may include a "by …" phrase after the verb. Generally, it is better to use the active voice in your writing. Occasionally, however, the passive is more effective when you want to emphasize what is done to the subject, as in this sentence: "They are beaten by their own fear…"

4. Revise this sentence:

   Passive voice: The game **was won by** the Tangerine War Eagles.

   Active voice:

5. How is author's purpose in a news article different from a theme in a novel?

Choices and Consequences Three

As you complete Part 2 of *Tangerine*, keep a record of the choices made by the characters. For some of the choices, you will be able to fill in the consequences right away. For other choices, you may not know a consequence until you have read more of the novel.

Monday, September 18– Friday, November 10
End of Part 2

Choice (include page number)	Who Made the Choice	Consequence(s)	Impact on Paul

Choices and Consequences Three

Monday, September 18– Friday, November 10
End of Part 2

Choice (include page number)	Who Made the Choice	Consequence(s)	Impact on Paul

Writing Prompt: Using notes in your double-entry journal above, identify which of the choices is the most significant, and explain why.

_____

_____

_____

_____

_____

_____

_____

_____

_____

Novel Structure: Conflict and Plot

SUGGESTED LEARNING STRATEGIES: Double-Entry Journal, Graphic
Organizer, Notetaking, Predicting, Think-Pair-Share, Word Map

1. A novel is composed of many **conflicts** and plots. The major
conflict involves the main character and drives the main plot. In the
graphic below, state the main conflict of *Tangerine*, and detail the
components of that conflict.

> **LITERARY TERMS**
> A **conflict** is a struggle
> between opposing forces;
> for example, man versus
> self, man versus man, man
> versus nature, or man
> versus society.

Main Conflict

> **Individual vs. Self**

2. In *Tangerine*, each of the other types of conflicts is represented in a
subplot. Give specifics that characterize each type of conflict.

Additional Conflicts

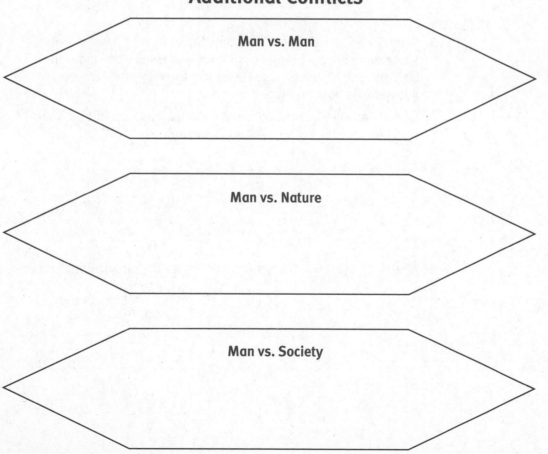

> **Man vs. Man**

> **Man vs. Nature**

> **Man vs. Society**

Saving the Grove

WORD CONNECTIONS

Complete the analogy with a word that shows the same relationship.

Grove : tree ::
house : _____

What relationship does this analogy show?

1. Before beginning Part 3, **scan** the section and note the length of the entries for this time period. In your double-entry journal, explain why you think Paul wrote this much at this time.

2. Reread the first sentence for Monday, November 20. Then **predict** what will happen when the science-project group comes to Paul's house.

_____

_____

_____

_____

_____

_____

3. Read the entries through Thursday, November 23, Thanksgiving. **Summarize** in your journal what Paul witnessed from under the bleachers on November 21. Then pose three interpretive level **questions** in your journal.

4. Revisit Activity 3.3. How does the weather Paul describes in the chapters match what you know about Florida?

_____

_____

_____

5. How does Bloor use the setting to advance the plot of *Tangerine*?

_____

_____

_____

_____

Real Life: Bully-Proofing

SUGGESTED LEARNING STRATEGIES: Close Reading, Double-Entry Journal, Drafting, Graphic Organizer, Marking the Text, RAFT, Sharing and Responding, Self-Editing, Word Map, Previewing

1. As you read "Bullying in Schools" and "Taming Wild Girls," mark the text by circling the examples of bullying and by highlighting or underlining solutions to the problem.

2. After reading both articles, complete the graphic organizer below by writing examples of bullying in the news and in the real world.

3. Finally, revisit your marked "Bullying in Schools" and "Taming Wild Girls" texts. List any solutions you find. Think of other solutions and list them as well.

Examples of Bullying in the Real World

Bully/Victim	Action

Solutions from "Bullying in Schools" and "Taming Wild Girls" and My Solutions for Bullying

My Notes

Article

BULLYING IN SCHOOLS
Fighting the Bully Battle

by Hilda Clarice Quiroz, June Lane Arnette, Ronald D. Stephens

What is school bullying?

Bullying is a form of violence that hurts others. School bullying happens at school or during school-sponsored activities when a student or group of students intentionally and repeatedly uses their power to hurt other individuals or groups. Bullies' power can come from their physical strength, age, financial status, popularity, social status, technology skills, or by association (the people they know, who they hang out with, who their family is).

What do bullies do?

They can bully in direct ways, such as:

- hitting, tripping, shoving, pinching, excessive tickling;
- verbal threats, name calling, racial slurs, insults;
- demanding money, property, service; and
- stabbing, choking, burning and shooting.

They can also bully in indirect ways, such as:

- rejecting, excluding, isolating;
- ranking or rating, humiliating;
- manipulating friends and relationships;
- writing hurtful or threatening e-mails and postings on web sites; and
- blackmailing, terrorizing, and proposing dangerous dares.

Do boys and girls bully in different ways?

Traditionally, boys tended to bully in direct and physical ways, and girls tended to bully in emotional or indirect ways. However, influences, such as media, technology and new forms of social power, are beginning to blur the gender lines.

Other things to know about bullying:

- Some students are bullies; others are targets of bullying.

- A student can be both a target and a bully at the same time.

- Some students are bystanders; bystanders can be either passive or active.

- Some acts of bullying at school can result in suspension and/or expulsion.

- Bullying breaks the law when it becomes stealing, assault and battery, extortion, sexual harassment, hate crimes and other criminal acts.

- Administrators, teachers, school staff, students and parents must accept the responsibility to recognize, report and/or intervene with bullying when it occurs.

- Bullying that goes unchecked tends to escalate into more serious forms of bullying or even criminal behavior.

My Notes

Real Life: Bully-Proofing

GRAMMAR & USAGE

Use commas to separate items in a series in your writing. A **series** is a list of three or more items, the last two of which are joined by *and, or,* or *nor.*

Remember:

• Use commas after each item in the series, including the item before *and, or,* or *nor.*

• Do not use commas if each of the items is connected by *and, or,* or *nor.*

Identify the series of phrases in the second paragraph on this page.

My Notes

What can students do about school bullying?

There are a variety of ways students can be involved with bullying. A student can be a **bully** or the **target** of bullying. A student may even be **both a target and a bully** at the same time. Some students are bystanders. Some students may not be aware of bullying at their school and still be affected by the problems it creates.

A student who is a target of bullying needs to know that bullies rarely stop what they are doing on their own. In fact, it is more likely that over time a bully will find more serious ways to hurt people. This is why it is important for a target of bullying to tell a responsible and caring adult at school what is happening and to ask for their help. In the meantime, targets can reduce the chances of being harmed by avoiding the times and places they are typically bullied, hang out in safe places at school, and stay close to good friends. It is important to keep reporting bullying until help is provided.

A student who bullies in return for being bullied becomes one more bully at school. Some students make the mistake of thinking that carrying a weapon, joining a gang, or planning serious acts of retaliation will solve the problem. More often than not the act of revenge seriously hurts more than just the target— it hurts the bully, the target and innocent bystanders.

Students who are bystanders to bullying must realize that they can either be a part of the problem or part of the solution. Bystanders are a powerful majority at any school. Bystanders have the power to help create safe and comfortable schools for themselves and other students. They can use their social power and personal actions to promote respect. They can carry out anti-bullying activities and campaigns. Bystanders should be warned against trying to protect a student or group of students who are being bullied. Peers who intervene risk retaliation or harm. The most important thing they can do is to report bullying when they see it happening to others.

A student who is a bully needs help and support to admit the behavior is hurtful and wrong. It is important for students who bully to find respectful ways to express their power when they are with others. Like the target of bullying, a bully can ask for the help of a caring and responsible adult or agree to accept the help when it is offered.

Taming Wild Girls

by Jeffrey Kluger

You can tell things aren't going to end well the moment the little cluster of girls starts to talk. Amanda, a junior at Lower Dauphin Middle School in Hummelstown, Pa., is in the cafeteria, commiserating with her friends about a monster test they all just took. Her friends are sure they tanked it, but Amanda has no such worries. "I aced it," she says airily, "but that's just me." As she gets up to clear her tray, the other girls exchange narrowed looks. "Let's trip her," one suggests. Another one nods, goes after Amanda and in an instant sends her sprawling.

The scene is a nasty one—or it would be if the girls meant any harm. But they don't. There is no real tray, no real cafeteria, and Amanda's tumble was a planned pratfall. The students are merely role-playing, acting out a Kabuki version of the girl-on-girl aggression they are increasingly finding in their school. The teachers noticed it too and have taken steps to stop it.

"O.K.," says Pam Eberly, a health and physical-education teacher who helped the girls stage the exercise. "What happened here? Who was the bully? Who were the bystanders? And what could you have done so that things turned out differently?"

The role playing at Lower Dauphin is part of a new program called Club Ophelia that the school initiated to stem the problem of violence among its girls. And Club Ophelia is just one of a few programs in the U.S. that educators are putting in place to tame a group of girls who—to hear teachers and psychologists tell it—have suddenly found their feral side.

The take-no-prisoners pitilessness teenage girls can show one another is nothing new. Pitch-perfect movies such as *Mean Girls* and *Thirteen* elevated awareness of the behavior, while shelves of advice books help parents and girls get through those angry years. But while the kids may be acquiring better tools to deal with cliques and cattishness, few are skilled at surviving a darker part of the schoolgirl power struggles: physical violence.

Popular stereotype doesn't always make room for the idea of violent girls, but they are there—and they are acting out. In 2003, according to the Centers for Disease Control, more than 40% of boys admitted to having carried a gun or a knife or been in at least one physical fight in the previous year. But the girls were not far behind, at 25%. And when the violence is girl-on-girl, it can get especially

My Notes

GRAMMAR & USAGE

In present tense, the verb form changes (singular or plural) to match the number of the subject (singular or plural). Be sure to make the **verb agree** with the **subject**, not with a noun in a prepositional phrase that follows the subject and happens to be closer to the verb.

Notice this example:

...the little *cluster* of girls *starts* the talk. (The verb *starts* agrees with the singular subject *cluster*, not with the plural word *girls* in the prepositional phrase.)

As you write your problem-solution letter on page 218, check your sentences to be sure that your verb forms agree with the subjects, not with some other word.

Real Life: Bully-Proofing

ugly. Deborah Prothrow-Stith, co-author of *Sugar & Spice and No Longer Nice: How We Can Stop Girls' Violence* and professor of public health at the Harvard School of Public Health, meets with teachers and administrators around the country and is taken aback by what she hears. "Principals talk about not only the increased number of girl fights but also the savagery" she says. "One of them told me, 'We never had to call an ambulance here until girls started fighting.'"

Experts agree that girls can be a handful, but they can't agree on why. One explanation is the Kill Bill culture—a reference to the famously bloody movie and its famously lethal female protagonist. If generations of boys found their mojo imitating the likes of Bruce Lee and James Bond, why shouldn't girls be equally juiced at the sight of a jumpsuited, sword-wielding Uma Thurman? ENTERTAINMENT WEEKLY (a sister publication of TIME) recently ran an online list of Hollywood's 15 best "Butt-Kicking Babes," from the pugilistic Hilary Swank to the gun-toting Charlie's Angels. A few of the stars were of older vintage, but most made their screen bones in the last generation.

Then there is the Internet. Girls have traditionally practiced not so much physical aggression as relational aggression—battles of cutting words, frosty looks and exclusion from cliques. E-mail makes it easy for the verbal part of that fragging to go on around the clock. Says Cheryl Dellasega, a humanities professor at Penn State's College of Medicine and creator of the Ophelia clubs: "They go back and forth on the computer all night, and the next day they're ready to fight."

Whatever the cause of all the combat, it is groups such as Club Ophelia that are making the peace. Dellasega founded the clubs in 2002 after the publication of her first book, *Surviving Ophelia*, about the struggles girls face growing up. One of the principles behind the groups is that girls tend to be tenacious about their anger, with resentments continuing to simmer long after the fisticuffs have ended. Most boys, always thought of as brawlers, are raised from birth on the idea of avoiding fights or at least ending them with a handshake. Girls need to learn the same lessons. More than 400 teachers and guidance counselors have taken Dellasega's workshops, and groups are sprouting up nationwide.

An Ophelia group consists of about 30 girls, two adult counselors and five or six mentors, who are one or two grades above the other girls and sometimes Ophelia graduates themselves. Teachers and administrators pick the participants, looking for girls who are aggressors, victims or enabling bystanders. The groups meet in 12 weekly sessions of 90 min. each. Most meetings begin with cooperation exercises such as forming hand-holding circles with all the girls' arms crisscrossing in the middle, and then trying to untangle without releasing hands. Sullen teens and tweens would not seem the best candidates for such an exercise, but at Lower Dauphin, they go at it gamely. "This is not for speed," Eberly reminds them. "Go slowly and listen to one another."

After the exercise and role playing, the girls retreat to the school's art room, where they work together on creative projects and brainstorm nonviolent solutions to hypothetical situations the instructors present them with. They also discuss powerful—and peaceable— women they admire. The list the teachers compile includes Oprah Winfrey, J. K. Rowling and Laura Bush. The girls' nominees mostly include teachers and guidance counselors and often their mothers.

Ophelia is not the only program doing that work. As long ago as 1986, the Seattle-based Committee for Children introduced its Second Step program, a classroom-based regimen that teaches anger management and impulse control. The program, which has been tested in a remarkable 25,000 schools, is aimed at younger kids—ages 4 to 14— and makes no distinction between boys and girls. But nowadays, says Joan Cole Duffell, the Committee's director of partnership development, girls "are beginning to express anger in ways more similar to boys."
Other, independent groups are appearing elsewhere, such as Images of Me, a girls-only self-awareness program in District Heights, Md., that teaches mediation and communication skills.

Nobody pretends that programs or mentoring can roll back the girls' behavior all the way—nor should it. Says Erika Karres, a retired teacher who once worked in the North Carolina school system: "You have to teach kids that it's good to have anger because it helps you get things out." The trick, of course, is learning to master the difference between assertiveness and aggressiveness, confidence and swagger.

Real Life: Bully-Proofing

Compose a business letter that discusses the problem of bullying and suggests possible solutions. Write about a specific example of bullying from one of the texts you have read or from your experience.

Address the letter to someone who can help change this serious situation. Using the **RAFT** graphic organizer, fill in the role you will assume, the audience, and a topic. If you choose a situation from *Tangerine*, use the voice of Paul or another character. If you use a situation from one of the articles or from your own experience, you may choose another voice under the Role category.

Role	
Audience	
Format	Business letter
Topic	

First, review the business letter format you used in Unit 2 (Activity 2.12). Use the format of a business letter and the framework of a problem-solution essay. In your letter, describe the bullying situation, explain why it is a serious problem, offer possible solutions, and make a plea for the person or group to whom you are writing to help make a change.

1. **Describe the problem:** Thesis: Exactly what is the problem and why is it a problem? Give reasons or causes and describe the effects of this problem. This is your introduction paragraph.

2. **Propose a Solution:** Describe your proposed solution and give details, perhaps focusing on one or two solutions the reader can help you with. Be sure your solution addresses the causes and effects and is logical and enforceable.

3. **Defend Your Proposal:** Why is yours the best solution? Imagine why someone might say your solution won't work, and disprove those reasons with a thoughtful analysis of your plan's strengths.

4. **Call to Action:** Remind the audience of the problem, your solution, and why your solution will work. You might tell the reader how he or she can help solve the problem. This could serve as your conclusion.

5. Edit your letter carefully. Check especially for subject-verb agreement in your sentences. Remember that a letter with grammar errors or other mistakes loses credibility with its audience.

SUGGESTED LEARNING STRATEGIES: Close Reading, Double-Entry Journal, Marking the Text, Oral Reading

Poetry

To an Athlete Dying Young

by A. E. Housman

The time you won your town the race
We chaired you through the market-place;
Man and boy stood cheering by,
And home we brought you shoulder-high.

To-day, the road all runners come,   5
Shoulder-high we bring you home,
And set you at your threshold down,
Townsman of a stiller town.

Smart lad, to slip betimes away
From fields where glory does not stay,
And early though the laurel grows
It withers quicker than the rose.

Eyes the shady night has shut
Cannot see the record cut,
And silence sounds no worse than cheers   15
After earth has stopped the ears:

Now you will not swell the rout
Of lads that wore their honours out,
Runners whom renown outran
And the name died before the man.   20

So set, before its echoes fade,
The fleet foot on the sill of shade,
And hold to the low lintel up
The still-defended challenge-cup.

And round that early-laurelled head   25
Will flock to gaze the strengthless dead,
And find unwithered on its curls
The garland briefer than a girl's.

ABOUT THE AUTHOR
British poet A. E. Housman (1859-1936) spent most of his life as a teacher and a scholar. His poems are known for capturing deep feeling.

My Notes

LITERARY TERMS
An **allusion** is a reference to a well-known person, place, event, or practice from literature or history.

Choices and Consequences Four

As you read the last section of *Tangerine*, keep a record of the choices made by the characters. Complete the consequences and the impact on Paul.

Monday, November 20–Wednesday, December 6
End of Part 3

Choice (include page number)	Who Made the Choice	Consequences	Impact on Paul

Monday, November 20–Wednesday, December 6
End of Part 3

Choice (include page number)	Who Made the Choice	Consequence(s)	Impact on Paul

Writing Prompt: Using the notes in your double-entry journal, identify which of the choices is the most significant, and explain why.

_____

_____

_____

_____

_____

_____

_____

Paul's Report to the Police

SUGGESTED LEARNING STRATEGIES: Drafting, Summarizing/
Paraphrasing, Discussion Groups

GRAMMAR & USAGE

Prepositional phrases begin with a preposition and end with a noun or pronoun. For example, "to the police" is a prepositional phrase. When a prepositional phrase is used as an adjective, it is called an **adjectival phrase**.

Example:

The report to the police described the incident. ("to the police" serves as an adjective modifying "report")

Prepositional phrases can also modify a verb, an adjective, or an adverb. Used in this way, they become **adverbial phrases**.

Examples:

He **lost** his skateboard *at the park*. ("at the park" modifies the verb "lost")

Saraya was **thrilled** *about her birthday present*. ("about her birthday present" modifies the adjective "thrilled")

Summer swimming classes start **early** *in the morning*. ("in the morning" modifies the adverb "early")

1. Reread the entry for Tuesday, December 5, *later*. Paul says, "I started with the basic facts, a paragraph or two, but I couldn't stop there." On a separate sheet of paper, write two paragraphs of the basic facts using Paul's voice. In other words, write what you think Paul would have written and the way Paul would have written it.

2. Then, Paul says, "I started writing about Luis, and what he meant to the people around him, and how they depended on him, and why they looked up to him." Write what you think Paul wrote in this part of the report. In other words, write about Luis in the way you think Paul would have described Luis.

3. Next, Paul says, "Then I tried to write the same thing about Erik: What did he mean to the people around him? How did they depend on him? Why did they look up to him?" Write what you think Paul wrote in this part of his report. Answer the questions about Erik that Paul says he answered in the report.

4. Read what you have written. Think about the audience for the report — the police. Think about the form of the writing — a report of the facts. Think about the purpose of the report — what it is that Paul wants to communicate to the police. Do you think that what you have written does that? Have you based your report on the facts given in the novel?

5. After thinking about the audience and purpose of the report, how would you organize this piece of writing so that it has an introduction with a thesis, a body, and conclusion? What information would make up your introduction? What would your thesis be? What would your conclusion consist of?

6. Truth is an important concept in *Tangerine*. Discuss with a group the ways various characters confess truths. Then collaborate on a thematic statement about truth.

What Is a Brother?

Exploring Brotherhood

In your double-entry journal, respond to these prompts:

1. How does the author use the imagery, or motif, of sight to show Paul's growing awareness and understanding of himself and his family?

2. Write a literal and a figurative definition of *brother*. Then explore Paul's insights about the idea of brothers and brotherhood.

WORD CONNECTIONS

Critique comes from a Greek root meaning "to judge" or "able to discern." This root is also in *crisis*, *critic*, *criticize*, and *criteria*.

Evaluating the Book's Covers

Revisit Activity 3.4 in which you previewed the book by analyzing the front and back covers.

3. Review the information on the covers, and consider what alterations or modifications you would make—and why—if you were redesigning the covers. Create an original book jacket incorporating some of your ideas. You might want to give the novel a new title, design a more visually appealing cover, include reviews of the novel from your classmates, and so on.

Front Cover: Revised Title, Visual Representation	Back Cover: Brief Synopsis of the Novel, Brag Page, and Review/Critique

Writing an Analytical Essay

SUGGESTED LEARNING STRATEGIES: **Marking the Text, Prewriting, Drafting, Revising, Sharing and Responding**

Now that you have read the novel *Tangerine*, write a multi-paragraph literary analysis essay in which you analyze the choices made by Paul's parents, by Paul, or by another character in the novel. Consider the impact of these choices on Paul. For example, you might focus on how the character's choices affect Paul's life, his self-concept, and his relationships with his peers and/or family members.

Steps

Prewriting

1. Collect your four Choices and Consequences charts. Highlight all the choices made by Paul in one color, the choices made by other characters in other colors. Select the character whose choices you are going to write about. Identify the effects of these choices on Paul. You might also consult your notes in your double-entry journal.

2. Select three or more of the character's highlighted choices that you think have significant consequences for Paul.

Planning

3. Place these choices in some type of order. You may cut them out of the sheets and experiment with arranging them in these organizational patterns:

   ▶ least consequence to greatest consequence

   ▶ types of choices made

   ▶ significance of the choices

   ▶ time order.

4. Which organizational pattern seems most logical to you? Paste or tape the choices on a sheet of paper in the order in which you want to discuss them in your essay.

5. Complete "The Choices _____ Makes" outline (page 226).

Drafting

6. Review all your notes before beginning a draft of the essay. If you are writing your essay by hand, try to write legibly since you will be sharing your draft within your writing group. In your introduction, include the title and author of the novel. You might also include a brief summary of the novel and introduce the concept of choices and the impact of a person's choices on another person's life. Your thesis sentence should state an opinion, without using "I," about how _____'s choices affect Paul.

7. As you continue to draft the essay, discuss the choices you have selected. Try to explain why the character you selected made these choices. Most importantly, give details and include specific examples from the novel to show how this choice affected Paul and what the long-term consequences were for him and his family. Properly cite page numbers in parentheses whenever you quote directly from the text. Use an appropriate format to integrate quotes into your essay, and use effective transitions to maintain the flow of ideas.

8. Write a conclusion that includes an evaluation of the character's choices and the consequences. Consider some of the following questions: Overall, how was Paul affected? How might he have turned out differently if the character had made different choices? Do you think the character meant well? Why or why not?

9. Remember to use transition words as you move through your discussion of each of the choices. Be sure to use transitions that reflect your organizational choice: least consequence to greatest, chronological order, significance of the choices, types of choices made.

Revising Through Sharing and Responding

10. Share your draft in your writing group, and use the Scoring Guide provided with this assignment to evaluate one another's work and ensure that it meets or exceeds the expectations. Use the feedback provided from your writing group, and revise your essay accordingly.

11. Review your draft and revise it for sentence variety. Where possible, revise sentences to include appositives, adverbial and adjectival phrases, and adverbial and adjectival clauses.

Editing for Publication

12. Read through your draft silently and mark your text to correct errors in grammar, punctuation, spelling. Use available resources to help you produce an error-free essay.

13. Create an appropriate title for your essay and prepare a publishable draft for submission.

Writing an Analytical Essay

The Choices _____ **Makes**

Before you begin your draft, complete the outline below to explain and evaluate your character's choices. Then, using the information from the outline and your other notes, begin writing a draft of your essay.

I. A choice made by _____ and how it affects Paul:

    A. Describe the choice.

    B. Why this choice is made: _____

    C. How Paul reacts to the choice and its effect on him.

II. Another choice made by _____ and how it affects Paul:

    A. Describe the choice.

    B. Why this choice is made: _____

    C. How Paul reacts to the choice and its effect on him.

III. Another choice made by _____ and how it affects Paul:

    A. Describe the choice.

    B. Why this choice is made: _____

    C. How Paul reacts to the choice and its effect on him.

SCORING GUIDE

Scoring Criteria	Exemplary	Proficient	Emerging
Ideas	The content shows a sophisticated response to the prompt by insightfully and clearly: • analyzing the choices made by the character • explaining the reasons for those choices • explaining the impact of the choices on Paul's life. Specific examples from the text directly support the claims made in the essay.	The content shows an adequate response to the prompt by: • identifying the choices made by the character • explaining the reasons for the choices • explaining the impact the choices have on Paul's life. Examples from the text support the claims made in the essay.	The content does not appropriately respond to the the prompt. The essay does not make clear connections among the choices made by the character, the reasons for the choices, and/or the impact they have on Paul. Analysis may be replaced by plot summary. Examples from the text are vague or missing.
Organization	The essay is well organized and includes: • a strong introduction with a hook and clear thesis • coherent body paragraphs with a defined organizational pattern • an insightful conclusion.	The essay is organized and includes: • an introduction with a hook and thesis • detailed body paragraphs with a defined organizational pattern • an effective conclusion.	The essay is disorganized and is missing one or more of the following: • an introduction with a thesis • developed body paragraphs with a defined organizational pattern • an adequate conclusion.
Use of Language	Word choice is effective and descriptive throughout the essay. Essay is written in third person point-of-view. It contains no "I" statements.	Word choice is appropriate and, at times, descriptive. Most of the essay is written in third person point-of-view. It avoids "I" statements.	Word choice is forced, vague, and/or repetitive. It detracts from the paper. Essay does not maintain third person point-of-view and contains "I" statements.

Writing an Analytical Essay

SCORING GUIDE

Scoring Criteria	Exemplary	Proficient	Emerging
Conventions	Direct quotations are punctuated and formatted properly. Writing contains few or no errors in spelling, punctuation, capitalization, or grammar.	Direct quotations may contain minor punctuation or formatting errors. Spelling, punctuation, capitalization, or grammar mistakes do not detract from the essay.	Direct quotations contain many punctuation or formatting errors. Spelling, punctuation, capitalization, or grammar mistakes detract from meaning and/or readability.
Evidence of Writing Process	Extensive evidence reflects the various stages of the writing process.	Evidence reflects the various stages of the writing process.	Little or no evidence reflects the stages of the writing process.
Additional Criteria			

Comments: _____

_____

_____

_____

_____

Learning Focus:

Real-World Solutions

Realistic fiction, such as *Holes* and *Tangerine*, challenges readers to identify with characters and their conflicts by creating situations that seem relevant and real to the audiences. When stories are told in first-person **point of view,** we are especially drawn to identify with the main characters and their situations. Their problems become ours, and we hope to see them resolved in a beneficial way. This connection between you—the reader—and the main character is part of what makes reading relevant and meaningful to the real world. Just as the fictional world focuses on **conflict and resolution,** the real world is full of problems that need solutions.

Working collaboratively to address real-world problems is a challenge for everyone. Alone, we are not able to work as efficiently or effectively to solve problems as we are if we work together. To prepare for the academic and work challenges that lie ahead for you, it is important that you practice working in a group to **research** and present solutions to real-world problems. This idea of working collaboratively sets the stage for effective actions in relation to real-world problems. But beyond the research is the important next step, which is the presentation of information. This act of communicating a problem and its solutions expands your influence beyond your small group to a larger audience of potential activists. This communication is a good reason to strive for quality and careful presentation of your work.

Working with technology is an important part of research and presentation in the 21st century. Much information is readily available via the Internet. While this access has made research easier in some ways, it has also made it much more difficult in other ways. You must be able to ask the right questions as you work with search engines and be careful evaluators of resources before you include those resources as part of your research. It is increasingly important not just to be able to access information online, but also to **evaluate the sources** for **accuracy, reliability, validity, currency,** and **authority.** When the research is complete, the Internet also offers many avenues for you to communicate your information to a large and receptive audience. As your experience with technology grows, your potential to influence a wider audience with your ideas also grows.

Brainstorming for a Research Project

ACADEMIC VOCABULARY

Research is finding and collecting information about a specific topic.

On the chart below, list the types of problems that occurred in *Tangerine*. Create a comprehensive list so that you have many research options for Embedded Assessment 2, "Researching and Presenting a Problem and Solutions."

Next, in your research group, select and circle two or three issues from each side that you might want to research for your presentation. You will decide which issue to present after you research the problems you have selected. Some issues may have a great deal of related research information available while others may not. Your interest and the information you find will guide your final selection of topic.

Problems in *Tangerine*

Social Issues	Environmental Issues
1. Sibling rivalry	1. The impact of housing developments on the environment

Domain Suffixes

Some Internet sites may contain more valid information than others. One way to know whether a Web site is valid is by its domain suffix. The domain name is the Web address, or Internet identity. The domain suffix, the three letters that follow the "dot," is the category in which that Web site falls. The most commonly used domain suffixes are defined below.

Domain Suffix	Definition/Description
.com	Stands for "commercial." Usually, Web sites with this suffix intend to make some sort of profit from their Internet services. Typically these are the Web sites that sell goods or services.
.org	Stands for "organization." Primarily used by not-for-profit groups such as charities and professional organizations.
.net	Stands for "network." Used by Internet service providers or Web-hosting companies.
.edu	Stands for "education." Used by major universities or educational organizations or other institutions.
.gov	Stands for "government." Used by U.S. government sites.

Every Web site has its place and its purpose. Use the information about domain suffixes to answer the questions below:

1. Which domain suffix(es) would you look for in Web sites when conducting research for Embedded Assessment 2?

2. Which domain suffix(es) would you look for when conducting research on a new law that is being passed?

3. Which domain suffix(es) would you look for when researching the best kind of cell phone to purchase next?

4. What domain suffix(es) would you look for when researching a new Internet provider for your parents to use?

Creating an Annotated Bibliography

GRAMMAR & USAGE

When using direct quotations from a source, you must place the quoted words inside quotation marks. You must also provide a **parenthetical citation**, which includes the author's name and the page number of the quotation in parentheses after the quoted material.

Now that you have read *Tangerine*, you are familiar with the major conflicts in the novel. Novels often deal with real-life issues and problems. Identify two of these problems to research, and create an annotated bibliography as you evaluate your sources. An **annotated bibliography** provides both the citation information and a brief explanation or summary of the source as well.

Working with your research group, choose two topics from the list that your class compiled. Using the Internet and library or media sources, research the topics. Use your research questions as a guide. Find at least three useful sources for each topic and create your annotated bibliography as follows:

1. On a notecard for each source, provide the complete bibliographical citation. See the sample below.

   • Use the Internet or a print reference to review the Modern Language Association (MLA) format for a citation.

2. Skip a line after the citation and briefly annotate your source with the following:

   • A brief synopsis of the content of the site

   • An evaluation of the usefulness of the information

   • A summary of the information in the source that can be used in the research project.

Sample annotated bibliography entry:

Stephenson, Nate. "Florida Muck Fires." U.S. Environmental Update. 12 Aug 2005.

   Environmental Concern Administration. 31 May 2006

http://www.nameofwebsite.org

Stephenson persuades the reader of the frequency and danger of muck fires, urging citizens to put pressure on state and local governments to prevent and fight the fires. The site represents the point of view of more extreme environmental groups.

This initial research will help you select your specific problem to research and determine how much information is readily available. Your group will use these sources as you prepare your problem-solution presentation.

Researching and Presenting a Problem and Solutions

SUGGESTED LEARNING STRATEGIES: **Marking the Text, KWHL Chart, Visualizing**

Assignment

Work with your research group to describe a real-life problem as it is presented in the novel *Tangerine*. For this assignment, you will conduct research on your problem and propose solutions to the problem using the reference materials that you located. Your final product will be a visual display in the form of digital slides or a trifold project display board, which will be viewed by an audience.

Steps

Prewriting

1. Write a thorough description of the problem as it exists in the novel and the real world. This description is your problem statement. Provide enough background and context for someone who has not read the novel to understand the problem. Be sure to cite page numbers from the novel when you refer to specific portions of the text. Ask a parent, guardian, sibling, or anyone else who has not read the novel to read your description of the problem in the book. Ask him or her to mark any places where he or she was confused or thought the text was unclear. Revise the problem statement accordingly and prepare a publishable draft for later submission.

Planning

2. Create a Research Plan for your chosen topic. You might begin by creating a KWHL chart to identify what you already know, what you need to know, and how you'll learn more. Make a list of the sources you expect to consult and what you hope or expect to learn about your topic from each. Use the **Research Plan Guide** on the next page to outline your work and construct your presentation.

   ▶ When developing your proposed solution, be sure to base your conclusions on reliable and relevant research.

   ▶ Your proposed solution must explain the topic and provide relevant reasons for your solution. Makes notes about facts and visuals that support your proposed solution. You will need this information to justify your conclusions.

Researching and Presenting a Problem and Solutions

Research Plan Guide

The problem we are researching/our title:

Why we chose this problem:

The format in which we will present our problem/solutions (PowerPoint or Trifold Presentation Board):

How this problem relates to the novel *Tangerine*:

(Be sure to include information from your research on the following points in your presentation. Take notes and cite your sources for the points in your presentation.)

Why this issue is a problem:

The effects of this problem on society today:

Possible solutions:

One of the best solutions:

Visuals (illustrations, charts/data, artwork, graphics) for our display:

Our annotated bibliography:

Our Sources Review:

Keep in mind that you may need to refine your research question. As you collect information, organize your notes to help you clarify your understanding of the topic.

3. Use the following **Sources Review** chart to check the reliablility of your sources. If you are using other sources than the Internet, many of the questions will still apply. If a question does not apply, just mark "N/A" in the appropriate box. A "yes" answer to many of the questions indicates that your source has a high degree of reliability and is a good source.

Criteria	Question	#1	#2	#3
Accuracy	Is the site free from grammatical and typographical errors?			
	Do the links and graphics operate properly?			
	Was the information verified by a third party?			
Validity or Objectivity	Does the information appear to be well researched?			
	Is there a bibliography or list of sources?			
	Is there a statement about the purpose of the site?			
	Is there a place to note and communicate errors on the site?			
	Does the site appear to be free from bias or a single position?			
Authority	Are the author's name and qualifications clearly identified?			
	Does the URL address match the site's name?			
	Does the site identify itself as a .gov site in its address?			
	Does the author appear to be well qualified to write on the subject?			
	Does this site identify itself as an .edu site in its address?			
Currency and Uniqueness	Does the date the site was last updated appear?			
	Has the site been updated recently?			
	Are any parts of the site "under construction"?			
	Are the majority of the articles on the site a part of that site (as opposed to links to other sites)?			
Coverage	Does the site seem to cover the topic fully?			
	Are there other, related topics discussed on the site?			
	Is there a resources section with links to other sites?			

Drafting

4. After reviewing at least three sources and discussing the information collected, write responses to the following questions by referring to specific parts of the sources you located and to the novel *Tangerine:*

   ▶ What conclusions has your group drawn about how the problem you identified manifests itself in the real world?

   ▶ What conclusions have you reached about the solutions that already exist for this problem?

   ▶ What creative solutions can you offer to the problem?

   ▶ Use an appropriate format to integrate quotes into your presentation. Use effective transitions to integrate your quotes and maintain the flow of ideas.

Revising and Editing for Presentation

5. Prepare a publishable draft of your annotated list of sources, which you will put on the back of the trifold display or at the end of a digital slide show. Your annotated bibliography should contain the following:

   ▶ properly cited sources

   ▶ a summary of the information included from each source

   ▶ a description of how valuable this source proved to be in providing information for your topic.

6. Create a trifold or digital presentation that contains the following:

   ▶ a description of the problem in the novel

   ▶ a description of the problem in the real world

   ▶ a description of possible solutions in the real world and an explanation of how these solutions would work for the problems in the novel

   ▶ visuals (pictures, drawings, or graphic representations) that enhance your presentation.

Remember to use technology and media ethically.

Revisit the Scoring Guide to ensure you are meeting specific criteria.

Your project will be displayed in a gallery fashion with the other projects from your classmates. You will not present the information orally, so your display must clearly reveal the problem and solutions. Your classmates will view your project, provide comments, and write questions regarding your display as they circulate throughout the classroom. After the gallery walk, your group will have time to respond to any questions or comments posed by your classmates.

TECHNOLOGY TIP If you are doing research on the Internet, meet with your teacher or your school's media specialist to gain ideas for search terms you might use to find information related to your topic.

SCORING GUIDE

Scoring Criteria	Exemplary	Proficient	Emerging
Presentation	The description of the problem from the novel is accurate and carefully crafted to provide a context that enables the reader to thoroughly understand the problem and the solutions proposed. The research presented makes meaningful connections between how the problem is represented in the novel and how it exists in the real world.	The description of the problem from the novel is accurate and provides a context that enables the reader to understand the problem and the solutions proposed. The research presented makes relevant connections between how the problem is represented in the novel and how it exists in the real world.	The description of the problem from the novel is inaccurate or vague, does not establish a context for the reader, and/or does not propose solutions. The research presented is limited and does not make relevant connections between how the problem is represented in the novel and how it exists in the real world.
Evidence of Research	There is extensive evidence of research conducted. The solutions proposed display a knowledgeable understanding of the problem and a thoughtful exploration of successful solutions that integrate appropriate quotes.	There is evidence of research conducted. The solutions proposed display an understanding of the problem and a consideration of possible solutions and appropriate quotes.	There is minimal evidence of research conducted. If a solution is proposed, it displays a limited understanding of the research on the problem and/or does not promote a possible solution.

SCORING GUIDE

Scoring Criteria	Exemplary	Proficient	Emerging
Annotated Bibliography	The annotated bibliography contains the following: • properly cited sources • a well-written summary of the relevant information contained in the source • a reflective description of how the source informed the research.	The annotated bibliography contains the following: • sources cited with a few errors • a summary of the information contained in the source • a description of how the source informed the research.	The annotated bibliography may be missing one or more of the following: • sources cited correctly (multiple errors in conventions and/or spelling) • a summary of the information contained in the source • a description of how the source informed the research.
Evidence of Collaboration	The group works collaboratively to design a presentation that effectively communicates to the intended audience.	The group works collaboratively to design a presentation that adequately communicates to its audience.	The group does not work collaboratively to design a presentation that communicates to an audience.
Additional Criteria			

Comments: _____

_____

_____

_____

_____

_____

Reflection

An important aspect of growing as a learner is to reflect on where you have been, what you have accomplished, what helped you to learn, and how you will apply your new knowledge in the future. Use the following questions to guide your thinking and to identify evidence of your learning. Use separate notebook paper.

Thinking about Concepts

1. Using specific examples from this unit, respond to the Essential Questions:
   - What is the relationship between choices and consequences?
   - How does research contribute to the discovery of solutions?

2. Consider the new academic vocabulary from this unit (Imagery, Point of View, Literary Analysis, Problem/Solution Essay, Research) as well as academic vocabulary from previous units and select 3-4 terms of which your understanding has grown. For each term, answer the following questions:
   - What was your understanding of the word before you completed this unit?
   - How has your understanding of the word evolved throughout the unit?
   - How will you apply your understanding in the future?

Thinking about Connections

3. Review the activities and products (artifacts) you created. Choose those that most reflect your growth or increase in understanding.

4. For each artifact that you choose, record, respond to, and reflect on your thinking and understanding, using the following questions as a guide:
   a. What skill/knowledge does this artifact reflect, and how did you learn this skill/knowledge?
   b. How did your understanding of the power of language expand through your engagement with this artifact?
   c. How will you apply this skill or knowledge in the future?

5. Create this reflection as Portfolio pages—one for each artifact you choose. Use the model in the box for your headings and commentary on questions.

Thinking About Thinking
Portfolio Entry

Concept:

Description of Artifact:

Commentary on Questions:

Reflecting on
My Choices

Essential Questions

? Why is it important to revisit, reflect on, and revise previously written texts?

? What influences a writer's choices during the revision process?

Unit Overview

By this time of the year, you are able to reflect upon the choices you have made in your writing, in addition to setting new goals for the remainder of the year. The portfolio you are developing provides multiple opportunities for reflection and revision. This unit includes activities and tasks that will allow you to revisit, reflect on, and transform previous assignments in order for you to understand the role that purpose, audience, and structure can have in the revision process.

Reflecting on My Choices
Contents

Goals

▶ To revisit and evaluate previously written texts

▶ To recognize how audience and format influence voice

▶ To understand the difference between revising and editing

ACADEMIC VOCABULARY

Voice

Revision

Global Revision

Learning Focus:

A Writer's Choices

Writers make many choices when creating texts. They can write in formal or informal voices. They can choose to present their ideas in **narrative** or **expository** modes. They can craft sentences that are either short or long in structure. As a writer yourself, you make many choices. For instance, have you ever really stopped to consider the choices you make when you write a note to your friend compared to when you write an essay for an assignment at school? Effective writers always consider the purpose and intended audience of their writing.

Effective writers also learn to revisit and revise their writing to improve it. They reflect upon the changes they make to become aware of specific techniques they use during the writing process. Some of the revision techniques you may be familiar with are highlighting text, adding and deleting words or phrases, replacing or rearranging ideas, writing notes in the margins, and combining sentences. In this unit, you will be given the opportunity to employ all of these revision techniques to texts you have previously written.

Listed below are essential terminology and strategies that writers use during revision and reflection about their writing:

▶ **Audience:** the intended readers of the written text

▶ **Voice:** the distinctive language that conveys the writer's personality; it includes sentence structure, diction, and tone to match the intended audience

▶ **Tone:** the writer's attitude toward his or her subject

▶ **Diction:** a writer's word choice

▶ **RAFT:** A writing strategy that analyzes various **R**oles, **A**udiences, **F**ormats, and **T**opics available to a writer

▶ **Revision:** rewriting text to improve ideas, organization, use of language, coherence, and fluency

▶ **Editing:** proofreading for errors in standard writing conventions, such as grammar, spelling, punctuation, and capitalization.

Independent Reading: In *Tangerine*, you read about a character who makes some difficult choices. Find a novel or nonfiction book (biography or autobiography) that interests you, and pay attention to the choices the characters make. As you read, think about how the choices in the two books are similar and different and how they compare to choices you may make in real life.

Previewing the Unit

Essential Questions

1. Why is it important to revisit, reflect on, and revise previously written texts?

_____

_____

_____

_____

2. What influences a writer's choices during the revision process?

_____

_____

_____

_____

Unit Overview and Learning Focus

Predict what you think this unit is about. Use the words or phrases that stood out to you when you read the Unit Overview and the Learning Focus.

_____

_____

_____

_____

_____

Embedded Assessment

What knowledge must you have (what do you need to know)? What skills must you have (what will you need to do to complete the Embedded Assessment successfully)?

_____

_____

_____

_____

Revisiting Choices

SUGGESTED LEARNING STRATEGIES: Graphic Organizer, Quickwrite, Think-Aloud, Think-Pair-Share

1. During the course of this school year, you have had the opportunity to make many different choices. These might have been simple choices of what to wear or eat, or larger ones dealing with relationships or school. Put a checkmark next to any of the following choices you made during the year. There are spaces for a few other choices you may have made.

_____	I chose to play a new sport this year.
_____	I chose to cut or color my hair differently.
_____	I chose a new circle of friends this year.
_____	I chose to wear a different brand of clothes this year.
_____	I chose to take a new elective this year.
_____	I chose to start a new hobby this year.
_____	I chose to take my schoolwork more seriously this year.
_____	I chose to play a new instrument this year.
_____	I chose to take on a new job: babysitting, lawn mowing, other.
_____	I chose to be friendlier this year.
_____	I chose to do volunteer work this year.
_____	
_____	
_____	

Revisiting Choices

In Pairs

2. Share one of your choices and its effects with a partner. Then share another choice with another partner. Add choices to the preceding list that you discover as you talk with others.

_____

_____

_____

_____

_____

_____

_____

_____

_____

3. **Quickwrite:** Select one of the choices you explored and write a paragraph explaining your attitude (were you pleased with this choice or did you regret it?) and the effect of your choice (how did it impact you and/or your friends or family?). Include a reflection evaluating whether you would make this choice again.

_____

_____

_____

_____

_____

_____

_____

_____

_____

_____

4. Interview a few people about choices they have made this year. After a person has identified some choices, ask him or her about the effect of those choices. Take careful notes on the graphic organizer so you can refer to them later.

Ask Each of These People	"What was one of the most important choices that you made this year?"	"What has been the effect of that choice on you, your friends, or family?"
Classmate		
Classmate		

Revisiting Choices

Ask Each of These People	"What was one of the most important choices that you made this year?"	"What has been the effect of that choice on you, your friends, or family?"
Friend		
Parent or Guardian		

5. Overall, were most people you interviewed happy with the outcome
of their choices, or were they disappointed? Did you get a sense that
most people would change their choices if they could? Explain.

_____

_____

_____

_____

_____

_____

_____

_____

_____

_____

_____

_____

_____

6. **Thesis Statement:** Based on your quickwrite and your interview
with others about choice, write a thesis sentence that makes a
generalization about the choices people make and the impact of
choices on their lives.

_____

_____

_____

_____

_____

Revisiting Writing

1. Consider all the writing you have done this year. List the titles and
a description of each asssignment on the graphic organizer below.
You may need more room. An example is given below.

Unit/Activity	Title of Writing Assignment	Description
1	E.A. 1: Revising a Personal Narrative About Choice	Narrative Essay

2. Using the list you have created, choose texts that you have written or performed this year that fit into each of the following categories. Write the titles in or near the appropriate circles.

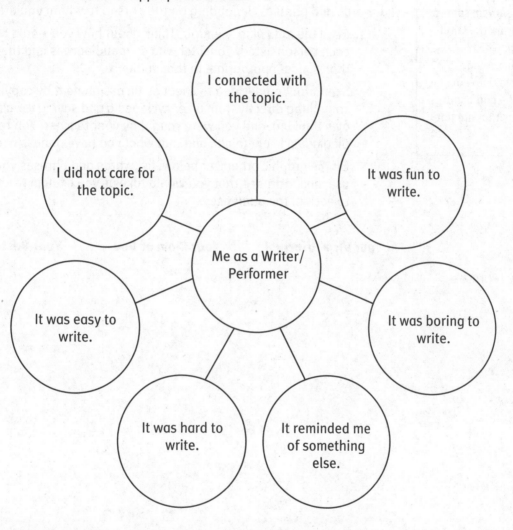

3. Reflective Prompt: Select one of the circles above and explain why you chose to put that text into that category.

_____

_____

_____

_____

_____

_____

Choosing Your Voice

SUGGESTED LEARNING STRATEGIES: Graphic Organizer, Prewriting, Drafting, Word Map

WORD CONNECTIONS

The word *plagiarism* comes into English from the Latin word *plagium*, which means "a kidnapping." Plagiarism is taking—or "kidnapping"—and using ideas or words that are not your own.

How do you change the way you speak for different audiences? Think about the way you talk and the words you use when you speak to your parents or your teacher or your best friend. Why do you use different words and phrases depending on the person to whom you are speaking?

1. Read the following scenario. Think about how you would respond to each person listed. Consider who your audience is and the language that is most appropriate to that audience.

Scenario: You decided to cheat on an assignment by copying something directly from an encyclopedia and saying it was your own thinking, and you were caught by your teacher. You realize that plagiarism is unethical, and that what you have done is wrong.

On the graphic organizer below, list words and phrases you would use, and attitudes that you would take as you explain what happened to each of the audiences.

	Your Vice-Principal	Your Mom or Dad	Your Best Friend
Words/Phrases	Yes Mam		
Attitude			

2. Now, using the ideas you have generated, write a first draft of your explanations to the three different audiences on separate paper.

3. With a partner, small group, or the whole class, choose one of your explanations and read it aloud. Your listeners will guess the identity of your intended audience.

4. In groups or as a whole class, reflect on the following questions and record your responses.

- What kinds of words and phrases were used for the different audiences?

_____

_____

_____

_____

_____

- Which words conveyed the voice you used for each audience?

_____

_____

_____

_____

_____

- Which audience was easiest to address? Why?

_____

_____

_____

_____

_____

RAFT Brainstorming

Role	Audience	Format	Topic

Reviewing Revision

SUGGESTED LEARNING STRATEGIES: Brainstorming, Graphic Organizer, Quickwrite, Word Map

Revision Survey

1. What is the difference between revising and editing?

_____

_____

_____

_____

_____

2. Why is revision important in your writing process?

_____

_____

_____

_____

_____

_____

3. Describe the most effective revision technique that you have used in the past. What effect did it have on your final version?

_____

_____

_____

_____

_____

_____

4. What revision strategies do you know about, but rarely use?

_____

_____

_____

_____

_____

> **WORD CONNECTIONS**
>
> *Revision* contains the Latin root *-vis-* (also spelled *-vid-*). The root *-vis-* or *-vid-*, which means "see" or "look," also appears in *vision, visualize, visible, visitor, televise, advise, video*, and many other English words.
>
> The Latin prefix *re-* means "back" or "again."

Reviewing Revision

Global Revision—Large-Scale	Local Revision—Small-Scale

Editing and Proofreading

ACADEMIC VOCABULARY

A global revision means looking at the writing as a whole—perhaps even rethinking purpose, audience, and message—and making changes to the entire document.

Quickwrite: Using your brainstorming cluster, write about a significant choice you had to make. Describe the factors that went into making that decision.

_____

_____

_____

_____

_____

_____

_____

_____

Revision: Replacing "Dead Words"

SUGGESTED LEARNING STRATEGIES: **Marking the Text, Revisiting Prior Work, Deleting, Substituting, Word Map**

Read the following paragraph and underline the "dead words." Then rewrite the paragraph replacing the dead words with more lively, energetic words. After you have revised your wording, think about the effect of the revised paragraph.

"Hey Mike, I just heard something really interesting," said Kate.

"Jennie thinks you're nice and cute too." Mike was happy when

he heard this. He dropped his stuff and looked happily at Kate.

Then he began to move around in an excited way. He went down

the hallway fast and said, "Wow." He accidentally ran into the

principal in the doorway. The principal was unhappy and told

Mike to calm down. Mike said he was sorry and moved away from

Mr. Johnson. Then he turned and walked sadly back to Kate, and

she said, "Let's go find Jennie."

WORD CONNECTIONS

Create an analogy to show the same relationship as tombstone : graveyard.

Tombstone : graveyard ::

_____ : _____

What relationship does this analogy show?

Revision: Deleting Wordiness

My Notes

There is/there are

1. Rewrite the sentences below to eliminate wordiness. By omitting *there is* and *there are* wherever you can, you not only reduce wordiness but also provide sentence variety.

   a. There is no way I can stay in this room.

   _____

   b. There is nothing better than pumpkin pie.

   _____

   c. There were ten mounted police in the parade.

   _____

   d. There are four laws that should be obeyed.

   _____

   e. When there is a problem, you can avoid it by speaking up.

   _____

Forms of *to be*

2. Forms of the verb *to be* are the most lifeless verbs in English. Whenever you can, replace forms of *to be* with action verbs.

   a. John is in need of a good meal.

   _____

   b. There is fighting every day between my two cats, Rosie and Gil.

   _____

   c. The crowd was wild with enthusiasm.

   _____

   d. The birds were in the air at the sound of the gunshot.

   _____

   e. To be a good friend, you must listen carefully.

   _____

GRAMMAR & USAGE

The verb *to be* is the most common verb in the English language; however, it can often lead to passive voice or lifeless writing. Here is the verb *to be* in its many forms:

Present tense: I *am*, you *are*, he/she/it *is*, we *are*, they *are*.

Past tense: I *was*, you *were*, he/she/it *was*, we *were*, they *were*.

Perfect forms: *have been, has been, had been, will have been*

3. With a partner, examine the words and phrases below. Explain what makes them wordy, and discuss how to revise them.

pink in color	terrible tragedy
small in size	end result
true facts	various differences
period in time	free gift
past memories	very unique
of cheap quality	in a confused state
often times	past history
future plans	for the reason that
honest in character	

4. Clichés can also contribute to wordiness.

5. Read the paragraph below. With your writing group, highlight as many examples of wordiness as you can find. Then, on separate paper rewrite the paragraph, eliminating the wordiness without changing the meaning of the sentences.

In this day and age, anyone and everyone who has the ability to sing and dance needs to try to audition for a talent show. Everyone is aware of the fact that at this point in time the average, ordinary person can make millions if he is able to be discovered. There are lots of really talented people. If you snooze, you lose. There are lots of ways to begin to develop your talents. If you are able, join a community musical theater group. This very unique experience can prepare an amateur singer and dancer for stage performances. The aspiring performer may be coached by a professional singer and/or dancer. Performing in front of an audience is a key to success. At the end of the day, to have more experience on stage is a way of avoiding nervousness.

WORD CONNECTIONS

Write an analogy to show the same relationship as talent show : performers :: _____ : _____.

What type of relationship does the analogy show?

Revision: Combining Sentences

My Notes

Sentence Variety

Writing that contains many sentences of the same short pattern bores both the writer and the reader for two reasons:

- Repetition of a single, simple sentence pattern draws attention to itself, *not* to the ideas in the paper.
- Simple, short sentences cannot show the relationships that exist among ideas of differing importance.

To create rhythm and interest in your writing, use a combination of simple, complex, and compound sentences.

Using Appositives

Examine the sentences below to distinguish between the patterns. Notice that the second pattern displays more complexity and variety. What grammar technique is used to combine the ideas presented in the choppy sentences?

Choppy: Diana is a famous ballet dancer. Diana loves to perform on stage.

Combined: Diana, a famous ballet dancer, loves to perform on stage.

Watch as your teacher models use of appositives—and the correct punctuation—to combine ideas into a tighter, more effective sentence.

- I liked *Monsters Inc.* because the monsters were afraid of the little girl. The film is a classic.

- I saw the play *Crow*. The costumes for the play were all dark and feathery to imitate crows.

WORD CONNECTIONS

The root *-pos-* in **appositive** comes from a Latin word meaning "to place." An appositive is placed next to the word it explains. Other words with this root include *opposite*, *juxtapose, impose, compose, dispose,* and *transpose.*

The Latin prefix *ad-* means "near." It may change spelling to fit with the word it is attached to, as in *appositive*, where it is spelled *ap-*.

Working with a partner or in a small group, combine the following sentences, making the idea in one of them an appositive:

1. Marsha is in great demand as a writer and performer. She is a poet and dancer.

2. Ariana packed her favorite shoes. She had red boots, black heels, and sandals.

3. The house sold for over a million dollars. The small, white cottage sat on a hill.

4. Tucker is a trucker. Tucker's truck is stuck in the muck. Tucker is from Winnemucka.

5. John works for one of the big studios. He is a film editor. John likes his job.

Using Subordination

What is a subordinate clause?

What are some of the markers that signal a subordinate clause?

What has to be in place for a subordinate clause to work effectively?

Revision: Combining Sentences

GRAMMAR & USAGE

A sentence that contains one independent clause and at least one subordinate clause is a **complex sentence**.

In writing complex sentences, choose a subordinating conjunction that shows the relationship between the independent and the subordinate clauses:

Contrast: *although, even though, though, while*

Time: *after, as long as, as soon as, before, when, whenever, since, until, while*

Reason or consequence: *as, because, if, provided that, since, so that, unless*

When you begin a sentence with a subordinate clause, follow the clause with a comma. Many subordinate clauses are adverbial clauses. An adverbial clause functions as an adverb and modifies a verb to tell how, when, why, how much, or to what extent.

Use subordinate clause markers (subordinating conjunctions) to combine the following simple sentences to create **complex sentences**.

1. John was tired. John was proud of his performance.

2. Joan smiled to herself. Joan thought of her mother's jokes and smiled.

3. The boa constrictor only ate one mouse a week. The boa constrictor was young.

4. Marina has been traveling. Her travels started at the beginning of the week.

5. Marty found a wallet. He found it after school. Marty walks home from school.

6. Jane has practiced singing for weeks. She is going to sing at her sister's wedding. Jane is finally ready to sing.

7. Some people prefer fast-food hamburgers. I like to eat hamburgers. I prefer them cooked at home on the barbeque.

Revisit a draft that you created earlier in the unit and locate a section of your writing that contains short, choppy sentences. Revise that section of text by combining sentences using subordinate adverbial clauses or appositives and the correct punctuation.

Revising Structure: Rearranging a Text

SUGGESTED LEARNING STRATEGIES: **Think Aloud, Word Map**

Rearrange the sentences in the following paragraph in a logical, easy-to-follow sequence.

Even though my dog cannot run very well anymore, I still love him. My dog, a yellow Labrador retriever, is crippled. I was really frightened. Crying, I held Speedy's fragile body in my arms while my dad drove to the animal hospital. He lost his ability to run well five years ago when he ran into the street and a car hit him. But he did not die. His front leg got badly broken in three places. The vet had to amputate the leg and said, "He was a very lucky puppy." He gets along just fine with only three legs. But we don't call him Speedy anymore. Now his name is Limpy. I am glad he is still a part of our family.

What would be an appropriate title for this piece? Explain.

_____

_____

_____

_____

_____

_____

_____

_____

_____

_____

Making Revision Choices

SUGGESTED LEARNING STRATEGIES: **Revisiting Prior Work,
Marking the Draft, Sharing and Responding**

Assignment

Your assignment is to revise a piece of your writing using the revision
techniques you have learned throughout the year. After you have completed
your revision, write a reflection on the changes you made to the piece and the
ways that these changes improved your piece.

Steps:

Planning

1. Look back at the writing that you have completed this year or worked
   on in this unit. Identify one piece that you would like to revise for this
   assessment.

2. As you read through your piece, make notes to yourself about potential
   areas for revision. Write a revision plan in which you identify the
   strengths and weaknesses of the piece and the specific elements you
   plan to revise.

3. Present the selected piece and your revision plan to your writing group.
   The task of the writing group is to help each writer refine his or her
   improvement plan and identify strategies for revision.

   ▶ The group will first read the paper aloud and respond to it. Each group
     member will write specific suggestions for how to improve the piece
     and will share his or her suggestions orally. Each group member will be
     responsible for turning in the suggestions he or she gives to the writer.

   ▶ The writer will take notes on what he or she hears and incorporate
     changes to the draft accordingly.

4. Include a prewriting technique (i.e., clustering, brainstorming, outlining,
   freewriting, and looping) to re-envision your purpose, audience, and
   tone.

Evaluating/Revising

5. Use specific revision techniques you have learned this year. You will need
   to show evidence that you have used these revision techniques by writing
   notes in the margins, and by marking your draft showing where you have
   deleted, added, rewritten, and rearranged content or sentences.

6. Put aside the original draft, and, without looking at it for now, draft a new text implementing your revision plans as you write. After you have finished a second draft, go back to your original and merge and rearrange ideas from the two texts to effectively reflect what you would like to say to your readers. Highlight changes you have made from the original text. Revisit the Scoring Guide to ensure that you are meeting specific criteria.

Editing for Publication

7. Proofread your draft by reading your text carefully and correcting errors in grammar, punctuation, and spelling. Be sure that you have followed punctuation rules when combining sentences.

8. Reread your draft and create an appropriate title for it. Your publishable draft should be neat, polished, and revised to your satisfaction and the satisfaction of your writing group.

Reflecting

9. After completing your revision, write a reflection about the specific changes you made and the improvement those changes created in the original piece. Include several writing goals you hope to achieve in your next class writing experience.

Making Revision Choices

SCORING GUIDE

Scoring Criteria	Exemplary	Proficient	Emerging
Revision Plan	The revision plan thoroughly identifies and justifies why the piece was selected, details the specific areas that will be revised, and describes the strategies that will be used to improve the text.	The revision plan identifies why the piece was selected, details the specific areas that will be revised, and describes the strategies that will be used to improve the text.	The attempted revision does not identify why the piece was selected, detail the specific areas that will be revised, or describe the strategies that will be used to improve the text.
Improvement Through Revision	The revision reflects both word level and structural level revision techniques that effectively change and improve the original draft in content, style, and structure.	The revision reflects both word level and structural level revision techniques that improve the original draft in content and style.	The revision reflects minimal, if any, changes. Revisions, if made, do not significantly improve the draft.
Evidence of Collaboration	The writing group implements the following effective revision techniques: • attentive and active listening to drafts as they are read within the group • extensive written or oral recommendations • high level of engagement in discussion of writing strategies and ideas • active engagement in response to suggestions • effective, entire group involvement working to improve the text, explore ideas deeply, and research unfamiliar concepts bringing in outside resources.	The writing group displays the following behaviors that enable revision: • listening to drafts as they are read within the group • written or oral suggestions • discussion of writing strategies and ideas • suggestions are made • involvement of the entire group to improve the text using the resources provided.	The writing group displays one or more of the following behaviors: • unfocused or off-task behavior when writing is shared • generic and superficial responses • minimal response on the part of the writer while suggestions are given • little evidence that the group has worked well together, resulting in minimal feedback and changes to the draft.

SCORING GUIDE

Scoring Criteria	Exemplary	Proficient	Emerging
Reflection	The reflection insightfully explains what was changed and how revisions have improved the text, citing clear examples from the original and revised texts. Reflection includes several writing goals.	The reflection explains what was changed and how revisions have improved the text. Reflection includes some writing goals.	The reflection of what was changed and/or how revisions have improved the text is vague. Writing goals are unclear or missing.
Additional Criteria			

Comments: _____

_____

_____

_____

_____

_____

_____

_____

Reflection

An important aspect of growing as a learner is to reflect on where you have been, what you have accomplished, what helped you to learn, and how you will apply your new knowledge in the future. Use the following questions to guide your thinking and to identify evidence of your learning. Use separate notebook paper.

Thinking about Concepts

1. Using specific examples from this unit, respond to the Essential Questions:

   • Why is it important to revisit, reflect on, and revise previously written texts?

   • What influences a writer's choices during the revision process?

2. Consider the new academic vocabulary from this unit (**Voice, Revision, Global Revision**) as well as academic vocabulary from previous units and select 3–4 terms of which your understanding has grown. For each term, answer the following questions:

   • What was your understanding of the word before you completed this unit?

   • How has your understanding of the word evolved throughout the unit?

   • How will you apply your understanding in the future?

Thinking about Connections

3. Review the activities and products (artifacts) you created. Choose those that most reflect your growth or increase in understanding.

4. For each artifact that you choose, record, respond to, and reflect on your thinking and understanding, using the following questions as a guide:

   a. What skill/knowledge does this artifact reflect, and how did you learn this skill/knowledge?

   b. How did your understanding of the power of language expand through your engagement with this artifact?

   c. How will you apply this skill or knowledge in the future?

5. Create this reflection as Portfolio pages—one for each artifact you choose. Use the model in the box for your headings and commentary on questions.

Thinking About Thinking
Portfolio Entry

Concept:

Description of Artifact:

Commentary on Questions:

How We Choose
to Act

Essential Questions

? How does a speaker create and present an effective oral text?

? How do literary devices enhance a text?

Unit Overview

Every day, we choose how to act. These choices are sometimes conscious and sometimes unconscious. People make choices of which they are proud, and people choose to act in ways they later regret. In this unit, you will discover that almost every action, attitude, or emotion you display begins with a choice. You will discover that a performer makes choices about how to act before an audience. You will be introduced to pantomime, inflection, role playing, and other performance skills. In addition, you will learn to read and analyze poetry and to portray yourself and characters in individual and group performances.

Goals

- ▶ To learn to communicate in a variety of forms (verbal, nonverbal)
- ▶ To improve skills in oral reading and presentation
- ▶ To increase textual analysis skills and apply them to a variety of genres

ACADEMIC VOCABULARY

Oral Interpretation

Tone

Monologue

Narrative Poem

Poetic Devices

Learning Focus:

Performing with a Purpose

Sharing information and stories begins with oral communication. The **oral tradition** of telling and listening to stories has its modern expression in drama. Actors are not the only people, though, who communicate orally. The art of expressing yourself orally is probably one of the most important communication skills you can master. Performance is a way of honing your ability to communicate with others by making physical and vocal choices to convey a certain idea or purpose and feeling or tone. You already modify your voice depending on your purpose and audience, and you naturally use gestures and your face to create a certain effect.

Performance is simply the art of making purposeful and deliberate choices to express a text. **Oral interpretation** is the art of deciding on what a text means and then expressing that meaning through movement, gesture, facial expression, and the voice (**inflection**, **intonation**, and **emphasis**). You already know how to sound sarcastic, or excited, or sad, and you can use your face and your body to convey that tone as well as your voice. Couple that knowledge with a **monologue** that expresses a specific **tone** and you can bring your audience to laughter or to tears.

Working in a group to share and respond to writing at various stages of the writing process can help you to improve and revise your work. Working with a group to plan and execute a performance is another way of taking advantage of the give-and-take of thoughtful communication with others.

Independent Reading: In this unit, you will read several poems. To gain more experience with poetry, you might choose a poetry collection or a novel written in verse as your independent reading.

Previewing the Unit

Essential Questions

1. How does a speaker create and present an effective oral text?

2. How do literary devices enhance a text?

Unit Overview and Learning Focus

Predict what you think this unit is about. Use the words or phrases that stood out to you when you read the Unit Overview and the Learning Focus.

Embedded Assessment

What knowledge must you have (what do you need to know)? What skills must you have (what will you need to do to complete the Embedded Assessment successfully)?

Warming Up with Pantomime

Viewing *Hook*

1. As you watch the clip from the film *Hook*, list the foods that you envision the characters eating.

   Soup, Corn, Drumstick, apple, burger, cat

2. Refer to your list of foods as you watch the clip the second time. Circle the foods that you definitely see the second time you watch.

   Bannas, watermelon, chips, Yams

After watching the next clip, complete the questions below.

3. What choice does Peter have to make in order to see the food?

   He must imagine the food is there.

4. What might have happened if he had made a different choice?

   He wouldn't see the food

5. Why do you think the filmmakers choose to have some of the food seem realistic and other food appear unrealistic (multicolored, etc.)?

   The colors show childish attributes.

6. Have you ever needed to act in a way that caused you to stretch beyond your comfort zone as Peter does? Explain.

Pantomime

1. What is **pantomime**?

_____

_____

2. While you participated in the drama game, you had to pantomime an action. What did you do to help others to determine the action you were pantomiming? What other movements and facial expressions could you have included to make your pantomime even better? Use the graphic organizer below to reflect on your experience. Imagine another object or situation you could also pantomime and complete the organizer below to show how you could effectively pantomime it.

Object/Action Pantomimed	Movements and Facial Expressions Needed for Others to Guess the Action and the Food
A Different Object/Action I Could Pantomime	**Movements and Facial Expressions Needed for Others to Guess the Action/Object**

Emotional Choices

1. Sometimes the words we say are not as meaningful as the way we say them. Listen as your classmates say the same sentence in different ways. Identify the emotion each student is communicating. Record the sentences and the emotions below.

Sentence	Emotion 1	Emotion 2	Emotion 3	Emotion 4

2. With your small group, list additional emotions that are sometimes evident in people's actions and words.

_____

_____

_____

_____

_____

3. After listening to the sentences presented by each group, think about the emotions that you saw portrayed. What did you see and hear that communicated the emotion the speaker was feeling? Use the web on the next page to list evidence for the emotion based on what you *saw* and *heard*.

_____

_____

_____

_____

_____

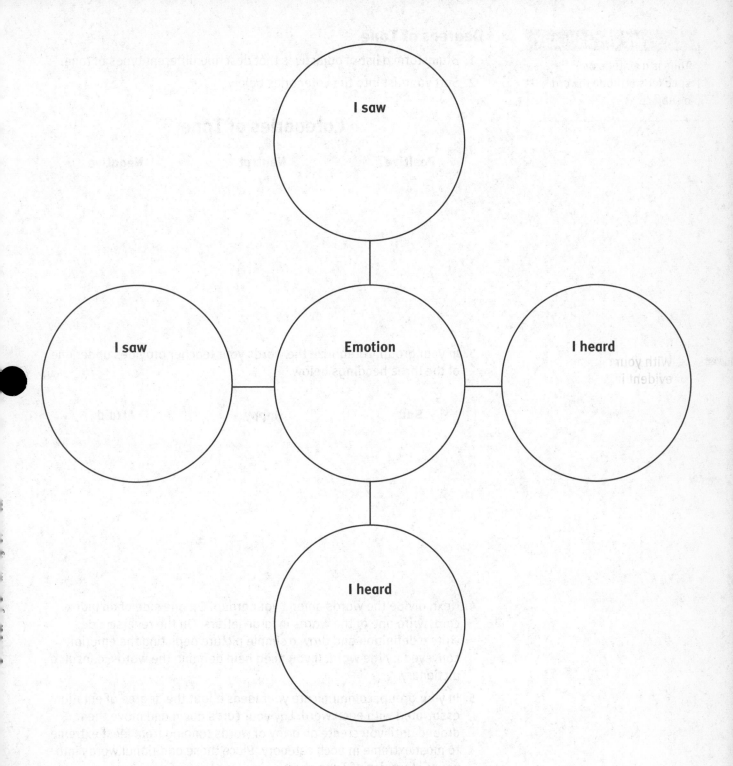

I saw

I saw

Emotion

I heard

I heard

A Linear Array of Tones

ACADEMIC VOCABULARY

Tone is a writer's or speaker's attitude toward a subject.

Degrees of Tone

1. Brainstorm a list of adjectives that describe different types of tone.
2. Sort your list into the categories below.

Categories of Tone

Positive	Neutral	Negative

3. In your group, categorize the words your teacher provides under one of the three headings below.

Sad	Happy	Afraid

4. Next, divide the words among your group. On one side of an index card, write one of the words in large letters. On the reverse side, write a definition and draw a simple picture depicting the emotion conveyed by the word. If you need help defining the words, consult a dictionary.

5. In your group, communicate your ideas about the degree of emotion associated with each word. Lay your cards down and move them around until you create an array of words ranging from least extreme to most extreme in each category. Place these additional words into your Categories of Tone chart.

Communicating Tone in Writing

6. Your teacher will assign you a topic for which you will craft a written response. You may respond based on a real or imagined experience. However, for this assignment, you are to write your piece using the emotion (tone) your teacher assigns to your group. Your experiences will be different, but your group will all write using the tone you have been assigned.

Topic:

_____

Assigned Tone:

_____

As you plan your response, brainstorm words you can include to portray your assigned tone. Use a thesaurus if needed.

7. Craft your response on your own paper. After you finish, highlight or underline the specific words you include that communicate your assigned tone. Save this text in your Working Folder.

Writing with Feeling

WORD CONNECTIONS

Complete the analogy to show a part-to-whole relationship.

headline : _____ :: table of contents : _____ .

1. Think about an event for which you felt a strong emotion. Write the event in the circle below, then use the space around the circle to create a cluster of words or phrases that recall the circumstances surrounding that emotional event.

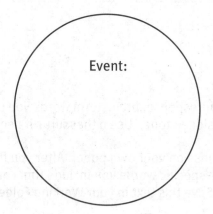

Event:

2. **Quickwrite:** Describe the circumstances and the reason for the strong emotion. Use some of the words from your cluster above.

_____

_____

_____

_____

3. **Writing Prompt:** Choose one of the headlines your teacher has provided. On separate paper, write an emotionally-charged fictional account of the event. Consider the emotions that are being felt, and show those emotions in your writing.

SUGGESTED LEARNING STRATEGIES: Oral Interpretation, Word Map

In this activity, you will practice **oral interpretation**. In your small group, practice saying each statement, putting emphasis on the underlined word. After you have practiced the statements, write a second sentence that clarifies the meaning. Use these examples to guide you.

- She said she didn't want to go to the <u>party</u>. (She didn't say anything about the game.)
- She <u>said</u> she didn't want to go to the party. (Didn't you hear her?)
- She said she <u>didn't</u> want to go to the party. (I can't believe she changed her mind.)

ACADEMIC VOCABULARY

An **oral interpretation** is a sharing of a literary work with an audience, with the reader expressing the emotions and intent of the printed text.

Group One
- <u>We</u> like rainy days. *Only they like rainy days they don't dislike*
- We <u>like</u> rainy days. *They like the rainy days they don't dislike*
- We like <u>rainy</u> days. *They like rainy days not clear days*
- We like rainy <u>days</u>. *they specifically like days not nights*

Group Two
- I <u>thought</u> you wanted pizza.
- I thought <u>you</u> wanted pizza.
- I thought you <u>wanted</u> pizza.
- I thought you wanted <u>pizza</u>.

Group Three
- <u>Are</u> you going straight to lunch?
- Are <u>you</u> going straight to lunch?
- Are you going <u>straight</u> to lunch?
- Are you going straight to <u>lunch</u>?

Group Four
- Do <u>we</u> really have a test tomorrow?
- Do we <u>really</u> have a test tomorrow?
- Do we really have a <u>test</u> tomorrow?
- Do we really have a test <u>tomorrow</u>?

ABOUT THE AUTHOR

Nikki Giovanni is a popular poet and professor of English. Over the years, she has won numerous writing awards. Her writing often focuses on individuals and their choices to make a difference.

GRAMMAR & USAGE

Poets use punctuation—or *absence* of punctuation—primarily for dramatic effect. In this poem, the only punctuation used is the points of **ellipsis** (...). Points of ellipsis often indicate an intentional omission of a word or phrase from the text. They may also be used to indicate an intentional silence of the speaker.

Poetry

CHOICES

by Nikki Giovanni

if i can't do
what i want to do
then my job is to not
do what i don't want
5   to do

it's not the same thing
but it's the best i can
do

if i can't have
10   what i want … then
my job is to want
what i've got
and be satisfied
that at least there
15   is something more
to want

since i can't go
where i need
to go … then i must … go
20   where the signs point
though always understanding
parallel movement
isn't lateral

when i can't express
25   what i really feel
i practice feeling
what i can express
and none of it is equal
i know
30   but that's why mankind
alone among the animals
learns to cry

1. Following your teacher's example, use the TP-CASTT strategy to analyze "Choices" by Nikki Giovanni.

TP-CASTT

Acronym	Directions for analysis	Response
T: Title	Ponder the title before reading the poem.	
P: Paraphrase	Restate the poem in your own words.	
C: Connotation	Contemplate the poem for word meanings beyond the literal.	(Think especially of the words *job* and *satisfied*.)
A: Attitude	Observe both the speaker's and the poem's tone.	
S: Shift	Note the shifts in person, place, and attitude.	
T: Title Revisited	Examine the title again, this time on an interpretive level.	
T: Theme	Determine the message about life implied in the poem.	

LITERARY TERMS

Inflection is a change in the tone or pitch of the voice.

Pitch is the highness or lowness of a voice in speaking.

Volume is the loudness or softness of a voice.

Tempo is the speed or rate of speaking.

Phrasing refers to dividing a speech into smaller parts, adding pauses for emphasis.

My Notes

2. Complete the following sentence starter:

   In "Choices," Nikki Giovanni discusses ....

   _____

   _____

3. How does the poem address the idea of choice?

   _____

   _____

4. What emotional words help you discover the tone of "Choices"?

   _____

   _____

5. You have practiced fluent oral reading by focusing on accuracy, tempo, and inflection. Using the inflection key below, mark the poem with your inflection choices. Then read the poem aloud, or listen to others read aloud, using your suggestions for inflection.

Inflection Key	
Pitch	Circle words to speak at a higher pitch.
Volume	Underline words or sentences to read louder. Double underline words to read softer.
Tempo	Write "slow" next to phrases or lines to read slowly.
Phrasing	Place a vertical line or slash to indicate a pause.

6. How do your inflection markings of "Choices" make the thoughts and emotions of the speaker clear to the audience?

   _____

   _____

7. Which other inflection choices, if any, might make an oral interpretation of "Choices" even better?

   _____

   _____

Poetry

My Notes

> **ABOUT THE AUTHOR**
> Robert Frost (1874-1963) was one of America's most popular twentieth-century poets. For much of his life, he lived on a farm in New Hampshire and wrote poems about farm life and the New England landscape. He wrote "Stopping by Woods on a Snowy Evening" in 1922, and he described it as his favorite work, calling it his "best bid for remembrance."

STOPPING BY WOODS ON A SNOWY EVENING

by Robert Frost

Whose woods these are I think I know,
His house is in the village though;
He will not see me stopping here
To watch his woods fill up with snow.

My little horse must think it queer
To stop without a farmhouse near
Between the woods and frozen lake
The darkest evening of the year.

He gives his harness bells a shake
To ask if there is some mistake.
The only other sound's the sweep
Of easy wind and downy flake.

The woods are lovely, dark and deep,
But I have promises to keep,
And miles to go before I sleep,
And miles to go before I sleep.

My Notes

Poetry

> **ABOUT THE AUTHOR**
> Samuel Allen, who also wrote under the pen name of Paul Vesey, was a lawyer and an educator as well as a poet. Allen earned a law degree from Harvard in 1941, and he later studied at the Sorbonne in Paris. His poems reflect his African American heritage and are noted for their artistic expression.

TO SATCH

by Samuel Allen

Sometimes I feel like I will never stop
Just go on forever
'Til one fine mornin'
I'm gonna reach up and grab me a handfulla stars
Throw out my long lean leg
And whip three hot strikes burnin' down the heavens
And look over at God and say
How about that!

DRIVING
to TOWN LATE *to* MAIL *a* LETTER

by Robert Bly

ABOUT THE AUTHOR

Robert Bly has published more than 30 books of poetry, essays, and translations. Bly honed his writing craft through two years at the Writers Workshop at the University of Iowa. After living in Norway, translating Norwegian poems into English, he started a literary magazine to publish poetry translations and essays on American poets. Bly's interest in myth, story telling, and meditation influence his work. His book *Iron John: A Book About Men* was an international best seller.

It is a cold and snowy night.
The main street is deserted.
The only things moving are swirls of snow.
As I lift the mailbox door, I feel its cold iron.
There is a privacy I love in this snowy night.
Driving around, I will waste more time.

My Notes

Poetry

> **ABOUT THE AUTHOR**
> Langston Hughes (1902-1967) was a prominent figure in the Harlem Renaissance. His poems, plays, and stories frequently focused on the African American experience, particularly on the struggles and feelings of individuals.

MOTHER to SON

by Langston Hughes

Well, son, I'll tell you:
Life for me ain't been no crystal stair.
It's had tacks in it,
And splinters,
5   And boards torn up,

And places with no carpet on the floor –
Bare.
But all the time
I'se been a-climbin' on,
10 And reachin' landin's,

And turnin' corners,
And sometimes goin' in the dark
Where there ain't been no light.
So boy, don't you turn back.
15 Don't you set down on the steps

'Cause you finds it's kinder hard.
Don't you fall now –
For I'se still goin, honey,
I'se still climbin',
And life for me ain't been no crystal stair.

IT HAPPENED IN MONTGOMERY

for Rosa Parks

by Phil W. Petrie

> **ABOUT THE AUTHOR**
> Phil W. Petrie is a freelance writer and former book publishing
> editor. He lives in Clarksville, Tennessee, and has written articles for
> numerous publications, including *Black Enterprise* and *The New Crisis*.

My Notes

Then he slammed on the brakes—
Turned around and grumbled.
But she was tired that day.
Weariness was in her bones.
And so the thing she's done yesterday, 5
And yesteryear,
On her workdays,
Churchdays,
Nothing-to-do-I'll-go-and-visit
Sister Annie Days— 10
She felt she'd never do again.
And he growled once more.
So she said:
"No sir...I'm stayin right here."
And he gruffly grabbed her, 15
Pulled and pushed her—
Then sharply shoved her through the doors.
The news slushed through the littered streets
Slipped into the crowded churches,
Slimmered onto the unmagnolied side of town. 20
While the men talked and talked and talked.
She—
Who was tired that day,
Cried and sobbed that she was
glad she'd done it. 25
That her soul was satisfied.
That Lord knows,
A little walkin' never hurt anybody;
That in one of those unplanned, unexpected
Unadorned moments— 30
A weary woman turned the page
of History.

Choosing to Apply an Understanding of Inflection

1. Your teacher will assign a poem to your group. Work with your group to analyze your poem using TP-CASTT.

TP-CASTT

Acronym	Directions for analysis	Response
T: Title	Ponder the title before reading the poem.	
P: Paraphrase	Restate the poem in your own words.	
C: Connotation	Contemplate the poem for word meanings beyond the literal.	Choose two or three key words.
A: Attitude	Observe both the speaker's and the poem's tone.	
S: Shift	Note the shifts in speaker, place, attitude, etc.	
T: Title Revisited	Examine the title again, this time on an interpretive level.	
T: Theme	Determine the message about life implied in the poem.	

2. Research the author, subject, and/or historical setting of "Stopping by Woods on a Snowy Evening" to help you develop a deeper understanding of the poem.

3. As a group, decide how you would like to present your poem. Using your Inflection Key, mark the text to indicate the inflections you will use when delivering the poem. Rehearse your poem to be sure that you are reading with fluency and communicating the theme and tone effectively. Finally, perform your oral interpretation.

Discovering Meaning

SUGGESTED LEARNING STRATEGIES: **Discussion Groups, Summarizing/Paraphrasing**

The words below are from the poem "Casey at the Bat." In a group, define the words on the list your teacher assigns. Then, in your collaborative jigsaw groups, define all of the words.

Warm-up for Vocabulary Baseball: Study the definitions of all of the words before you play Vocabulary Baseball. Line numbers in parentheses give the location of the word in "Casey at the Bat" in Activity 5.10.

A

brilliant (1)

bearing (22)

patron (4)

doffed (doff) (23)

straggling (straggle) (5)

applauded (26)

clung (cling) (6)

B

writhing (writhe) (27)

preceded (precede) (9)

defiance (28)

latter (10)

sneer (28, 45)

stricken (11)

sphere (29)

C

multitude (11)

haughty (30)

melancholy (11)

grandeur (3)

wonderment (13)

unheeded (heed) (31)

despised (despise) (14)

D

muffled (muffle) (33)

occurred (occur) (15)

stern (34, 43)

lusty (17)

charity (37)

recoiled (recoil) (19)

visage (37)

E

tumult (38)

scornful (42)

spheroid (39)

awed (awe, *v.*) (42)

clenched (clench) (45)

shattered (shatter) (48)

favored (favor, *v.*) (49)

> ### WORD CONNECTIONS
>
> Prefixes can help you determine meaning. The following are common prefixes:
>
> *multi-* meaning "many"
>
> *pre-* meaning "before"
>
> *de-* meaning "remove from" or "reverse of"
>
> *un-* meaning "opposite of"
>
> *re-* meaning "again"

Discovering Meaning

Vocabulary Baseball

Play Ball! Choose a captain, a pitcher, and a scorekeeper for your team, and name your team. Your teacher is the umpire. Team members must define words as they are "pitched" or called out by the pitcher. Each correct answer will move a player forward one base. Words defined incorrectly are "outs." If the bases are loaded, the next player can try for a home run. The player must announce that he or she is trying for a home run before the word is pitched. The game is over when time is called or when all the words have been "pitched."

BATTER UP!

Vocabulary Word Bank

brilliant	despised	sphere	awed	multitude
patrons	occurred	haughty	clenched	melancholy
straggling	lusty	grandeur	shattered	writhing
clung	recoiled	unheeded	favored	defiance
preceded	bearing	muffled	wonderment	visage
latter	doffed	stern	sneer	tumult
stricken	applauded	charity	spheroid	defiance

Analyzing and Responding to "Casey at the Bat"

During Reading

Circle the words you learned for Vocabulary Baseball, as well as any other unfamiliar words. Use context clues to define these words as they are used in the poem. Write your own definitions in the My Notes space.

Poetry

My Notes

ABOUT THE AUTHOR

Ernest Lawrence Thayer (1863-1940) wrote light verse while he was on the editorial staff of the *San Francisco Examiner*. "Casey at the Bat," his best-known poem, became a popular choice for oral recitation in schools and theaters.

Casey at the Bat

by Ernest Lawrence Thayer

The outlook wasn't brilliant for the Mudville nine that day;
The score stood four to two, with but one inning more to play,
And then when Cooney died at first, and Burrows did the same,
A pall-like silence fell upon the patrons of the game.

A straggling few got up to go in deep despair. The rest   5
Clung to that hope which springs eternal in the human breast;
They thought, "If only Casey could but get a whack at that —
We'd put up even money now, with Casey at the bat."

But Flynn preceded Casey, as did also Jimmy Blake,
And the former was a <u>hoodoo</u>, while the latter was a fake;   10
So upon that stricken multitude grim melancholy sat;
For there seemed but little chance of Casey getting to the bat.

But Flynn let drive a single, to the wonderment of all,
And Blake, the much despised, tore the cover off the ball;
And when the dust had lifted, and men saw what had occurred,   15
There was Jimmy safe at second and Flynn a-hugging third

Then from five thousand throats and more there rose a lusty yell;
It rumbled through the valley, it rattled in the dell;
It pounded on the mountain and recoiled upon the flat,
For Casey, mighty Casey, was advancing to the bat.   20

There was ease in Casey's manner as he stepped into his place;
There was pride in Casey's bearing and a smile lit Casey's face.
And when, responding to the cheers, he lightly doffed his hat,
No stranger in the crowd could doubt 'twas Casey at the bat.

25   Ten thousand eyes were on him as he rubbed his hands with dirt.
Five thousand tongues applauded when he wiped them on his shirt.
Then while the writhing pitcher ground the ball into his hip,
Defiance flashed in Casey's eye, a sneer curled Casey's lip.

And now the leather-covered sphere came hurtling through the air,
30   And Casey stood a-watching it in haughty grandeur there.
Close by the sturdy batsman the ball unheeded sped —
"That ain't my style," said Casey. "Strike one!" the umpire said.

From the benches, black with people, there went up a muffled roar,
Like the beating of the storm-waves on a stern and distant shore;
35   "Kill him! Kill the umpire!" shouted someone on the stand;
And it's likely they'd have killed him had not Casey raised his hand.

With a smile of Christian charity great Casey's visage shone;
He stilled the rising tumult; he bade the game go on;
He signaled to the pitcher, and once more the spheroid flew;
40   But Casey still ignored it, and the umpire said "Strike two!"

"Fraud!" cried the maddened thousands, and echo answered "Fraud!"
But one scornful look from Casey and the audience was awed.
They saw his face grow stern and cold, they saw his muscles strain,
And they knew that Casey wouldn't let that ball go by again.

45   The sneer has fled from Casey's lip, the teeth are clenched in hate;
He pounds with cruel violence his bat upon the plate.
And now the pitcher holds the ball, and now he lets it go,
And now the air is shattered by the force of Casey's blow.

Oh, somewhere in this favored land the sun is shining bright,
50   The band is playing somewhere, and somewhere hearts are light,
And somewhere men are laughing, and little children shout;
But there is no joy in Mudville — mighty Casey has struck out.

After Reading

1. How might Casey be feeling, or what might he be thinking after such a public loss? Highlight words and phrases that indicate what Casey feels (and thinks), and then, based on information from the text, write your response below.

_____

_____

_____

2. What are the feelings and thoughts of the fans after the loss? Mark the text by underlining words and phrases that support your reponse, and then describe the feelings in the space below.

_____

_____

_____

3. Use the RAFT strategy to create and present a **monologue** about the loss at Mudville. You may choose from the suggestions listed below, or brainstorm more options for the role and audience category and respond accordingly. Write your monologue on separate paper.

WORD CONNECTIONS

Mono- , meaning "one," comes from the Greek, as does *logos*, which means "words, speech, or reason."

ACADEMIC VOCABULARY

A **monologue** is a speech or the written expression of thoughts by a character.

Role: What is your role as an author?	Audience: Who is the target audience for this text?	Format: What is the best format to capture your ideas?	Topic: What is the topic?
• Casey • Fan • Parent • Team member • Spectator from the crowd	• News reporter • Interviewer	• Monologue	• To respond to the events leading up to the loss at Mudville • To describe the feelings and thoughts experienced before, during, and after the loss

Role Playing

LITERARY TERMS

Persona refers to the voice or character speaking a role.

Preparing to Improvise

You and a partner will create and present an oral text. Assume the **persona** of a character and **improvise** a brief scene (one to two minutes) to role play. *Improvise* means "to respond or perform on the spur of the moment." Use appropriate emotion, expression, and pantomime.

1. First, review the scenarios listed below and choose one to role-play with a partner or two.

    *   A friend spreads gossip about another friend, and a major disagreement results.

    *   One friend informs the other that his or her hair is out of fashion and is embarrassing to the friend.

    *   It is past your curfew, and your parents greet you at the door.

    *   A child tells his or her mother that he or she has received an "A" in English class.

    *   A boy asks two girls out for the same event. The girls catch on and confront the boy.

    *   An early-morning argument erupts between siblings about taking too much time in the bathroom.

    *   A new kid is welcomed at school.

    *   Two friends are shopping at the mall, and one tells the other of a plan to shoplift.

2. Choose a partner, and take five to ten minutes to plan your scene. Decide who is playing which part and what each person is to say. You do not need to write out a script or thoroughly rehearse. This is intended to be an **improvisational** activity.

After the Performance: Reflection

3. Think about your improvised performance. Using the graphic organizer below, evaluate the use and effectiveness of gestures, facial expressions, inflection, and pantomine during the role play.

Element of Performance	Level of Use in My Performance	Effectiveness in My Performance
Gestures	Not at all	Not Effective
	A little	Somewhat Effective
	A fair amount	Effective
	To a great extent	Very Effective
Facial expressions	Not at all	Not Effective
	A little	Somewhat Effective
	A fair amount	Effective
	To a great extent	Very Effective
Inflection	Not at all	Not Effective
	A little	Somewhat Effective
	A fair amount	Effective
	To a great extent	Very Effective
Pantomime	Not at all	Not Effective
	A little	Somewhat Effective
	A fair amount	Effective
	To a great extent	Very Effective

Respond to these guiding questions on separate paper.

4. What element(s) of performance did you use effectively? Explain how they helped you achieve your purpose.

5. What element(s) of performance did you not use or use least effectively?

6. What would you do differently to make the scenario more effective if you performed it again?

Reader's Theatre

Before the Performance: Preparation

You will do a Reader's Theatre performance of "Casey at the Bat." To help you develop an effective performance, complete the organizer below based on the character you will play from "Casey at the Bat."

Character: _____

Element of performance I need to include:	Lines where I will include this element and what I will do:	Tone I intend to convey to the audience:
Gestures		
Facial expressions	smirk (use when Casey is at bat after first two strikes)	self-satisfied, haughty, arrogant
Inflection		
Pantomime		

After the Performance: Reflection

1. How well did your group work together in your performance?

_____

2. How do you think the audience felt about your performance?

_____

3. How do you know? Did most or all the audience appear to be listening? Why or why not?

_____

4. If you were to perform this poem again, what would you do to make the performance better?

_____

Reading a Monologue

SUGGESTED LEARNING STRATEGIES: **Marking the Text, Oral Reading, Quickwrite, Think-Pair-Share**

Monologue

> **ABOUT THE AUTHOR**
> Deborah Karczewski teaches high-school English and Drama. She wrote *Teens Have Feelings Too!* to give her drama students relevant and compelling practice material.

Eye Contact

from Teens Have Feelings Too!
by Deborah Karczewski

Oh — my — gosh! He's looking at me! He can't be looking at me. It's impossible. I'm nobody, and he's really really, really *somebody*! There is no way he's looking at me. Nope. Uh-uh.

(*Opens up a textbook*) OK, just look casual. Yup, I'm just reading. Just doing my homework like everyone else here in study hall. Same ol' routine. Now slowly look in his direction … He is looking at me! (*In a moment of surprised confusion, she raises her book up in front of her face.*) Oh man, why did I do that? Now I look like a dork! (*She slowly lowers the book.*) OK, calm down. Just thumb through the book. Now look super interested in this page. Good — very convincing … Now, just take a little teeny, tiny peek to see what he's doing. (*She glances, sees him, and waves nervously.*) Holy smoke, I think I'm going to faint! What do I do now? Do I wait till he says something? Maybe I should do something to let him know that … well… that it's OK with me if he has something to tell me. I mean, what if he's waiting for some kind of a sign that I'm … sort of … interested?

I know! I could ask him if he wrote down the math assignment. Yeah! No wait … there's no talking in study hall. Wouldn't you know it! This is the most major opportunity of my life, and I'm forced into silence. OK, I've got it! I'll write him a note! (*Reaches for her book bag.*) There's got to be some paper in here! The bell! Wait! Where did he go? (*Looks left and right. Disappointed, she slumps into her chair.*) Man, another moment ruined by the bell!

1

2

3

> **GRAMMAR & USAGE**
> Monologues, like poetry, use punctuation for dramatic effect. You can use punctuation as reading fluency and performance cues: periods and semicolons mark longer pauses, commas mark shorter pauses, exclamation points mark excitement or shock, and question marks indicate a confused tone.

My Notes

My Notes

Monologue

Snob

from Teens Have Feelings Too!
by Deborah Karczewski

1   I . . . am . . . like . . . speechless! How can anyone — anyone who matters, anyway — accuse *me* of being a *snob*? (Points

2   I mean, get real. I am the friendliest person in the entire class. Remember? I'm the one who handed out Godiva chocolates to the whole homeroom! I even gave one to that girl who wears the ripped jeans, and I don't even, like, know her name!

3   I know . . . you're just jealous! Look, I *would've* invited you to my pool party. Really, I would've, but I was trying — to protect you. And *this* is how you show your gratitude? I know you don't have that much money — not that it matters, heaven knows — and I didn't want you to have to worry about buying a new bathing suit, that's all. Here I am worrying about *your* feelings and *your* reputation . . . and how do you thank me? By calling me a *snob!*

4   . . .Well, just to show you who's the bigger person — I'm not talking about actual size, of course, 'cause you sure have me beat there — but just to show you who's the most un-snobby . . . I forgive you. My mama always tells me to forgive and forget . . . especially if the person is a poor, little chubby girl. It is up to us, those blessed in society, to set an example for those beneath us. *(Flips hair and saunters off.)*

Monologue

Roommate

from Teens Have Feelings Too!
by Deborah Karczewski

OK you little slug, here's the plan. If I have to be stuck with a little punk brother in my room, then you have to follow the rules. Got it? **1**

It's bad enough that I'm gonna have to be tortured by a stinky, whiny, bottle-sucking baby in the house, but to give up half of my room? . . . to the brat of the century? . . . Arghhh! *(Or some noise of frustration)* This is worse than being stung by killer wasps! It's like being eaten by cannibals while I'm still alive! It's … it's … like having to clean the litter box of a giant Bengal Tiger! **2**

So here's the rules, Turkey. One: observe the row of sock balls making a line down the middle of the floor. You stay on your side of the sock line. Understand? Well, OK … you can cross to go to the bathroom … but only once a night. **3**

Two: my stuff is *my* stuff. You touch *anything* and you're asking for it. See? **4**

Three: when I want my privacy, I'll put a sign on the outside of the door … something like … "Anyone Under This Height Stay Out!" If you want to come in, you can knock on the door and say, "Oh Great One, may I enter?" And maybe, just maybe . . . if you're good, I'll let ya. **5**

Hey, I know … let's give it a try. You go outside the bedroom door. Yeah, that's good. Now shut the door. That's right. OK, now say, "Oh Great One, may I enter?" *(Listens.)* I can't hear you. Say it louder … Hey, pinhead, I can't hear you! *(Pause, followed by a look of shock)* What's that? *(Talking sweetly through the door)* Dad? Oh, nothing, Dad. We're just playing a game! Sure, he can come in any time he wants, cute little guy! *(Pause)* Whew! That was a close one! **6**

Monologue

Mr. Perfect

from **Teens Have Feelings Too!**
by Deborah Karczewski

1   My little brother is heaven's gift to mankind. Oh yes. Just ask my parents. Oh yes. He's the perfect child. Might as well dub him a knight now — Why wait till he's older? Hey, why not give him an honorary degree now to save some time later? Yeah, how 'bout his picture on a postage stamp? I know — What about sainthood?

2   Jealous? Me? Now, why should I be jealous? I should be honored to live in the same house as our little prince. After all, Mr. Perfect always gets good grades … Mr. Perfect is so cute and adorable … Mr. Perfect's room is always clean … He even hugs and kisses and salivates all over the relatives. Yes, I am lucky to share his genes.

3   Every now and then, I forget how blessed I am. Silly me. Take yesterday for example: *someone* had taken my baseball glove without even asking and left it outside in the rain over night. But … oh … it was only an accident! Of course! How dense of me not to realize that! Or last week for example: Mr. Sunshine had left the top off of the trash can, which was an open invitation for every raccoon in the state. There was garbage all over the yard. But the little angel makes mistakes because he's so young, you see. And cleaning up the yard is a big job, too big for such a little guy like my brother. So, of course it makes sense that I would have to spend my Saturday scooping up old bones, rotten fruit crawling with ants, used kitty litter … of course!

4   I can't wait until Mr. Perfect moves up to my school next year. Maybe he has my parents wrapped around his obnoxious little finger … but High School … that's my territory. *(Evil, suggestive laugh)*

Monologue

Family Addition

from **Teens Have Feelings Too!**
by Deborah Karczewski

How can Mom be pregnant? This just can't be happening! First of all, she's way too old to be having another kid. And besides, there's already those two animals she calls my brothers! And — and that means that she and Dad — no, I'm not going to think about it! — 1

Where does she expect to put it — on the roof? If it's a boy, I'll be outnumbered even more! But if it's a girl, I'll be stuck with it in my room! A whiny, stinking, puking runt in my space! Not only will I not get any sleep, but everybody'll be in here all the time! That means I've got to constantly keep my room clean! This is torture! — 2

I can just imagine Mom barging in every hour to see if the little tadpole is OK. Don't you think she should trust me to know if the kid's all right? I mean, after helping raise two brothers, I'm practically an expert! And Mrs. Meyer down the street says I'm always the first girl she calls when she needs a baby-sitter. She's always going on about how patient I am … how little Cindy's always asking when I'll come back … — 3

Now that Cindy's a cute little kid. She's nothing like those two Neanderthals Mom calls my brothers. There's something special about a little girl … You can dress her up … brush her hair … play dolls … — 4

OK. Mom can have a baby on one condition: it's *got* to be a girl! — 5

Reading a Monologue

M o n o l o g u e

Too Young for...

from **Teens Have Feelings Too!**
by Deborah Karczewski

1   I hate that word! It gets me so mad — so angry — so … so furious! You know what's the most annoying word in my parents' vocabulary? "Tooyoungfor." You heard me. It's a brand new word … one word, three syllables. Tooyoungfor. (*Spells it.*) T-O-O-Y-O-U-N-G-F-O-R. I've been hearing it my whole life!

2   "You're tooyoungfor pierced ears."

3   "You're tooyoungfor shaving your legs."

4   "You're tooyoungfor makeup."

5   (*Scream of frustration such as*) Urgh! Today the slogan of the day is, "You're tooyoungfor dating."

6   I *told* them that it's not a real date. Man! I explained that it's just a bunch of us going out for fast food and a movie. What's wrong with that? OK, so maybe there's only four of us … and maybe two of 'em are guys … but can't guys be just friends? Well, OK, maybe an eleven o'clock movie is a little late … but it's not like I go out all the time! Give me a break! It's a one-shot deal!

7   I *should've* said, "Yeah? Well, Mom and Dad, I think you're tooyoungfor turning into such party-poopers! You're tooyoungfor becoming such old fogies! You're tooyoungfor turning into Grandma and Grandpa!"

8   … Why is it, I always think of the best things to say after *I've already lost the battle?*

Monologue

Party

from **Teens Have Feelings Too!**
by Deborah Karczewski

(*The actress is getting ready for a party. She can either provide props and music or mime her actions.*) 1

I hate my clothes! This one is too cutesy. I really have to look mature tonight. How 'bout this one? Nah, Dad would never let me out of the house in that one. Why doesn't he get with the times? OK … found it! Not too frilly … not too skimpy … makes me look a whole lot older … Bingo! 2

(*Dancing to music*) I am going to dance till my feet fall off. If the guys don't ask me, I'll ask them. I plan on dancing till my dad rings that doorbell, and even then I might not stop. These feet are gonna … wait! Shoes! Oh man, I hate my shoes! Should I go for comfort or for image? Heels? Wedges? Sandals? Straps? How 'bout this pair? Nah. Those'd weigh me down, and tonight I'm gonna fly! I'm gonna sail! I'm gonna twirl! Hold it … Ah! Shoe perfection! These'll look so major cool with this outfit! 3

I can't wait to see Valerie's face when she checks me out tonight. She always has to be the focus of every party. When she gets an eyeful of this outfit, her hair'll stand on end! Hair! I hate my hair! Ponytail? Too sporty. Slicked back? No — too lifeguard. Do I wear it up? No — too librarian. Pigtails? Heck no, I'd look like Pippi Longstocking. The casual wind-blown look? Hey, not bad. Not bad at all! Looks fun-loving, free spirited, ready-to-go … Oh yeah, this is the look all right. 4

Valerie Hoffman, eat your heart out! I've got the moves; I've got the dress; I've got the shoes; I've got the hair … I am it, girl! Valerie's gonna cry so hard that her mascara will run down her face like … like … Mascara? Makeup? Oh no, I hate my makeup! 5

Reading a Monologue

1. Your teacher will assign a monologue to your group. Read the monologue, and complete the following chart in preparation for your performance.

Title of Monologue	
Who is speaking?	
What is the purpose?	
What is the tone of the monologue?	
Who is the intended audience?	
Which choices cause a struggle for the speaker?	

WORD CONNECTIONS

The Latin root *-nota-* in **annotation**, means "to note." It is the basis of the English word *note* and also appears in *connote*, *denote*, *notable*, and *notary*.

The suffix *-ion* or *-tion* marks a noun.

2. With your group, decide what each group member's responsibilities will be: who will speak and who (if anyone) will pantomime. Discuss the inflections to use in your monologue. Mark the text to create a key to show the movements, gestures, and inflections you wish to use. Prepare to present your monologues by practicing them several times, incorporating the annotations of your marked text.

Reflection

Quickwrite: After hearing the monologues presented, write about a time when you chose the right path in a difficult situation. What would the consequences have been if you had chosen a different path? Discuss your response with a partner or as a class.

Creating and Presenting a Monologue

SUGGESTED LEARNING STRATEGIES: **Prewriting, Drafting, Graphic Organizer, Marking the Text, Sharing and Responding**

Assignment

Your assignment is to write, revise, rehearse, and present an original monologue that demonstrates your knowledge of pantomime, inflection, word emphasis, ways to show emotion, and the monologue form. You will select your topic, tone, and audience.

Steps

Prewriting

1. Review the texts and your personal reflections from this unit that address the concept of choice and the consequences of choices. You will write a monologue about a time when you made an important choice or decision. The speaker of the monologue, however, does not have to be you; you may want to adopt a persona. It could be someone who is affected by your choice or even a bystander who happens to observe the choice.

2. Using the graphic organizer, thoroughly plan each element of your monologue. When your organizer is complete, share your plan with a partner to discuss ideas before you create your first draft.

Describe a time when you made a significant choice, and explain the results of that choice.	
Who will be the speaker of the monologue? Why?	
Who is your intended audience? How will this audience affect what you write?	
What is the setting, and what descriptive words will you use to help your listeners visualize it?	
What is the purpose you are trying to communicate?	
What is the tone of the message? (tone = attitude)	
What words and phrases might help to illustrate the tone?	

Drafting

3. Revisit the monologues in Activity 5.13 to review the structure and format of this genre. Draft your monologue in the correct format, and incorporate your ideas from the graphic organizer. Consult the Scoring Guide to ensure that you are meeting the specific criteria. When your draft is complete, read it and clarify your ideas before sharing it within your writing group.

Sharing and Responding

4. Share your monologue in your writing group, and use the feedback to revise the following:

   ▶ clarity and coherence of ideas presented

   ▶ purpose and target audience

   ▶ consistent tone with appropriate word choice and language use.

5. After you have revised your draft, work with a partner to review and edit each other's work for grammar, punctuation, and spelling. You might choose to use resources (i.e., dictionary, thesaurus, grammar book, etc.) to assist you with this phase of the writing process.

6. To prepare for your presentation, mark your text to identify places where you want to include inflection, gestures, movements, facial expressions and various tones. Use the following guide to analyze your text and then to mark it.

Element to include	How I will mark the text to show this element:	Line numbers where I will use this element and *how* I will use the element:
Inflection	↗ Raise pitch. < Speak louder. > Speak softer. , Pause.	
Gestures	Draw or write how to gesture in the margins.	
Movement	Write down where and how to move.	
Facial Expression	Draw simple expressions in the margins.	
Tones to Emphasize	Describe the tone as a reminder (e.g. furious, mournful, anxious, etc.). Underline words to say in that tone.	

7. Describe the props and costumes (or props to pantomime) you plan to use at specific points in your presentation:

   ▶ Props to use:

   ▶ Props to pantomime:

   ▶ Costumes:

Rehearsal

8. Rehearse your monolgue with a partner. Practice your monologues several times using appropriate facial expressions, gestures, and movements. Give each other suggestions and constructive feedback regarding the performance and possible props or costumes. If necessary, revise your monologues once again based on comments from your partner and your own reflection on your rehearsal. Then complete the feedback graphic organizer to help refine your performances for the class. Check the box that describes your partner's performance in each area. Then offer suggestions for each area.

Suggestions to try:

▶ Inflections to consider:

▶ Gestures /Facial Expression/Movement to consider:

▶ To clarify the choice of the words (diction) you use, try:

▶ To achieve your purpose, try:

⤴ TECHNOLOGY TIP If you have access to a recording device, you may want someone to record your rehearsal so you can view your performance and make changes to improve it.

Feedback rubric for my partner: _____

	Exemplary	Proficient	Emerging
Inflection	Inflection changes to make the purpose clear and interesting.	Inflection changes when appropriate.	The inflection is sometimes unclear or flat.
Gestures/ Facial Expression/ Movement	Gestures, facial expression, and movement are appropriate to the monologue and enhance the performance.	Gestures, facial expression, and movement usually occur in the monologue when appropriate.	Gestures, facial expression, and movement is inconsistent or does not vary enough to make the performance effective.
Clarity of words	The diction fits the tone of the situation and makes the performance powerful for the audience.	The diction makes the purpose clear to the audience.	The diction needs more descriptive words to convey the emotion of the monologue.
Achievement of Purpose	The performer is able to elicit the emotional response desired from the audience.	The performer elicits a response from the audience.	The intended purpose of the monologue is unclear.

Performance

9. Make any needed changes to your monologue, and rehearse again if necessary.

10. Your teacher will inform you when you will present your monologue to the class. After all monologues have been presented, write a reflection addressing the effectiveness of your performance.

Reflection

11. Reread your monologue and think about your performance. Then, write a reflection, discussing the choices you made in creating your monologue, including the topic, tone, and revisions. In another paragraph discuss the elements of performance, including rehearsal, and your thoughts about how your performance affected your audience. In each paragraph, include a discussion of the most successful aspects and those aspects you might change if you had a chance to do it again.

SCORING GUIDE

Scoring Criteria	Exemplary	Proficient	Emerging
Ideas **Organization** **Use of Language**	The original monologue skillfully reveals the relationship between a choice and the consequence(s) of that choice by: • coherently communicating with a clear purpose to an intended audience • accurately using monologue structure and format • skillfully using language to convey tone.	The original monologue reveals a choice and the consequence(s) of that choice by: • communicating with a purpose to an intended audience • following monologue structure and format • using language to convey tone.	The original monologue fails to sufficiently reveal a choice and the consequence(s) of that choice. It may not include one or more of the following: • a purpose or intended audience • monologue structure or format • language to convey tone.
Performance	The performance includes the purposeful use of inflection and volume to emphasize and reinforce key words and ideas effectively in the monologue.	The performance includes appropriate use of inflection and volume to bring attention to key words and ideas in the monologue.	The performance includes limited use of inflection and volume to reinforce key words or ideas in the monologue.
Presentation	The performance includes extensive use of effective gestures, facial expressions, movements, props, and/or costumes to enhance the ideas presented in the monologue.	The performance includes adequate use of gestures, facial expressions, movements, props, and/or costumes to demonstrate the ideas presented in the monologue.	The performance includes minimal use of gestures, facial expressions, movements, props, and/or costumes to reinforece the ideas presented in the monologue.

Creating and Presenting a Monologue

SCORING GUIDE

Scoring Criteria	Exemplary	Proficient	Emerging
Reflection	The reflection clearly and descriptively explains: • choices on the topic, tone, and revisions during the creation the monologue • perspective on the most successful aspects of the performance and those aspects he/she wishes to improve.	The reflection explains: • choices on the topic, tone, and revisions during the creation of the monologue • perspective on the most successful aspects of the performance and those aspects he/she wishes to improve.	The reflection gives a minimal response to the writer's choices during the creation of the monologue or his/her perspective on the aspects of performance.
Additional Criteria			

Comments: _____

_____

_____

_____

_____

_____

_____

Learning Focus:

Writing Narrative Poetry

Do you remember the difference between prose and poetry? **Prose** is writing that is not in poetic or dramatic form. It includes essays, stories, articles, letters, memos, and so on. **Poetry** is often written in lines, and it makes use of imagery and language intended to appeal to the reader's emotions or imagination. Poetry can take several forms. You may be familiar with **free verse**, where the writer uses lines that do not have a regular rhythm or rhyme scheme. *Rhyme scheme* is the pattern the writer follows for rhyming words at ends of lines.

Another form of poetry is **narrative poetry,** which tells a story in verse. Narrative poems usually contain the same elements as short stories, such as setting, characters, conflict, and plot. Like a short story, the narrative poem has a beginning, middle, and end. "Casey at the Bat," which you read in Activity 5.10, is an example of a narrative poem.

Writing poetry is similar to writing prose in that you consider the purpose of your poem (your story), your audience, and the language and sensory details you want to use to communicate your story and paint a mental image for the reader. Familiarity with poetic devices, from rhyme schemes and figurative language, will help you compose your own narrative poems.

What Is a Narrative Poem?

My Notes

Five, Three, One

Name five things you know about narratives (Unit 1):

1. Conflict
2. It has to tell stories
3. Beggining
4. Middle
5. End

Name three things you know about poetry:

1. Rhyme
2. Stanzas
3. Good Stupe

Make one prediction about what a narrative poem is:

1. A poem about yorself

Little Red Riding Hood and the Wolf

by Roald Dahl

ABOUT THE AUTHOR
Roald Dahl (1916-1990) is best known for his mischievous children's stories, such as *James and the Giant Peach* and *Charlie and the Chocolate Factory*. His stories usually unfold with unexpected events and endings. Dahl also wrote screenplays and works for adults.

As soon as Wolf began to feel
That he would like a decent meal,
He went and knocked on Grandma's door.
When Grandma opened it, she saw
The sharp white teeth, the horrid grin,   5
And Wolfie said, "May I come in?"
Poor Grandmamma was terrified,
"He's going to eat me up!" she cried.
And she was absolutely right.
He ate her up in one big bite.   10
But Grandmamma was small and tough,
And Wolfie wailed, "That's not enough!
I haven't yet begun to feel
That I have had a decent meal!"
He ran around the kitchen yelping,   15
"I've got to have a second helping!"
Then added with a frightful leer,
"I'm therefore going to wait right here
Till Little Miss Red Riding Hood
Comes home from walking in the wood."   20
He quickly put on Grandma's clothes,
(Of course he hadn't eaten those).
He dressed himself in coat and hat.

My Notes

LITERARY TERMS
A **parody** is a humorous imitation of a literary work.

My Notes

He put on shoes, and after that
25 He even brushed and curled his hair,
Then sat himself in Grandma's chair.
In came the little girl in red.
She stopped. She stared. And then she said,

"What great big ears you have, Grandma."
30 "All the better to hear you with," the Wolf replied.
"What great big eyes you have, Grandma,"
said Little Red Riding Hood.
"All the better to see you with," the Wolf replied.

He sat there watching her and smiled.
35 He thought, I'm going to eat this child.
Compared with her old Grandmamma
She's going to taste like caviar.

Then Little Red Riding Hood said, "But Grandma,
what a lovely great big furry coat you have on."

40 "That's wrong!" cried Wolf. "Have you forgot
To tell me what BIG TEETH I've got?
Ah well, no matter what you say,
I'm going to eat you anyway."
The small girl smiles. One eyelid flickers.
45 She whips a pistol from her knickers.
She aims it at the creature's head
And *bang bang bang*, she shoots him dead.
A few weeks later, in the wood,
I came across Miss Riding Hood.
50 But what a change! No cloak of red,
No silly hood upon her head.
She said, "Hello, and do please note
My lovely furry wolfskin coat."

SUGGESTED LEARNING STRATEGIES: **Discussion Groups, Drafting, Graphic Organizer, Marking the Text, Rereading, TP-CASTT, Visualizing, Word Map**

Poetry

ABOUT THE AUTHOR

Rita Dove, born in 1952, became interested in writing poetry when she was in high school. She has since made a successful career as a poet. From 1993 to 1995 she was the Poet Laureate of the United States. Her poems explore family and history.

FIFTH GRADE AUTO-BIOGRAPHY

by Rita Dove

I was four in this photograph fishing
with my grandparents at a lake in Michigan.
My brother squats in poison ivy.
His Davy Crockett cap
sits squared on his head so the raccoon tail   5
flounces down the back of his sailor suit.

My grandfather sits to the far right
in a folding chair,
and I know his left hand is on
the tobacco in his pants pocket   10
because I used to wrap it for him
every Christmas. Grandmother's hips
bulge from the brush, she's leaning
into the ice chest, sun through the trees
printing her dress with soft   15
luminous paws.

I am staring jealously at my brother;
the day before he rode his first horse, alone.
I was strapped in a basket
behind my grandfather.   20
He smelled of lemons. He's died—

but I remember his hands.

Drawing the Poem

On separate paper, recreate the photograph described in "Fifth Grade Autobiography." Base your drawing on the images you highlighted as you marked the text. Write a brief reflection on how the imagery works toward creating a picture in your mind.

My Notes

A Picture Is Worth 1,000 Words

TP-CASTT

Acronym	Directions for analysis	Response
T: Title	Ponder the title before reading the poem.	
P: Paraphrase	Restate the poem in your own words.	
C: Connotation	Contemplate the poem for word meanings beyond the literal.	
A: Attitude	Observe both the speaker's and the poem's tone.	
S: Shift	Note the shifts in person, place, attitude, etc.	
T: Title Revisited	Examine the title again, this time on an interpretive level.	
T: Theme	Determine the message about life implied in the poem.	

Narrative Poetry: "The Highwayman"

SUGGESTED LEARNING STRATEGIES: Diffusing, Metacognitive
Markers, Rereading, Skimming/Scanning, Summarizing/Paraphrasing,
Think-Pair-Share, Word Map

Narrative Poetry

ABOUT THE AUTHOR

English poet Alfred Noyes (1880–1958) wrote more than
five volumes of poetry, many of them long narrative
poems or epic poems. He spent time in the United States
as a professor of literature at Princeton University from
1914 to 1923, and he also lived in Canada and the United
States during World War II.

The Highwayman [1]

by Alfred Noyes

Part One

The wind was a torrent of darkness upon the gusty trees,
The moon was a ghostly galleon[2] tossed upon cloudy seas,
The road was a ribbon of moonlight looping the purple moor,
And the highwayman came riding—
    Riding—riding—   5
The highwayman came riding, up to the old inn door.

He'd a French cocked hat on his forehead, a bunch of lace at his chin;
A coat of the claret[3] velvet, and breeches of fine doe-skin.
They fitted with never a wrinkle. His boots were up to the thigh.
And he rode with a jeweled twinkle,   10
    His pistol butts a-twinkle,
His rapier hilt a-twinkle, under the jeweled sky.

Over the cobbles he clattered and clashed in the dark inn-yard.
He tapped with his whip on the shutters, but all was locked and barred.
He whistled a tune to the window, and who should be waiting there   15

---

[1] **Highwayman** *n.* a man who robs travelers on the road
[2] **galleon** *n.* a large sailing ship with three masts
[3] **claret** *adj.* a deep, purplish red

My Notes

Lots of Metaphors
Tone: Dark

Narrative Poetry: "The Highwayman"

But the landlord's black-eyed daughter,
  Bess, the landlord's daughter,
Plaiting a dark red love-knot into her long black hair.

And dark in the dark old inn-yard a stable-wicket creaked
20 Where Tim the ostler[4] listened. His face was white and peaked.
His eyes were hollows of madness, his hair like mouldy hay,
But he loved the landlord's daughter,
  The landlord's red-lipped daughter.
Dumb as a dog he listened, and he heard the robber say—

25 "One kiss, my bonny sweetheart, I'm after a prize tonight,
But I shall be back with the yellow gold before the morning
light.
  Yet if they press me sharply, and harry[5] me through the day,
  Then look for me by moonlight,
    Watch for me by moonlight,
30 I'll come to thee by moonlight, though hell should bar the way."

He rose upright in the stirrups. He scarce could reach her hand,
But she loosened her hair in the casement.[6] His face burnt like a
brand
  As the black cascade of perfume came tumbling over his breast;
  And he kissed its waves in the moonlight,
35   (O, sweet, black waves in the moonlight!)
  Then he tugged at his rein in the moonlight, and galloped away
to the west.

Part Two

He did not come in the dawning. He did not come at noon;
And out of the tawny sunset, before the rise of the moon,
When the road was a gypsy's ribbon, looping the purple moor,
40 A red-coat troop came marching—
    Marching—marching—
King George's men came matching, up to the old inn-door.

They said no word to the landlord. They drank his ale instead.
  But they gagged his daughter, and bound her, to the foot of her
narrow bed.
45 Two of them knelt at her casement, with muskets[7] at their side!

---

[4] **ostler** *n.* someone employed in a stable to take care of horses
[5] **harry**, *v.* to harass or keep troubling
[6] **casement** *n.* a window that opens on hinges
[7] **muskets** *n.*, large guns widely used before rifles were invented

There was death at every window;
     And hell at one dark window;
For Bess could see, through her casement, the road that
he would ride.

They had tied her up to attention, with many a sniggering jest,
They had bound a musket beside her, with the barrel beneath
her breast!   50
"Now, keep good watch!" and they kissed her. She heard the
doomed man say—
Look for me by moonlight;
     Watch for me by moonlight;
I'll come to thee by moonlight, though hell should bar the way!

She twisted her hands behind her; but all the knots held good!   55
She writhed her hands till her fingers were wet with sweat or
blood!
They stretched and strained in the darkness, and the hours
crawled by like years,
     Till, now, on the stroke of midnight,
          Cold, on the stroke of midnight,
The tip of one finger touched it! The trigger at least was hers!   60

The tip of one finger touched it. She strove no more for the rest.
Up, she stood up to attention, with the muzzle beneath her
breast.
She would not risk their hearing, she would not strive again;
For the road lay bare in the moonlight;
     Blank and bare in the moonlight;   65
And the blood in her veins, in the moonlight, throbbed to
her love's refrain.

Tlot tlot; tlot tlot! Had they heard it? The horsehoofs, ringing
clear;
Tlot tlot, tlot tlot, in the distance? Were they deaf that they did
not hear?
Down the ribbon of moonlight, over the brow of the hill,
The highwayman came riding—   70
     Riding—riding—
The red-coats looked to their priming! She stood up, straight
and still.

Tlot tlot, in the frosty silence! *Tlot tlot,* in the echoing night!
Nearer he came and nearer. Her face was like a light.
Her eyes grew wide for a moment; she drew one last deep   75
breath,

My Notes

My Notes

Then her finger moved in the moonlight,
 Her musket shattered the moonlight,
Shattered her breast in the moonlight and warned him—with
her death.

He turned. He spurred to the west; he did not know who stood
 Bowed, with her head o'er the musket, drenched with her
80 own blood!
Not till the dawn he heard it, and his face grew grey to hear
How Bess, the landlord's daughter,
 The landlord's black-eyed daughter,
Had watched for her love in the moonlight, and died in the
darkness there.

85 Back, he spurred like a madman, shouting a curse to the sky,
With the white road smoking behind him and his rapier[8]
brandished high.
Blood-red were his spurs in the golden noon; wine-red was his
velvet coat;
When they shot him down on the highway,
 Down like a dog on the highway,
And he lay in his blood on the highway, with a bunch of lace
90 at his throat.

*And still of a winter's night, they say, when the wind is in the
trees,*
When the moon is a ghostly galleon tossed upon cloudy seas,
When the road is a ribbon of moonlight over the purple moor,
A highwayman comes riding—
95 *Riding—riding—*
A highwayman comes riding, up to the old inn-door.

Over the cobbles he clatters and clangs in the dark inn-yard.
*He taps with his whip on the shutters, but all is locked and
barred.*
*He whistles a tune to the window, and who should be waiting
there*
100 *But the landlord's black-eyed daughter,*
 Bess, the landlord's daughter,
Plaiting a dark red love-knot into her long black hair.

---

[8] **rapier**, *n.* a long, straight sword with a narrow blade and two edges

Consider the similarities and differences in the two narrative poems, "The Highwayman" and "Casey at the Bat." Revisit the two poems and complete the chart below.

Think about *diction*, which is the choice of words to express meaning, as you compare the poems.

WORD CONNECTIONS

Diction contains the Latin root *dict-*, meaning "say, declare, proclaim." The root appears in *dictionary*, *predict*, *contradict*, and *dictator*. The Latin suffix *–ion* means "being the result of."

"Casey at the Bat"	Element being compared	"The Highwayman"
	Diction that helps to convey meaning	
	Poetic elements	

Poetic Devices at Work

My Notes

Poetry

ABOUT THE AUTHOR

Of Mexican-American heritage, Gary Soto grew up in
Fresno, California. In high school, he discovered a love
of reading and knew he wanted to be a writer. He started
writing while in college. His poems, short stories, and
novels capture the vivid details of everyday life and have
won numerous awards and prizes.

ORANGES

by Gary Soto

The first time I walked
With a girl, I was twelve,
Cold, and weighted down
With two oranges in my jacket.
5   December. Frost cracking
Beneath my steps, my breath
Before me, then gone,
As I walked toward
Her house, the one whose
10 Porch light burned yellow
Night and day, in any weather.
A dog barked at me, until
She came out pulling
At her gloves, face bright
15 With rouge. I smiled,
Touched her shoulder, and led
Her down the street, across
A used car lot and a line
Of newly planted trees,
20 Until we were breathing
Before a drugstore. We

Entered, the tiny bell
Bringing a saleslady
Down a narrow aisle of goods.
I turned to the candies   25
Tiered like bleachers,
And asked what she wanted—
Light in her eyes, a smile
Starting at the corners
Of her mouth. I fingered   30
A nickel in my pocket,
And when she lifted a chocolate
That cost a dime,
I didn't say anything.
I took the nickel from   35
My pocket, then an orange,
And set them quietly on
The counter. When I looked up,
The lady's eyes met mine,
And held them, knowing   40
Very well what it was all
About.

Outside,
A few cars hissing past,
Fog hanging like old   45
Coats between the trees.
I took my girl's hand
In mine for two blocks,
Then released it to let
Her unwrap the chocolate.   50
I peeled my orange
That was so bright against
The gray of December
That, from some distance,
Someone might have thought   55
I was making a fire in my hands.

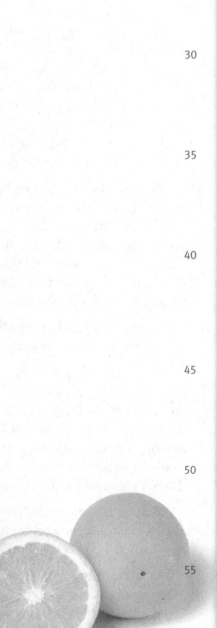

My Notes

ACTIVITY
5.18

Finding a Poem Anywhere

SUGGESTED LEARNING STRATEGIES: Discussion Groups, Marking the
Text, Predicting, Quickwrite, Think-Pair-Share, Graphic Organizer

My Notes

Short Story

Seventh Grade

by Gary Soto

On the first day of school, Victor stood in line half an hour before he came to a wobbly card table. He was handed a packet of papers and a computer card on which he listed his one elective, French. He already spoke Spanish and English, but he thought some day he might travel to France, where it was cool; not like Fresno, where summer days reached 110 degrees in the shade. There were rivers in France, and huge churches, and fair-skinned people everywhere, the way there were brown people all around Victor.

Besides, Teresa, a girl he had liked since they were in catechism classes at Saint Theresa's, was taking French, too. With any luck they would be in the same class. Teresa is going to be my girl this year, he promised himself as he left the gym full of students in their new fall clothes. She was cute. And good at math, too, Victor thought as he walked down the hall to his homeroom. He ran into his friend, Michael Torres, by the water fountain that never turned off.

They shook hands, *raza*-style, and jerked their heads at one another in a *saludo de vato*. "How come you're making a face?" asked Victor.

"I ain't making a face, *ese*. This is my face." Michael said his face had changed during the summer. He had read a *GQ* magazine that his older brother borrowed from the Book Mobile and noticed that the male models all had the same look on their faces. They would stand, one arm around a beautiful woman, and *scowl*. They would sit at a pool, their rippled stomachs dark with shadow, and *scowl*. They would sit at dinner tables, cool drinks in their hands, and *scowl*.

"I think it works," Michael said. He scowled and let his upper lip quiver. His teeth showed along with the ferocity of his soul. "Belinda Reyes walked by a while ago and looked at me," he said.

Victor didn't say anything, though he thought his friend looked pretty strange. They talked about recent movies, baseball, their parents, and the horrors of picking grapes in order to buy their fall clothes. Picking grapes was like living in Siberia, except hot and more boring.

"What classes are you taking?" Michael said, scowling.

"French. How 'bout you?"

"Spanish. I ain't so good at it, even if I'm Mexican."

"I'm not either, but I'm better at it than math, that's for sure."

A tinny, three-beat bell propelled students to their homerooms. The two friends socked each other in the arm and went their ways, Victor thinking, man, that's weird. Michael thinks making a face makes him handsome.

On the way to his homeroom, Victor tried a scowl. He felt foolish, until out of the corner of his eye he saw a girl looking at him. Umm, he thought, maybe it does work. He scowled with greater conviction.

In homeroom, roll was taken, emergency cards were passed out, and they were given a bulletin to take home to their parents. The principal, Mr. Belton, spoke over the crackling loudspeaker, welcoming the students to a new year, new experiences, and new friendships. The students squirmed in their chairs and ignored him. They were anxious to go to first period. Victor sat calmly, thinking of Teresa, who sat two rows away, reading a paperback novel. This would be his lucky year. She was in his homeroom, and would probably be in his English and math classes. And, of course, French.

The bell rang for first period, and the students herded noisily through the door. Only Teresa lingered, talking with the homeroom teacher.

"So you think I should talk to Mrs. Gaines?" she asked the teacher. "She would know about ballet?"

"She would be a good bet," the teacher said. Then added, "Or the gym teacher, Mrs. Garza."

Victor lingered, keeping his head down and staring at his desk. He wanted to leave when she did so he could bump into her and say something clever.

He watched her on the sly. As she turned to leave, he stood up and hurried to the door, where he managed to catch her eye. She smiled and said, "Hi, Victor."

He smiled back and said, "Yeah, that's me." His brown face blushed. Why hadn't he said, "Hi, Teresa," or "How was your summer?" or something nice?

As Teresa walked down the hall, Victor walked the other way, looking back, admiring how gracefully she walked, one foot in front of the other. So much for being in the same class, he thought. As he

My Notes

trudged to English, he practiced scowling.

In English they reviewed the parts of speech. Mr. Lucas, a portly man, waddled down the aisle, asking, "What is a noun?"

"A person, place, or thing," said the class in unison. "Yes, now somebody give me an example of a person—you, Victor Rodriguez."

"Teresa," Victor said automatically. Some of the girls giggled.

They knew he had a crush on Teresa. He felt himself blushing again.

"Correct," Mr. Lucas said. "Now provide me with a place."

Mr. Lucas called on a freckled kid who answered, "Teresa's house with a kitchen full of big brothers."

After English, Victor had math, his weakest subject. He sat in the back by the window, hoping that he would not be called on. Victor understood most of the problems, but some of the stuff looked like the teacher made it up as she went along. It was confusing, like the inside of a watch.

After math he had a fifteen-minute break, then social studies, and, finally, lunch. He bought a tuna casserole with buttered rolls, some fruit cocktail, and milk. He sat with Michael, who practiced scowling between bites.

Girls walked by and looked at him.

"See what I mean, Vic?" Michael scowled. "They love it."

"Yeah, I guess so."

They ate slowly, Victor scanning the horizon for a glimpse of Teresa. He didn't see her. She must have brought lunch, he thought, and is eating outside. Victor scraped his plate and left Michael, who was busy scowling at a girl two tables away.

The small, triangle-shaped campus bustled with students talking about their new classes. Everyone was in a sunny mood. Victor hurried to the bag lunch area, where he sat down and opened his math book. He moved his lips as if he were reading, but his mind was somewhere else. He raised his eyes slowly and looked around. No Teresa.

He lowered his eyes, pretending to study, then looked slowly to the left. No Teresa. He turned a page in the book and stared at some math problems that scared him because he knew he would have to do them eventually. He looked to the right. Still no sign of her. He stretched out lazily in an attempt to disguise his snooping.

Then he saw her. She was sitting with a girlfriend under a plum tree. Victor moved to a table near her and daydreamed about taking her to a movie. When the bell sounded, Teresa looked up, and their eyes met. She smiled sweetly and gathered her books. Her next class was French, same as Victor's.

They were among the last students to arrive in class, so all the good desks in the back had already been taken. Victor was forced to sit near the front, a few desks away from Teresa, while Mr. Bueller wrote French words on the chalkboard. The bell rang, and Mr. Bueller wiped his hands, turned to the class, and said, "*Bonjour.*"

"*Bonjour,*" braved a few students.

"*Bonjour,*" Victor whispered. He wondered if Teresa heard him.

Mr. Bueller said that if the students studied hard, at the end of the year they could go to France and be understood by the populace.

One kid raised his hand and asked, "What's 'populace'?"

"The people, the people of France."

Mr. Bueller asked if anyone knew French. Victor raised his hand, wanting to impress Teresa. The teacher beamed and said, "*Très bien. Parlez-vous français?*"

Victor didn't know what to say. The teacher wet his lips and asked something else in French. The room grew silent. Victor felt all eyes staring at him. He tried to bluff his way out by making noises that sounded French.

"La me vava me con le grandma," he said uncertainly.

Mr. Bueller, wrinkling his face in curiosity, asked him to speak up.

Great rosebushes of red bloomed on Victor's cheeks. A river of nervous sweat ran down his palms. He felt awful. Teresa sat a few desks away, no doubt thinking he was a fool. Without looking at Mr. Bueller, Victor mumbled, "Frenchie oh wewe gee in September."

Mr. Bueller asked Victor to repeat what he had said. "Frenchie oh wewe gee in September," Victor repeated.

Mr. Bueller understood that the boy didn't know French and turned away. He walked to the blackboard and pointed to the words on the board with his steel-edged ruler.

"*Le bateau,*" he sang.

"*Le bateau,*" the students repeated.

My Notes

My Notes

"Le bateau est sur l'eau," he sang.

"Le bateau est sur l'eau."

Victor was too weak from failure to join the class. He stared at the board and wished he had taken Spanish, not French. Better yet, he wished he could start his life over. He had never been so embarrassed. He bit his thumb until he tore off a sliver of skin.

The bell sounded for fifth period, and Victor shot out of the room, avoiding the stares of the other kids, but had to return for his math book. He looked sheepishly at the teacher, who was erasing the board, then widened his eyes in terror at Teresa who stood in front of him. "I didn't know you knew French," she said. "That was good."

Mr. Bueller looked at Victor, and Victor looked back. Oh please, don't say anything, Victor pleaded with his eyes. I'll wash your car, mow your lawn, walk your dog—anything! I'll be your best student, and I'll clean your erasers after school.

Mr. Bueller shuffled through the papers on his desk. He smiled and hummed as he sat down to work. He remembered his college years when he dated a girlfriend in borrowed cars. She thought he was rich because each time he picked her up he had a different car. It was fun until he had spent all his money on her and had to write home to his parents because he was broke.

Victor couldn't stand to look at Teresa. He was sweaty with shame. "Yeah, well, I picked up a few things from movies and books and stuff like that." They left the class together. Teresa asked him if he would help her with her French.

"Sure, anytime," Victor said.

"I won't be bothering you, will I?"

"Oh no, I like being bothered."

"Bonjour," Teresa said, leaving him outside her next class. She smiled and pushed wisps of hair from her face.

"Yeah, right, *bonjour,*" Victor said. He turned and headed to his class. The rosebushes of shame on his face became bouquets of love. Teresa is a great girl, he thought. And Mr. Bueller is a good guy.

He raced to metal shop. After metal shop there was biology, and after biology a long sprint to the public library, where he checked out three French textbooks.

He was going to like seventh grade.

A Poet Talks About Creating Poetry

SUGGESTED LEARNING STRATEGIES: Marking the Text, Word Map

Interview

QUESTIONS AND ANSWERS ABOUT POETRY

from A Fire in My Hands, by Gary Soto

Q *Where do your poems come from?*

A They come from my memory or from a story someone told me; they come from feelings and the inventive side of the mind. Most of the poems in this collection come from real experiences. But, like other artists, I treat the experiences with a measure of creativity.

Q *Then, not everything in your narrative poems is true?*

A No. But most poets who tell stories through verse believe that poems should be credible, that the experiences in them should be possible in life even if they did not happen to the poet. For instance, in "Learning to Bargain," my friend didn't really kill the cat. As I remember, he heaved a brick at it because it had knocked over his garbage can. Luckily, he missed. Still, I didn't like the idea of his trying to hurt the cat. I threatened to tell his mom if he ever did it again. In the poem, I make our actions more ominous. I say that he killed the cat and that I threatened to tell unless he paid me a dime. I wanted to show in the poem how people start conspiring at a very early age.

Q *Do all poems tell stories?*

A No. A lyric poem expresses the feelings or thoughts of the poem's speaker. (The speaker does not have to be the poet.) A lyric poem does not tell a complete story, as a narrative poem does. "October" is a lyric poem.

Q *Do you have to get inspired to write?*

A When I began writing fifteen years ago, I waited to be "inspired," which for me was a physical sensation — my body tingled. Now I get this feeling less frequently. I doodle a few phrases or lines, and a nice feeling settles on my shoulders. This is a sign that I'm ready to write. It's the same with an artist friend. Sometimes she doesn't know what she's going to paint until she sketches a few lines, maybe

My Notes

My Notes

a face, maybe an outline of a tree. Then, suddenly, like the flash of a camera, she has an idea and a feeling settles on her shoulders, too.

Q *When do you write?*

A Each poet has a routine. I write in the summer when I'm not teaching, and I write in the morning because my mind is clear and I can concentrate. After breakfast, I go out to my garage, which I've turned into a study, and write for two or three hours; then I have lunch, and do something else in the afternoon. When I'm stuck on a line, I go to the bench press in the backyard and do a quick set of reps, which is usually enough to get the blood and my imagination going.

Q *Do you have to change any of your words?*

A Since most poems are short, compared to other kinds of literature, every line needs a great deal of attention. I once worked on a single fourteen-line poem for a week, changing verbs, reworking line breaks, cutting out unnecessary words.

Q *Do you have a favorite poem?*

A Yes, but don't tell my other poems. My favorite is "Hitchhiking With a Friend and a Book That Explains the Pacific Ocean." The poem is about wonderment. I had never hitchhiked in my life when a friend, also named Gary, suggested that we hitchhike to the ocean. We stood at the edge of a road outside Fresno and waited and waited. Two hours later a truck driver picked us up, took us a short distance, and dropped us off near a dairy. After a short wait there, a man in a banged-up truck picked us up.

Q *Do you write the titles of your poems first?*

A I usually come up with a title when I'm about halfway through a poem. A title often hints to the reader what the poem is about. At times, however, poets will use wild titles that they may not wholly understand but may like for the way they sound or the way they look on the page.

Q *Why are poems difficult to understand?*

A Poetry is a concentrated form of writing; so much meaning is packed into such a little space. Therefore, each word in a poem is very important and is chosen very carefully to convey just the right meaning. For example, the word *tree* might *stand* for more

WORD CONNECTIONS

Complete the analogy to show a whole-to-part relationship.

Poem : _____ ::
_____ : quarter note

than a tree in an orchard. It might symbolize life itself, or it might symbolize the strength of your grandfather or your father. *Rain* may symbolize tears; *dusk* may symbolize approaching death.

Another reason why poetry can be difficult to understand is that you're not used to reading it. The more you read it, the better you get at understanding words and lines.

Q *Should I read a poem more than once?*

A Yes, by all means. Read it again and again. One poet remarked that "poetry is an act of attention" — you have to concentrate when you read a poem, just as you must concentrate when you're in the batter's box and your team needs you to bring in a player on second base.

I also like to think of a poem as a new person. Just because you say hello once doesn't mean that you never want to see this person again. Of course you do. A poem also needs to be seen again and again.

Q *Why don't your poems rhyme?*

A Most poets today don't use rhyme; they write "free verse" — poetry that has no regular rhyme or rhythm. Poetry has changed over the years, but poets' motives for writing poetry haven't changed. Most poets write because they feel something and want to share it with others.

Q *When did you decide to become a poet?*

A I decided to become a poet after I read a funny/sad poem by Edward Field called "Unwanted." It's about a lonely man who feels sad that no one wants him. He hangs a picture of himself at the post office next to posters of dangerous criminals. He wants people to recognize him and love him. I was inspired by this poem and identified with it because it seemed to speak about my own life. I read the poem over and over, and even typed it out to see what it looked like. I read this poet's book and began to read other poets. After a while, I decided to write my own poems, and I have been doing it ever since.

My Notes

My Notes

Poetry

Learning to Bargain

by Gary Soto

Summer. Flies knitting
Filth on the window,
A mother calling a son home . . .
I'm at that window, looking

5   Onto the street: dusk,
A neighbor kid sharpening
A stick at the curb.
I go outside and sit
Next to him without saying

10 A word. When he looks
Up, his eyes dark as flies . . .
I ask about the cat, the one dead
Among weeds in the alley.
"Yeah, I did it," he admits,

15 And stares down at his feet,
Then my feet. "What do you want?"
"A dime," I say. Without
Looking at me, he gets
Up, goes behind his house,

20 And returns with two Coke bottles.
"These make a dime." He sits
At the curb, his shoulders
So bony they could be wings
To lift him so far. "Don't tell."

25 He snaps a candy into halves
And we eat in silence.

Transformation of Text

SUGGESTED LEARNING STRATEGIES: Marking the Text, Oral
Interpretation, Rereading, Revising, Skimming/Scanning, Sharing And
Responding

Narrative

Disease, Dis-ease

by Kelsey Frost (student)

Shuffle. Shuffle. His feet were dragging across the asphalt. He looked around as if searching for something. A trace of confusion crossed his weary face.

"Nancy?" he asked as he spotted me on the porch of the restaurant.

"Come on. She's inside," I replied as I beckoned him towards me. Frustration and more confusion were visible on his face as he walked towards me. "We're stopping to eat," I explained.

Why is it so hard for Gramie to accept that it is getting worse? I wondered somberly. A year ago he could still tell you about some of his times in the military, but now the only thing that really got him talking was the mention of our president. Horrible. It is a horrible, horrible disease. For years it was slow moving, more like a slug, but now it had started to speed up, as if the slug had been caught on the foot of a passerby.

We should not have split him from my grandmother, but she needed time to talk to my mom, so he rode in the other car. He had been starting to get worse when he was away from home, and when he was away from her. Both together were too much, I guess. It hurt to see that confused look on his face, but I knew that I would have to get used to it. It was now a fact that my grandfather's memory and motor skills were deteriorating. Just being separated from his wife for the two-hour drive to the beach was enough to scare and confuse him.

Inside the little Otis Café, in the miniscule town of Otis, Oregon, we started examining our menus.

"Honey," my grandma began, "do you want this sandwich, or the hash browns?"

She pointed at the two descriptions on his laminated menu. My granddad paused for a moment. He glanced over the words, only partially taking them in.

My Notes

Transformation of Text

"That one," he said, pointing his finger at the sandwich on the menu. He smiled weakly, almost timidly at my grandmother, and she returned the gesture.

She is so firmly implanted in his brain, that he trusts her with all his heart, I thought as I watched them from across the booth. My own order fixed in my brain, I glanced around the one-room building for a waitress. The blond, overweight one made her way towards our family. She was one of the few Otisians…Otisites? Maybe? Anyway, she was one of the few people who lived in the town of Otis.

"Are you ready to order?" she asked rather blandly.

"Yes, I would like the cheese burger," I replied, since she was looking at me. Scribble, scribble, on her notepad. She took my menu.

"Can I have the hash browns, with some sour cream on the side?"

"I will take the hash browns also."

"I want the Reuben sandwich."

"I'll have the split pea soup with a house salad. Blue cheese dressing on the side, and he will have the turkey sandwich," Gramie finished, also ordering for her husband while patting his knee. Scribble, scribble on the pad again, the rest of the menus were gathered, and the waitress walked behind the counter.

Plates came, bearing the nourishment greatly needed by all. Conversation ceased as we all dove into our food. Pleasure, warmth, many things rushed into me at once. Thoughts of the ocean floated into my mind, in anticipation of where we would be in the next half-hour. We ordered a scrumptious strawberry-rhubarb pie to go, and my grandmother reached for the bill.

Tonight's dessert, I deduced.

Gramie stood up to go to the restroom, and my grandpa tried to follow her like the shadow that he had become.

"Granddad, you can just stay here. She's going to the bathroom," I tried to explain. He sank back down in the booth with frustrated a sigh. *It must be horrible not to understand what is going on so often,* I thought as I watched him. We all headed out to the parking lot again, and Granddad made his way towards his car.

"Dad, you're riding with Jeff, remember? Mom and I want girls' time together," my mom reminded him.

"Loy, you are going in that car, with Jeff," my grandmother also re-informed him as she pointed across the parking lot. That look crossed his face. The "*what are you trying to get me to do, and why the hell can I not understand you?*" look. The look that makes you want to cry when you see it on an adult. He followed my father to the car, and slowly lowered himself in. The rest of us clambered into the other car and pulled the doors to follow.

Just stopping to eat showed me what the rest of his life would be like, at best. Confused, but still loving. Happy, but frustrated at times. In the six months since I had seen him last, I could tell that the slug was happy with the ride it had hitched, and that it would not let go. Those minutes taught me just how real it was becoming, and so I was forced to say it, it just bubbled out.

"It's worse isn't it—the Alzheimer's?

Poetry

Dis-ease

Shuffle. Shuffle.
His feet dragging across the asphalt, like wood on sandpaper
"Nancy?" he asked…
"Come on, she's inside. We're stopping for lunch,"
Confusion and frustration
Crossed his weary face.
Before he could tell you tales of the military,
Now only the troubles of our presidency.
Horrible, horrible disease.
It had been a slow-moving slug,
But now the slug was caught on a passerby.

He should not have been split
From my grandma,
Her face was so firmly in his brain,
His heart was in her hands.
We were on our way to the glittering ocean.
But first a café.
Laminated menus, we picked our food.
Cheese burger,
Hash browns,

Transformation of Text

Reuben sandwich,
Split pea soup,
Salad,
Turkey sandwich.
The blond, overweight waitress
Scribbled on the notepad,
Took the menus.
Food.
Pleasure, warmth, everything rushed at me at once.
Thought of the ocean floated in my mind, like a butterfly.

We rose, and exited the café.
He tried to follow my grandma,
Like the shadow the slug made him.
Ushered to the other car by us all,
A look crossed his face,
The "What are you trying to get me to do,
And why the hell can I not understand you?" look.
Almost makes you cry.

The slug was happy with the ride it had hitched,
And it determined his life thereafter.
Confused but loving,
Happy but frustrated.
All boiled down to one thing…
Alzheimer's.

Reflection

Though my narrative story and my poem were very similar in their contents, I noticed a few differences in using the two forms. In a story, I could go into so much more detail, but it almost felt like I had to. If I did not, the story would have been monotonous while at the same time a little too uninformative. In poem form, though, I had to cut some details out so that it would not simply sound like an average story. Everything had to be sifted through to find the most descriptive sections, though this form did give more opportunities to use poetic devices like metaphors and personification. In the end, the poem seemed to convey more emotions, while the story provided a more accurate and understandable account of what happened that day.

Creating a Narrative Poem

SUGGESTED LEARNING STRATEGIES: Prewriting, Drafting, Sharing and Responding, Self-Editing

Assignment

Your assignment is to write a narrative poem that recounts a fictional or true event dealing with the concept of choice. The poem must demonstrate your knowledge of narrative elements and poetic devices.

Steps

Prewriting

1. Brainstorm ideas for a narrative poem about the concept of choice. These ideas may come from any of the following areas:
   - ▶ your own life
   - ▶ a narrative that you have already written
   - ▶ stories that you have heard about other people
   - ▶ fictional stories you have read or watched
   - ▶ myths and fairy tales.

   Be sure to look back at the material you have created in previous activities.

Drafting

2. Once you have decided on a topic/idea, in small groups review the elements of narrative writing that you have learned: sequence of events, dialogue, details, characters, setting, description, etc.

3. Use a prewriting strategy to create a plan incorporating these elements into a narrative poem. Write the first draft.

Revising

4. Share your first draft within your writing groups. Solicit feedback to guide your revision.
   - ▶ Identify places in your narrative poem where you can refine the structure to enhance its ideas and style.
   - ▶ Review your **Poetic Devices** chart and consider revising the poem to enhance descriptions through poetic devices: metaphors, similes, imagery, symbols, or other devices with which you are comfortable.
   - ▶ Revise your narrative poem to create appropriate line breaks and stanzas. Consider adding a refrain or a pattern of repeated words and phrases.
   - ▶ Consult the Grammar Handbook or a classroom reference book to review correct usage of relative pronouns and pronoun-antecedent agreement. Revise your draft as needed.
   - ▶ Revisit the Scoring Guide to further aid revisions.

Creating a Narrative Poem

Editing for Publication

5. Proofread your draft to identify mistakes in grammar, punctuation, and spelling. Edit your draft to correct errors.

6. Review your draft and select an appropriate title for your narrative poem.

7. Prepare a publishable draft of your narrative poem.

SCORING GUIDE

Scoring Criteria	Exemplary	Proficient	Emerging
Organization	The poem uses narrative structure and elements of plot creatively to address the concept of choice. The poem skillfully blends the organization of a narrative with the structure of a poem (title, stanzas, and line breaks) to reinforce the idea of choice.	The poem uses a narrative structure and elements of plot to address the concept of choice. The poem contains an original title, stanzas, and line breaks.	The poem does not use narrative structure or elements of plot to address the concept of choice. The poem may be missing one or more of the following: an original title, appropriate stanzas, or purposeful line breaks.
Use of Language	The poem contains skillful use of poetic devices that enhance and support larger ideas presented in the text.	The poem contains adequate use of poetic devices to enhance and support the larger ideas of choice presented in the text.	The poem contains few, if any, poetic devices to enhance the ideas presented in the text.
Evidence of the Writing Process	There is extensive evidence that the poem reflects the various stages of the writing process. The poem demonstrates thoughtful planning, purposeful revision, and careful editing in preparation for publication.	There is evidence that the poem reflects the stages of the writing process. The poem demonstrates planning, revision, and editing to produce a draft that is ready for publication.	There is little or no evidence that the poem reflects the stages of the writing process. The poem does not demonstrate evidence of planning, revision, and editing. The draft is not ready for publication.
Additional Criteria			

Comments: _____

_____

_____

_____

_____

Reflection

An important aspect of growing as a learner is to reflect on where you have been, what you have accomplished, what helped you to learn, and how you will apply your new knowledge in the future. Use the following questions to guide your thinking and to identify evidence of your learning. Use separate notebook paper.

Thinking about Concepts

1. Using specific examples from this unit, respond to the Essential Questions:
   - How does a speaker create and present an effective oral text?
   - How do literary devices enhance a text?

2. Consider the new academic vocabulary from this unit (Oral Interpretation, Tone, Monologue, Narrative Poem, Poetic Devices) as well as academic vocabulary from previous units and select 3-4 terms of which your understanding has grown. For each term, answer the following questions:
   - What was your understanding of the word before you completed this unit?
   - How has your understanding of the word evolved throughout the unit?
   - How will you apply your understanding in the future?

Thinking about Connections

3. Review the activities and products (artifacts) you created. Choose those that most reflect your growth or increase in understanding.

4. For each artifact that you choose, record, respond to, and reflect on your thinking and understanding, using the following questions as a guide:
   a. What skill/knowledge does this artifact reflect, and how did you learn this skill/knowledge?
   b. How did your understanding of the power of language expand through your engagement with this artifact?
   c. How will you apply this skill or knowledge in the future?

Create this reflection as Portfolio pages—one for each artifact you choose. Use the model in the box for your headings and commentary on questions.

> ## Thinking About Thinking
> ### Portfolio Entry
>
> Concept:
>
> Description of Artifact:
>
> Commentary on Questions:

Grammar Handbook

Part 1: Parts of Speech Overview

Nouns

A noun is a word that denotes a person, place, or thing. In a sentence, nouns answer the questions *who* and *what*.

Example: The *dog* ran after the *ball*.

In the sentence above, there are two nouns, *dog* and *ball*. A noun may be concrete (something you can touch, see, etc.), like the nouns in the example above, or a noun may be abstract, as in the sentences below.

Example 1: She possesses *integrity*.
Example 2: He was searching for *love*.

The abstract concepts of *integrity* and *love* in the sentences above are both nouns. Nouns may also be proper.

Example 1: She visited *Chicago* every year.
Example 2: *Thanksgiving* is in *November*.

Chicago, Thanksgiving, and *November* are all proper nouns, and they should be capitalized.

Pronouns

A pronoun is a word that takes the place of a noun in a sentence.

Example: *She* decided to go to a movie.

In the sentence above, *she* is the pronoun. Like nouns, pronouns may be used either as subjects or as objects in a sentence.

Example: *She* planned to ask *him* for an interview.

In the example above, both *she* and *him* are pronouns; *she* is the subject of the sentence while *him* is the object. Every subject pronoun has a corresponding object form, as shown in the table below.

Subject and Object Pronouns	
Subject Pronouns	*Object Pronouns*
I	Me
We	Us
You	You
She	Her
He	Him
It	It
They	Them

Articles

Articles include *a*, *an*, and *the*. They precede a noun or a noun phrase in a sentence.

> **Example 1:** They wanted *a* house with *a* big porch.
> **Example 2:** He bought *the* blue sweater on sale.

In example 1, the article *a* precedes the noun *house*, and *a* also precedes the noun phrase *big porch*, which consists of an adjective (big) and the noun it describes (porch). In example 2, the article *the* precedes the noun phrase *blue sweater*, in which *sweater* is the noun and *blue* the adjective.

Adjectives

An adjective is a word that modifies, or describes, a noun or pronoun. Adjectives may precede nouns, or they may appear after a form of the reflexive verb *to be* (*am, are, is, was,* etc.).

> **Example 1:** We live in the *red brick* house.
> **Example 2:** She is *tall* for her age.

In example 1, two consecutive adjectives, *red* and *brick*, both describe the noun *house*. In example 2, the adjective *tall* appears after the reflexive verb *is* and describes the subject, *she*.

Verbs

A verb is a word that denotes action, or a state of being, in a sentence.

> **Example 1:** Beth *rides* the bus every day.
> **Example 2:** Paul *was* an avid reader.

In example 1, *rides* is the verb; it describes what the subject, Beth, does. In example 2, *was* describes Paul's state of being and is therefore the verb.

There may be multiple verbs in a sentence, or there may be a verb phrase consisting of a verb plus a helping verb.

> **Example 1:** She *turned* the key and *opened* the door.
> **Example 2:** Jackson *was studying* when I saw him last.

In example 1, the subject *she* performs two actions in the sentence, *turned* and *opened*. In example 2, the verb phrase is *was studying*.

Some words in a sentence may look like verbs but act as something else, like a noun; these are called verbals.

Adverbs

Just as adjectives modify nouns, adverbs modify, or further describe, verbs. Adverbs may also modify adjectives. (Many, though not all, adverbs end in *-ly*.)

> **Example 1:** He waved *wildly* to get her attention.
> **Example 2:** The shirt he wore to the party was *extremely* bright.

In the first example, the adverb *wildly* modifies the verb *waved*. In the second example, the adverb *extremely* modifies the adjective *bright*, which describes the noun *shirt*. While nouns answer the questions *who* and *what*, adverbs answer the questions *how*, *when*, *why*, and *where*.

Conjunctions

A conjunction is a word that joins two independent clauses, or sentences, together.

> **Example 1:** Ellen wanted to take drive into the city, *but* the cost of gasoline was too high.
> **Example 2:** Richard planned to study abroad in Japan, *so* he decided to learn the language.

In the examples above, both *but* and *so* are conjunctions. They join two complete sentences with the help of a comma. *And, but, for, or, nor, so,* and *yet* can all act as conjunctions.

Prepositions

Prepositions work in combination with a noun or pronoun to create phrases that modify verbs, nouns/pronouns, or adjectives. Prepositional phrases convey a spatial, temporal, or directional meaning.

Example 1: Ivy climbed *up* the brick wall *of* the house.

There are two prepositional phrases in the example above: *up the brick wall* and *of the house*. The first prepositional phrase is an adverbial phrase, since it modifies the verb by describing where the ivy climbed. The second phrase further modifies the noun *wall* (the object of the first prepositional phrase) and describes which wall the ivy climbs.

Below is a list of prepositions in the English language:

Aboard, about, above, across, after, against, along, amid, among, around, at, before, behind, below, beneath, beside, between, beyond, by, down, during, except, for, from, in, into, like, near, of, off, on, onto, out, over, past, since, through, throughout, to, toward, under, underneath, until, unto, up, upon, with, within, without.

Part 2: Count and Noncount Nouns

Countable Nouns

Countable nouns refer to things that we can count. Such nouns can take either singular or plural form.

Concrete nouns may be countable.

There are a dozen *flowers* in the vase.
He ate an *apple* for a snack.

Collective nouns are countable.

She attended three *classes* today.
London is home to several *orchestras*.

Some proper nouns are countable.

There are many *Greeks* living in New York.
The *Vanderbilts* would throw lavish parties at their Newport summer mansion.

Uncountable Nouns

Uncountable nouns refer to things that we cannot count. Such nouns take only singular form.

Abstract nouns are uncountable.

The price of *freedom* is constant vigilance.
Her writing shows *maturity* and *intelligence*.

Some concrete nouns are uncountable (when understood in their undivided sense).

The price of *oil* has stabilized recently.
May I borrow some *rice*?

Using Articles with Countable and Uncountable Nouns

A countable noun always takes either the indefinite (*a, an*) or definite (*the*) article when it is singular. When plural, it takes the definite article if it refers to a definite, specific group and no article if it is used in a general sense.

> *The guest* of honor arrived late.
> You are welcome as *a guest* in our home.
> *The guests* at your party yesterday made a lot of noise.
> *Guests* are welcome here anytime.

Uncountable nouns never take the indefinite article (*a* or *an*), but they do take singular verbs. *The* is sometimes used with uncountable nouns in the same way it is used with plural countable nouns, that is, to refer to a specific object, group, or idea.

> *Information* is a precious commodity in our computerized world.
> *The information* in your files is correct.
> *Sugar* has become more expensive recently.
> Please pass me *the sugar*.

Part 3: Using Pronouns Clearly

Because a pronoun REFERS BACK to a noun or TAKES THE PLACE OF that noun, you have to use the correct pronoun so that your reader clearly understands which noun your pronoun is referring to. Therefore, pronouns should:

1. Agree in number

If the pronoun takes the place of a singular noun, you have to use a singular pronoun.

> If a student parks a car on campus, he or she has to buy a parking sticker.
> (**NOT:** If a student parks a car on campus, they have to buy a parking sticker.)

Remember: the words **everybody, anybody, anyone, each, neither, nobody, someone, a person**, etc. are singular and take singular pronouns.

> Everybody ought to do his or her best. (NOT: their best)
> Neither of the girls brought her umbrella. (NOT: their umbrellas)

NOTE: Many people find the construction "his or her" wordy, so if it is possible to use a plural noun as your antecedent so that you can use "they" as your pronoun, it may be wise to do so. If you do use a singular noun and the context makes the gender clear, then it is permissible to use just "his" or "her" rather than "his or her."

2. Agree in person

If you are writing in the "first person" (I), don't confuse your reader by switching to the "second person" (you) or "third person" (he, she, they, it, etc.). Similarly, if you are using the "second person," don't switch to "first" or "third."

> When a person comes to class, he or she should have his or her homework ready.
> (**NOT:** When a person comes to class, you should have your homework ready.)

3. Refer clearly to a specific noun.

Don't be vague or ambiguous.

> **NOT:** Although the motorcycle hit the tree, it was not damaged. (Is "it" the motorcycle or the tree?)
> **NOT:** I don't think they should show violence on TV. (Who are "they"?)
> **NOT:** Vacation is coming soon, which is nice. (What is nice, the vacation or the fact that it is coming soon?)
> **NOT:** George worked in a national forest last summer. This may be his life's work. (What word does "this" refer to?)
> **NOT:** If you put this sheet in your notebook, you can refer to it. (What does "it" refer to, the sheet or your notebook?)

Pronoun Case

Pronoun case is really a very simple matter. There are three cases.

- Subjective case: pronouns used as subject.
- Objective case: pronouns used as objects of verbs or prepositions.
- Possessive case: pronouns which express ownership.

Pronouns as Subjects	Pronouns as Objects	Pronouns that show Possession
I	me	my (mine)
you	you	your (yours)
he, she, it	him, her, it	his, her (hers), it (its)
we	us	our (ours)
they	them	their (theirs)
who	whom	whose

The pronouns **this, that, these, those**, and **which** do not change form.

Some problems of case:

1. In compound structures, where there are two pronouns or a noun and a pronoun, drop the other noun for a moment. Then you can see which case you want.

> **Not:** Bob and me travel a good deal.
> (Would you say, "me travel"?)
> **Not:** He gave the flowers to Jane and I.
> (Would you say, "he gave the flowers to I"?)
> **Not:** Us men like the coach.
> (Would you say, "us like the coach"?)

2. In comparisons. Comparisons usually follow *than* or *as*:

> He is taller than I (am tall).
> This helps you as much as (it helps) me.
> She is as noisy as I (am).

Comparisons are really shorthand sentences which usually omit words, such as those in the parentheses in the sentences above. If you complete the comparison in your head, you can choose the correct case for the pronoun.

> **Not:** He is taller than me.
> (Would you say, "than me am tall"?)

3. In formal and semiformal writing:

Use the subjective form after a form of the verb *to be*.

> **Formal:** It is I.
> **Informal:** It is me.

Use *whom* in the objective case.

> **Formal:** To whom am I talking?
> **Informal:** Who am I talking to?

Part 4: Appositives

An appositive is a noun or pronoun — often with modifiers — set beside another noun or pronoun to explain or identify it. Here are some examples of appositives (the **noun or pronoun will be in blue**, the **appositive will be in boldface**).

> Your **friend Bill** is in trouble.
> My brother's **car**, **a sporty red convertible with bucket seats**, is the envy of my friends.
> The chief **surgeon**, **an expert in organ-transplant procedures**, took her nephew on a hospital tour.

An appositive phrase usually follows the word it explains or identifies, but it may also precede it.

> **A bold innovator**, Wassily Kadinsky is known for his colorful abstract paintings.
> **The first state to ratify the U. S. Constitution**, Delaware is rich in history.
> **A beautiful collie**, Skip was my favorite dog.

Punctuation of Appositives

In some cases, the noun being explained is too general without the appositive; the information is essential to the meaning of the sentence. When this is the case, do not place commas around the appositive; just leave it alone. If the sentence would be clear and complete without the appositive, then commas are necessary; place one before and one after the appositive. Here are some examples.

> The popular US **president John Kennedy** was known for his eloquent and inspirational speeches.

Here we do not put commas around the appositive, because it is essential information. Without the appositive, the sentence would be, "The popular US president was known for his eloquent and inspirational speeches." We wouldn't know which president was being referred to.

> John Kennedy, **the popular US president**, was known for his eloquent and inspirational speeches.

Here we put commas around the appositive because it is not essential information. Without the appositive, the sentence would be, "John Kennedy was known for his eloquent and inspirational speeches." We still know who the subject of the sentence is without the appositive.

Part 5: What is the Difference Between Adjectives and Adverbs?

The Basic Rules: Adjectives

Adjectives modify nouns. To modify means to change in some way. For example:

- "I ate a meal." *Meal* is a noun. We don't know what kind of meal; all we know is that someone ate a meal.
- "I ate an enormous lunch." *Lunch* is a noun, and *enormous* is an adjective that modifies it. It tells us **what kind of** meal the person ate.

Adjectives usually answer one of a few different questions: "What kind?" or "Which?" or "How many?" For example:

- "The *tall* girl is riding a *new* bike." *Tall* tells us **which** girl we're talking about. *New* tells us **what kind of** bike we're talking about.
- "The *tough* professor gave us the *final* exam." *Tough* tells us **what kind of** professor we're talking about. *Final* tells us **which** exam we're talking about.
- "*Fifteen* students passed the midterm exam; *twelve* students passed the final exam." *Fifteen* and *twelve* both tell us **how many** students; *midterm* and *final* both tell us **which** exam.

So, generally speaking, adjectives answer the following questions: **Which? What kind of? How many?**

The Basic Rules: Adverbs

Adverbs modify verbs, adjectives, and other adverbs. (You can recognize adverbs easily because many of them are formed by adding *-ly* to an adjective, though that is not always the case.) The most common question that adverbs answer is **how**.

Let's look at verbs first.

- "She sang *beautifully*." *Beautifully* is an adverb that modifies *sang*. It tells us **how** she sang.
- "The cellist played *carelessly*." *Carelessly* is an adverb that modifies *played*. It tells us **how** the cellist played.

Adverbs also modify adjectives and other adverbs.

- "That woman is *extremely* nice." *Nice* is an adjective that modifies the noun *woman*. *Extremely* is an adverb that modifies *nice*; it tells us **how** nice she is. **How** nice is she? She's extremely nice.
- "It was a *terribly* hot afternoon." *Hot* is an adjective that modifies the noun *afternoon*. *Terribly* is an adverb that modifies the adjective *hot*. **How** hot is it? Terribly hot.

So, generally speaking, adverbs answer the question **how**. (They can also answer the questions **when**, **where**, and **why**.)

Part 6: Participles

A participle is a verbal that is used as an adjective and most often ends in *-ing* or *-ed*. The term *verbal* indicates that a participle, like the other two kinds of verbals, is based on a verb and therefore expresses action or a state of being. However, since they function as adjectives, participles modify nouns or pronouns. There are two types of participles: present participles and past participles. Present participles end in *-ing*. Past participles end in *-ed*, *-en*, *-d*, *-t*, or *-n*, as in the words *asked*, *eaten*, *saved*, *dealt*, and *seen*.

- The *crying* baby had a wet diaper.
- *Shaken*, he walked away from the *wrecked* car.
- The *burning* log fell off the fire.
- *Smiling*, she hugged the *panting* dog.

A participial phrase is a group of words consisting of a participle and the modifier(s) and/or (pro)noun(s) or noun phrase(s) that function as the direct object(s), indirect object(s), or complement(s) of the action or state expressed in the participle, such as:

Example: Removing his coat, Jack rushed to the river.

The participial phrase functions as an adjective modifying *Jack*.
Removing (participle)
his coat (direct object of action expressed in participle)

Example: Delores noticed her cousin **walking along the shoreline.**

The participial phrase functions as an adjective modifying *cousin*.
walking (participle)
along the shoreline (prepositional phrase as adverb)

> **Example:** Children **introduced to** music <u>early</u> develop strong intellectual skills.

The participial phrase functions as an adjective modifying *children*.
introduced (to) (participle)
music (direct object of action expressed in participle)
<u>early</u> (adverb)

> **Example: Having been a gymnast,** Lynn knew the importance of exercise.

The participial phrase functions as an adjective modifying *Lynn*.
Having been (participle)
a gymnast (subject complement for Lynn, via state of being expressed in participle)

Placement: In order to prevent confusion, a participial phrase must be placed as close to the noun it modifies as possible, and the noun must be clearly stated.

- *Carrying a heavy pile of books,* his foot caught on a step.
- *Carrying a heavy pile of books,* he caught his foot on a step.

In the first sentence there is no clear indication of who or what is performing the action expressed in the participle carrying. Certainly foot can't be logically understood to function in this way. This situation is an example of a <u>**dangling modifier**</u> error since the modifier (the participial phrase) is not modifying any specific noun in the sentence and is thus left "dangling." Since a person must be doing the carrying for the sentence to make sense, a noun or pronoun that refers to a person must be in the place immediately after the participial phrase, as in the second sentence.

Punctuation: When a participial phrase begins a sentence, a comma should be placed after the phrase.

- *Arriving at the store,* I found that it was closed.
- *Washing and polishing the car,* Frank developed sore muscles.

If the participle or participial phrase comes in the middle of a sentence, it should be set off with commas only if the information is not essential to the meaning of the sentence.

- Sid, *watching an old movie,* drifted in and out of sleep.
- The church, *destroyed by a fire,* was never rebuilt.

Note that if the participial phrase is essential to the meaning of the sentence, no commas should be used:

- The student *earning the highest grade point average* will receive a special award.
- The guy *wearing the chicken costume* is my cousin.

If a participial phrase comes at the end of a sentence, a comma usually precedes the phrase if it modifies an earlier word in the sentence but not if the phrase directly follows the word it modifies.

- The local residents often saw Ken wandering through the streets.
  (The phrase modifies *Ken*, not *residents*.)
- Tom nervously watched the woman, alarmed by her silence.
  (The phrase modifies *Tom*, not *woman*.)

Points to remember

1. A participle is a verbal ending in *-ing* (present) or *-ed, -en, -d, -t,* or *-n* (past) that functions as an adjective, modifying a noun or pronoun.

2. A participial phrase consists of a participle plus modifier(s), object(s), and/or complement(s).

3. Participles and participial phrases must be placed as close to the nouns or pronouns they modify as possible, and those nouns or pronouns must be clearly stated.

4. A participial phrase is set off with commas when it:
   (a) comes at the beginning of a sentence
   (b) interrupts a sentence as a nonessential element
   (c) comes at the end of a sentence and is separated from the word it modifies.

Part 7: Prepositions for Time, Place, and Introducing Objects

One point in time

On is used with days:

- I will see you **on** Monday.
- The week begins **on** Sunday.

At is used with noon, night, midnight, and with the time of day:

- My plane leaves **at** noon.
- The movie starts **at** 6 p.m.

In is used with other parts of the day, with months, with years, with seasons:

- He likes to read **in** the afternoon.
- The days are long **in** August.
- The book was published **in** 1999.
- The flowers will bloom **in** spring.

Extended time

To express extended time, English uses the following prepositions: **since, for, by, from–to, from–until, during, (with)in**

- She has been gone **since** yesterday. *(She left yesterday and has not returned.)*
- I'm going to Paris **for** two weeks. *(I will spend two weeks there.)*
- The movie showed **from** August **to** October. *(Beginning in August and ending in October.)*
- The decorations were up **from** spring **until** fall. *(Beginning in spring and ending in fall.)*
- I watch TV **during** the evening. *(For some period of time in the evening.)*
- We must finish the project **within** a year. *(No longer than a year.)*

Place

To express notions of place, English uses the following prepositions: to talk about the point itself: **in,** to express something contained: **inside,** to talk about the surface: **on,** to talk about a general vicinity, **at**.

- There is a wasp **in** the room.
- Put the present **inside** the box.
- I left your keys **on** the table.
- She was waiting **at** the corner.

Higher than a point

To express notions of an object being higher than a point, English uses the following prepositions: **over, above.**

- He threw the ball **over** the roof.
- Hang that picture **above** the couch.

Lower than a point

To express notions of an object being lower than a point, English uses the following prepositions: **under, underneath, beneath, below.**

- The rabbit burrowed **under** the ground.
- The child hid **underneath** the blanket.
- We relaxed in the shade **beneath** the branches.
- The valley is **below** sea-level.

Close to a point

To express notions of an object being close to a point, English uses the following prepositions: **near, by, next to, between, among, opposite.**

- She lives **near** the school.
- There is an ice cream shop **by** the store.
- An oak tree grows **next to** my house
- The house is **between** Elm Street and Maple Street.
- I found my pen lying **among** the books.
- The bathroom is **opposite** that room.

To introduce objects of verbs

English uses the following prepositions to introduce objects of the following verbs.

At: glance, laugh, look, rejoice, smile, stare

- She took a quick glance **at** her reflection.
  (*exception with* **mirror**: She took a quick glance **in** the mirror.)
- You didn't laugh **at** his joke.
- I'm looking **at** the computer monitor.
- We rejoiced **at** his safe rescue.
- That pretty girl smiled **at** you.
- Stop staring **at** me.

Of: approve, consist, smell

- I don't approve **of** his speech.
- My contribution to the article consists **of** many pages.
- He came home smelling **of** garlic.

Of (or about): dream, think

- I dream **of** finishing college in four years.
- Can you think **of** a number between one and ten?
- I am thinking **about** this problem.

For: call, hope, look, wait, watch, wish

- Did someone call **for** a taxi?
- He hopes **for** a raise in salary next year.
- I'm looking **for** my keys.
- We'll wait **for** her here.

- You go buy the tickets and I'll watch **for** the train.
- If you wish **for** an "A" in this class, you must work hard.

Part 8: Identifying Independent and Dependent Clauses

When you want to use commas and semicolons in sentences and when you are concerned about whether a sentence is or is not a fragment, a good way to start is to be able to recognize dependent and independent clauses. The definitions offered here will help you with this.

Independent Clause

An independent clause is a group of words that contains a subject and verb and expresses a complete thought. An independent clause is a sentence.

> Jim studied in the Sweet Shop for his chemistry quiz.

Dependent Clause

A dependent clause is a group of words that contains a subject and verb but does not express a complete thought. A dependent clause cannot be a sentence. Often a dependent clause is marked by a **dependent marker word**.

> **When** Jim studied in the Sweet Shop for his chemistry quiz . . . (What happened when he studied? The thought is incomplete.)

Dependent Marker Word

A dependent marker word is a word added to the beginning of an independent clause that makes it into a dependent clause.

> **When** Jim studied in the Sweet Shop for his chemistry quiz, it was very noisy.

Some common dependent markers are: **after, although, as, as if, because, before, even if, even though, if, in order to, since, though, unless, until, whatever, when, whenever, whether,** and **while.**

Connecting Dependent and Independent Clauses

There are two types of words that can be used as connectors at the beginning of an independent clause: coordinating conjunctions and independent marker words.

1. Coordinating Conjunction

The seven coordinating conjunctions used as connecting words at the beginning of an independent clause are **and, but, for, or, nor, so,** and **yet.** When the second independent clause in a sentence begins with a coordinating conjunction, a comma is needed before the coordinating conjunction:

> Jim studied in the Sweet Shop for his chemistry quiz, **but** it was hard to concentrate because of the noise.

2. Independent Marker Word

An independent marker word is a connecting word used at the beginning of an independent clause. These words can always begin a sentence that can stand alone. When the second independent clause in a sentence has an independent marker word, a semicolon is needed before the independent marker word.

> Jim studied in the Sweet Shop for his chemistry quiz; **however,** it was hard to concentrate because of the noise.

Some common independent markers are: **also, consequently, furthermore, however, moreover, nevertheless,** and **therefore.**

Some Common Errors to Avoid

Comma Splices

A comma splice is the use of a comma between two independent clauses. You can usually fix the error by changing the comma to a period and therefore making the two clauses into two separate sentences, by changing the comma to a semicolon, or by making one clause dependent by inserting a dependent marker word in front of it.

> **Incorrect:** I like this class, it is very interesting.

> **Correct:** I like this class. It is very interesting.
> - (or) I like this class; it is very interesting.
> - (or) I like this class, and it is very interesting.
> - (or) I like this class because it is very interesting.
> - (or) Because it is very interesting, I like this class.

Fused Sentences

Fused sentences happen when there are two independent clauses not separated by any form of punctuation. This error is also known as a run-on sentence. The error can sometimes be corrected by adding a period, semicolon, or colon to separate the two sentences.

> **Incorrect:** My professor is intelligent I've learned a lot from her.

> **Correct:** My professor is intelligent. I've learned a lot from her.
> - (or) My professor is intelligent; I've learned a lot from her.
> - (or) My professor is intelligent, and I've learned a lot from her.
> - (or) My professor is intelligent; moreover, I've learned a lot from her.

Sentence Fragments

Sentence fragments happen by treating a dependent clause or other incomplete thought as a complete sentence. You can usually fix this error by combining it with another sentence to make a complete thought or by removing the dependent marker.

> **Incorrect:** Because I forgot the exam was today.

> **Correct:** Because I forgot the exam was today, I didn't study.
> - (or) I forgot the exam was today.

Part 9: Parallel Structure

Parallel structure means using the same pattern of words to show that two or more ideas have the same level of importance. This can happen at the word, phrase, or clause level. The usual way to join parallel structures is with the use of coordinating **conjunctions** such as "and" or "or."

Words and Phrases

With the -ing form (gerund) of words:

> **Parallel:** Mary likes hiking, swimming, and bicycling.

With infinitive phrases:

> **Parallel:** Mary likes **to hike**, **to swim**, and **to ride** a bicycle.
> OR
> Mary likes to **hike**, **swim**, and **ride** a bicycle.

(Note: You can use "to" before all the verbs in a sentence or only before the first one.)

Do not mix forms.

Example 1

Not Parallel:

Mary likes hik**ing**, swimm**ing**, and **to ride** a bicycle.

Parallel:

Mary likes hik**ing**, swimm**ing**, and rid**ing** a bicycle.

Example 2

Not Parallel:

The production manager was asked to write his report quick**ly**, accurate **ly**, and **in a detailed manner**.

Parallel:

The production manager was asked to write his report quick**ly**, accurate**ly**, and thorough**ly**.

Example 3

Not Parallel:

The teacher said that he was a poor student because he wait**ed** until the last minute to study for the exam, complet**ed** his lab problems in a careless manner, and **his motivation was** low.

Parallel:

The teacher said that he was a poor student because he wait**ed** until the last minute to study for the exam, complet**ed** his lab problems in a careless manner, and lack**ed** motivation.

Clauses

A parallel structure that begins with clauses must keep on with clauses. Changing to another pattern or changing the voice of the verb (from active to passive or vice versa) will break the parallelism.

Example 1

Not Parallel:

The coach told the players **that they should get** a lot of sleep, **that they should not eat** too much, and <u>to do</u> some warm-up exercises before the game.

Parallel:

The coach told the players **that they should get** a lot of sleep, **that they should not eat** too much, and **that they should do** some warm-up exercises before the game.

OR

Parallel:

The coach told the players that they should **get** a lot of sleep, not **eat** too much, and **do** some warm-up exercises before the game.

Example 2

Not Parallel:

The salesman expected **that he would present** his product at the meeting, **that there would be** time for him to show his slide presentation, and **that questions would be asked** by prospective buyers. **(passive)**

Parallel:

The salesman expected **that he would present** his product at the meeting, **that there would be** time for him to show his slide presentation, and **that prospective buyers would ask** him questions.

Lists After a Colon

Be sure to keep all the elements in a list in the same form.

Example 1

Not Parallel:
The dictionary can be used for these purposes: to find **word meanings, pronunciations, correct spellings,** and **looking up irregular verbs**.

Parallel:
The dictionary can be used for these purposes: to find **word meanings, pronunciations, correct spellings,** and **irregular verbs**.

Proofreading Strategies to Try:

- Skim your paper, pausing at the words "and" and "or." Check on each side of these words to see whether the items joined are parallel. If not, make them parallel.
- If you have several items in a list, put them in a column to see if they are parallel.
- Listen to the sound of the items in a list or the items being compared. Do you hear the same kinds of sounds? For example, is there a series of "-ing" words beginning each item? Or do your hear a rhythm being repeated? If something is breaking that rhythm or repetition of sound, check to see if it needs to be made parallel.

Part 10: Introduction and General Usage in Defining Clauses

Relative pronouns are **that, who, whom, whose, which, where, when,** and **why.** They are used to join clauses to make a complex sentence. Relative pronouns are used at the beginning of the subordinate clause which gives some specific information about the main clause.

> This is the house *that* Jack built.
> I don't know the day *when* Jane marries him.
> The professor, *whom* I respect, was tenured.

In English, the choice of the relative pronoun depends on the type of clause it is used in. There are two types of clauses distinguished: *defining (restrictive)* relative clauses and *non-defining (non-restrictive)* relative clauses. In both types of clauses the relative pronoun can function as a subject, an object, or a possessive.

Relative Pronouns in Defining Clauses

Defining relative clauses (also known as *restrictive relative clauses*) provide some essential information that explains the main clause. The information is crucial for understanding the sentence correctly and cannot be omitted. Defining clauses are opened by a relative pronoun and **ARE NOT** separated by a comma from the main clause.

The table below sums up the use of relative pronouns in defining clauses:

Function in the sentence	Reference to				
	People	Things/concepts	Place	Time	Reason
Subject	who, that	which, that			
Object	(that, who, whom)	(which, that)	where	when	why
Possessive	whose	whose, of which			

Examples

Relative pronoun used as a subject:

This is the house *that* had a great Christmas decoration.
It took me a while to get used to people *who* eat popcorn during the movie.

Relative pronoun used as an object:

1. As can be seen from the table, referring to a person or thing, the relative pronoun **may be omitted** in the object position:

   This is the man (who / that) I wanted to speak to and whose name I'd forgotten.

   The library didn't have the book (which / that) I wanted.

   I didn't like the book (which / that) John gave me.

   This is the house *where* I lived *when* I first came to the US.

2. In American English, *whom* is not used very often. **Whom** is more formal than *who* and is very often omitted in **speech**:

   Grammatically Correct: The woman to *whom* you have just spoken is my teacher.

   Common in Speech: The woman (*who*) you have just spoken to is my teacher.

However, *whom* may not be omitted if preceded by a preposition:

   I have found you the tutor <u>for</u> *whom* you were looking.

Relative pronoun used as a possessive:

Whose is the only possessive relative pronoun in English. It can be used with both people and things:

   The family *whose* house burnt in the fire was immediately given a suite in a hotel.
   The book *whose* author is now being shown in the news has become a bestseller.

General remarks: That, Who, Which compared

The relative pronoun *that* can only be used in defining clauses. It can also be substituted for *who* (referring to persons) or *which* (referring to things). *That* is often used in speech; *who* and *which* are more common in written English.

   William Kellogg was the man *that* lived in the late 19th century and had some weird ideas about raising children. (spoken, less formal)

   William Kellogg was the man *who* lived in the late 19th century and had some weird ideas about raising children. (written, more formal)

Although your computer may suggest to correct it, referring to things, *which* may be used in the defining clause to put additional emphasis on the explanation. Again, the sentence with *which* is more formal than the one with *that*: Note that since it is the defining clause, there is NO comma used preceding *which*:

   The café *that* sells the best coffee in town has recently been closed. (less formal)
   The café *which* sells the best coffee in town has recently been closed. (more formal)

Some special uses of relative pronouns in defining clauses

that / who

Referring to people, both *that* and *who* can be used. *That* may be used to refer to someone in general:

> He is the kind of person *that/who* will never let you down.
> I am looking for someone *that/who* could give me a ride to Chicago.

However, when a particular person is being spoken about, *who* is preferred:

> The old lady *who* lives next door is a teacher.
> The girl *who* wore a red dress attracted everybody's attention at the party.

that / which

There are several cases when *that* is more appropriate and is preferred to *which*.

After the pronouns *all, any(thing), every(thing), few, little, many, much, no(thing), none, some(thing)*:

> The police usually ask for every detail *that* helps identify the missing person. - *that* used as the subject
> Marrying a congressman is *all* (that) she wants. - that used as the object

After verbs that answer the question **WHAT?** For example, *say, suggest, state, declare, hope, think, write*, etc. In this case, the whole relative clause functions as the object of the main clause:

> Some people *say* (that) success is one percent of talent and ninety-nine percent of hard work.
> The chairman *stated* at the meeting (that) his company is part of a big-time entertainment industry.

After the noun modified by an adjective *in the superlative degree*:

> This is the *funniest* story (that) I have ever read! - *that* used as the object

After ordinal numbers, e.g., *first, second, etc.*:

> The first draft (that) we submitted was really horrible. - *that* used as the object

If the verb in the main clause is a form of *BE*:

> This is a claim that has absolutely no reason in it. - *that* used as the subject

Relative Pronouns in Non-Defining Clauses

Non-defining relative clauses (also known as non-restrictive, or parenthetical, clauses) provide some additional information which is not essential and may be omitted without affecting the contents of the sentence. All relative pronouns EXCEPT "that" can be used in non-defining clauses; however, the pronouns MAY NOT be omitted. Non-defining clauses ARE separated by commas.

The table below sums up the use of relative pronouns in non-defining clauses:

Function in the sentence	Reference to				
	People	Things/concepts	Place	Time	Reason
Subject	who	which			
Object	who, whom	which	where	when	why
Possessive	whose	whose, of which			

a. **Relative pronoun used as a subject:**

The writer, **who** lives in this luxurious mansion, has just published his second novel.

b. **Relative pronoun used as an object:**

The house at the end of the street, **which** my grandfather built, needs renovating.

c. **Relative pronoun used as a possessive:**

William Kellogg, **whose** name has become a famous breakfast foods brand-name, had some weird ideas about raising children.

Some Special Uses of Relative Pronouns in Non-Defining Clauses

a. **which**
If you are referring to the previous clause as a whole, use *which*:
My friend eventually decided to get divorced, **which** upset me a lot.

b. **of whom, of which**
Use *of whom* for persons and *of which* for things or concepts after numbers and words such as *most, many, some, both, none*:
I saw a lot of new people at the party, <u>some</u> **of whom** seemed familiar.
He was always coming up with new ideas, <u>most</u> **of which** were absolutely impracticable.

Part 11: Sentence Types and Punctuation Patterns

To punctuate a sentence, you can use and combine some of these patterns.

Pattern One: Simple Sentence

This pattern is an example of a simple sentence:

Independent clause [.]

Example: Doctors are concerned about the rising death rate from asthma.

Pattern Two: Compound Sentence

This pattern is an example of a compound sentence with a coordinating conjunction:

Independent clause [,] coordinating conjunction **independent clause** [.]

There are seven coordinating conjunctions: **and, but, for, or, nor, so, yet.**

Example: Doctors are concerned about the rising death rate from asthma, but they don't know the reasons for it.

Pattern Three: Compound Sentence

This pattern is an example of a compound sentence with a semicolon.

Independent clause [;] independent clause [.]

Example: Doctors are concerned about the rising death rate from asthma; they are unsure of its cause.

Pattern Four: Compound Sentence

This pattern is an example of a compound sentence with an independent marker.

Independent clause [;] <u>independent marker</u> [,] independent clause [.]

Examples of independent markers are the following: **therefore, moreover, thus, consequently, however, also.**

Example: Doctors are concerned about the rising death rate from asthma; <u>therefore</u>, they have called for more research into its causes.

Pattern Five: Complex Sentence

This pattern is an example of a complex sentence with a dependent marker.

<u>*Dependent marker*</u> dependent clause [,] Independent clause [.]

Examples of dependent markers are as follows: **because, before, since, while, although, if, until, when, after, as, as if.**

Example: *Because* doctors are concerned about the rising death rate from asthma, they have called for more research into its causes.

Pattern Six: Complex Sentence

This pattern is an example of a complex sentence with a dependent marker following the independent clause.

Independent clause <u>dependent marker</u> dependent clause [.]

Example: Doctors are concerned about the rising death rate from asthma <u>because</u> it is a common, treatable illness.

Pattern Seven

This pattern includes an independent clause with an embedded <u>non-essential</u> clause or phrase. A non-essential clause or phrase is one that can be removed without changing the meaning of the sentence or making it ungrammatical. In other words, the non-essential clause or phrase gives additional information, but the sentence can stand alone without it.

First part of an independent clause [,] non-essential clause or phrase, rest of the independent clause [.]

Example: Many doctors, including both pediatricians and family practice physicians, are concerned about the rising death rate from asthma.

Pattern Eight

This pattern includes an independent clause with an embedded <u>essential</u> clause or phrase. An essential clause or phrase is one that cannot be removed without changing the overall meaning of the sentence.

First part of an independent clause essential clause or phrase rest of the independent clause [.]

Example: Many doctors who are concerned about the rising death rate from asthma have called for more research into its causes.

Part 12: Making Subjects and Verbs Agree

1. When the subject of a sentence is composed of two or more nouns or pronouns connected by *and*, use a plural verb.

   She and **her friends** <u>are</u> at the fair.

2. When two or more singular nouns or pronouns are connected by *or* or *nor*, use a singular verb.

   The book or **the pen** <u>is</u> in the drawer.

3. When a compound subject contains both a singular and a plural noun or pronoun joined by *or* or *nor*, the verb should agree with the part of the subject that is nearer the verb.

   The boy or **his friends** <u>run</u> every day.
   His friends or **the boy** <u>runs</u> every day.

4. *Doesn't* is a contraction of *does not* and should be used only with a singular subject. *Don't* is a contraction of *do not* and should be used only with a plural subject. The exception to this rule appears in the case of the first person and second person pronouns *I* and *you*. With these pronouns, the contraction *don't* should be used. [Note that formal writing generally avoids the use of contractions.]

   He doesn't <u>like</u> it.
   They don't <u>like</u> it.

5. Do not be misled by a phrase that comes between the subject and the verb. The verb agrees with the subject, not with a noun or pronoun in the phrase.

   One of the boxes <u>is</u> open
   The people who listen to that music <u>are</u> few.
   The team captain, as well as his players, <u>is</u> anxious.
   The book, including all the chapters in the first section, <u>is</u> boring.
   The woman with all the dogs <u>walks</u> down my street.

6. The words *each*, *each one*, *either*, *neither*, *everyone*, *everybody*, *anybody*, *anyone*, *nobody*, *somebody*, *someone*, and *no one* are singular and require a singular verb.

   Each of these hot dogs <u>is</u> juicy.
   Everybody <u>knows</u> Mr. Jones.
   Either <u>is</u> correct.

7. Nouns such as *civics*, *mathematics*, *dollars*, *measles*, and *news* require singular verbs.

   The news <u>is</u> on at six.

   Note: The word **dollars** is a special case. When talking about an amount of money, it requires a singular verb, but when referring to the dollars themselves, a plural verb is required.

   Five dollars <u>is</u> a lot of money.
   Dollars <u>are</u> often used instead of rubles in Russia.

8. Nouns such as *scissors*, *tweezers*, *trousers*, and *shears* require plural verbs. (There are two parts to these things.)

   These scissors <u>are</u> dull.
   Those trousers <u>are</u> made of wool.

9. In sentences beginning with *there is* or *there are*, the subject follows the verb. Since *there* is not the subject, the verb agrees with what follows.

There **are** many questions.
There **is** a question.

10. Collective nouns are words that imply more than one person but that are considered singular and take a singular verb, such as: *group*, *team*, *committee*, *class*, and *family*.

The team **runs** during practice.
The committee **decides** how to proceed.
The family **has** a long history.
My family **has never been able to agree**.

In some cases, a sentence may call for the use of a plural verb when using a collective noun.

The crew **are preparing** to dock the ship.

This sentence is referring to the individual efforts of each crew member.

11. Expressions such as *with*, *together with*, *including*, *accompanied by*, *in addition to*, or *as well* do not change the number of the subject. If the subject is singular, the verb is too.

The President, accompanied by his wife, **is** traveling to India.
All of the books, including yours, **are** in that box.

Sequence of Tenses

Simple Present: They walk.

Present Perfect: They have walked.

Simple Past: They walked.

Past Perfect: They had walked.

Future: They will walk.

Future Perfect: They will have walked.

Problems in sequencing tenses usually occur with the perfect tenses, all of which are formed by adding an auxiliary or auxiliaries to the past participle, the third principal part.

ring, rang, rung
walk, walked, walked

The most common auxiliaries are forms of "be," "can," "do," "may," "must," "ought," "shall," "will," "has," "have," "had," and they are the forms we shall use in this most basic discussion.

Present Perfect

The present perfect consists of a past participle (the third principal part) with "has" or "have." It designates action which began in the past but which continues into the present or the effect of which still continues.

1. Betty taught for ten years. (simple past)
2. Betty has taught for ten years. (present perfect)

The implication in (1) is that Betty has retired; in (2), that she is still teaching.

1. John did his homework. He can go to the movies.
2. If John has done his homework, he can go to the movies.

Infinitives, too, have perfect tense forms when combined with "have," and sometimes problems arise when infinitives are used with verbs such as "hope," "plan," "expect," and "intend," all of which usually point to the future (I wanted to go to the movie. Janet meant to see the doctor.) The perfect tense sets up a sequence by marking the action which began and usually was completed before the action in the main verb.

1. I am happy to have participated in this campaign!
2. John had hoped to have won the trophy.

Thus the action of the main verb points back in time; the action of the perfect infinitive has been completed.

The past perfect tense designates action in the past just as simple past does, but the action of the past perfect is action completed in the past before another action.

1. John raised vegetables and later sold them. (past)
2. John sold vegetables that he had raised. (past perfect)

The vegetables were raised before they were sold.

1. Renee washed the car when George arrived (simple past)
2. Renee had washed the car when George arrived. (past perfect)

In (1), she waited until George arrived and then washed the car. In (2), she had already finished washing the car by the time he arrived.

In sentences expressing condition and result, the past perfect tense is used in the part that states the condition.

1. If I had done my exercises, I would have passed the test.
2. I think George would have been elected if he hadn't sounded so pompous.

Future Perfect Tense

The future perfect tense designates action that will have been completed at a specified time in the future.

1. Saturday I will finish my housework. (simple future)
2. By Saturday noon, I will have finished my housework. (future perfect)

Part 13: Using Active Versus Passive Voice

In a sentence using **active voice**, the subject of the sentence performs the action expressed in the verb.

The dog *bit* the boy.

The arrow points from the subject performing the action (the dog) to the individual being acted upon (the boy). This is an example of a sentence using the active voice.

Scientists *have conducted* **experiments** to test the hypothesis.

Sample active voice sentence with the subject performing the action described by the verb.

Watching a framed, mobile world through a car's windshield *reminds* me of watching a movie or TV.

The active voice sentence subject (watching a framed, mobile world) performs the action of reminding the speaker of something.

Each example above includes a sentence subject performing the action expressed by the verb.

Examples:

	Active	Passive
Simple Present	• The company ships the computers to many foreign countries.	• Computers are shipped to many foreign countries
Present Progressive	• The chef is preparing the food.	• The food is being prepared.
Simple Past	• The delivery man delivered the package yesterday.	• The package was delivered yesterday.
Past Progressive	• The producer was making an announcement.	• An announcement was being made.
Future	• Our representative will pick up the computer.	• The computer will be picked up.
Present Perfect	• Someone has made the arrangements for us.	• The arrangements have been made for us.
Past Perfect	• They had given us visas for three months.	• They had been given visas for three months.
Future Perfect	• By next month we will have finished this job.	• By next month this job will have been finished.

Part 14: Irregular Verbs: Overview and List

In English, regular verbs consist of three main parts: the root form (present), the (simple) past, and the past participle. Regular verbs have an *-ed* ending added to the root verb for both the simple past and past participle. Irregular verbs do not follow this pattern, and instead take on an alternative pattern.

The following is a partial list of irregular verbs found in English. Each listing consists of the present/ root form of the verb, the (simple) past form of the verb, and the past participle form of the verb.

List of Irregular Verbs in English

Present	Past	Past Participle	Present	Past	Past Participle
be	was, were	been	deal	dealt	dealt
become	became	become	do	did	done
begin	began	begun	drink	drank	drunk
blow	blew	blown	drive	drove	driven
break	broke	broken	eat	ate	eaten
bring	brought	brought	fall	fell	fallen
build	built	built	feed	fed	fed
burst	burst	burst	feel	felt	felt
buy	bought	bought	fight	fought	fought
catch	caught	caught	find	found	found
choose	chose	chosen	fly	flew	flown
come	came	come	forbid	forbade	forbidden
cut	cut	cut	forget	forgot	forgotten

Present	Past	Past Participle	Present	Past	Past Participle
forgive	forgave	forgiven	see	saw	seen
freeze	froze	frozen	seek	sought	sought
get	got	gotten	sell	sold	sold
give	gave	given	send	sent	sent
go	went	gone	shake	shook	sent
grow	grew	grown	shine	shone	shone
have	had	had	sing	sang	sung
hear	heard	heard	sit	sat	sat
hide	hid	hidden	sleep	slept	slept
hold	held	held	speak	spoke	spoken
hurt	hurt	hurt	spend	spent	spent
keep	kept	kept	spring	sprang	sprung
know	knew	known	stand	stood	stood
lay	laid	laid	steal	stole	stolen
lead	led	led	swim	swam	swum
leave	left	left	swing	swung	swung
let	let	let	take	took	taken
lie	lay	lain	teach	taught	taught
lose	lost	lost	tear	tore	torn
make	made	made	tell	told	told
meet	met	met	think	thought	thought
pay	paid	paid	throw	threw	thrown
quit	quit	quit	understand	understood	understood
read	read	read	wake	woke (waked)	woken (waked)
ride	rode	ridden	wear	wore	worn
run	ran	run	win	won	won
say	said	said	write	wrote	written

Commonly Confused Verbs

LIE versus LAY

Lie vs. Lay Usage		
Present	Past	Past Participle
lie, lying (to tell a falsehood)	I lied to my mother.	I have lied under oath.
lie, lying (to recline)	I lay on the bed because I was tired.	He has lain in the grass.
lay, laying (to put, place)	I laid the baby in her cradle.	We have laid the dishes on the table.

Example sentences:

After **laying** down his weapon, the soldier **lay** down to sleep.

Will you **lay** out my clothes while I **lie** down to rest?

SIT versus SET

Sit vs. Set Usage		
Present	Past	Past Participle
sit (to be seated or come to resting position)	I sat in my favorite chair.	You have sat there for three hours.
set (to put or place)	I set my glass on the table.	She has set her books on my desk again.

Example sentence:

Let's **set** the table before we **sit** down to rest.

RISE versus RAISE

Rise vs. Raise Usage		
Present	Past	Past Participle
rise (steady or customary upward movement)	The balloon rose into the air.	He has risen to a position of power.
raise (to cause to rise)	They raised their hands because they knew the answer.	I have raised the curtain many times.

Example sentence:

The boy **raised** the flag just before the sun **rose.**

Part 15: Capitalization and Punctuation

A Little Help with Capitals

If you have a question about whether a specific word should be capitalized that doesn't fit under one of these rules, try checking a dictionary to see if the word is capitalized there.

Use capital letters in the following ways:

The first words of a sentence

When he tells a joke, he sometimes forgets the punch line.

The pronoun "I"

The last time I visited Atlanta was several years ago.

Proper nouns (the names of specific people, places, organizations, and sometimes things)

Worrill Fabrication Company
Golden Gate Bridge
Supreme Court
Livingston, Missouri
Atlantic Ocean
Mothers Against Drunk Driving

Family relationships (when used as proper names)

I sent a thank-you note to Aunt Abigail, but not to my other aunts.
Here is a present I bought for Mother.
Did you buy a present for your mother?

The names of God, specific deities, religious figures, and holy books

God the Father
the Virgin Mary
the Bible
the Greek gods
Moses
Shiva
Buddha
Zeus

Exception: Do not capitalize the non-specific use of the word "god."

The word "polytheistic" means the worship of more than one god.

Titles preceding names, but not titles that follow names

She worked as the assistant to Mayor Hanolovi.
I was able to interview Miriam Moss, mayor of Littonville.

Directions that are names (North, South, East, and West when used as sections of the country, but not as compass directions)

The Patels have moved to the Southwest.
Jim's house is two miles north of Otterbein.

The days of the week, the months of the year, and holidays (but not the seasons used generally)

Halloween
October
Friday
winter
spring
fall

Exception: Seasons are capitalized when used in a title.

The Fall 1999 Semester

The names of countries, nationalities, and specific languages

Costa Rica
Spanish
French
English

The first word in a sentence that is a direct quote

Emerson once said, "A foolish consistency is the hobgoblin of little minds."

The major words in the titles of books, articles, and songs (but not short prepositions or the articles "the," "a," or "an," if they are not the first word of the title)

One of Jerry's favorite books is *The Catcher in the Rye*.

Members of national, political, racial, social, civic, and athletic groups

> Green Bay Packers
> African-Americans
> Democrats
> Friends of the Wilderness
> Chinese

Periods and events (but not century numbers)

> Victorian Era
> Great Depression
> Constitutional Convention
> sixteenth century

Trademarks

> Pepsi
> Honda
> IBM
> Microsoft Word

Words and abbreviations of specific names (but not names of things that came from specific things but are now general types)

Freudian	UN
NBC	french fries
pasteurize	italics

Comma

Use a comma to join two independent clauses by a comma and a coordinating conjunction (*and, but, or, for, nor, so*).

> Road construction can be inconvenient, but it is necessary.

> The new house has a large fenced backyard, so I am sure our dog will enjoy it.

Use a comma after an introductory phrase, prepositional phrase, or dependent clause.

> To get a good grade, you must complete all your assignments.

> Because Dad caught the chicken pox, we canceled our vacation.

> After the wedding, the guests attended the reception.

Use a comma to separate elements in a series. Although there is no set rule that requires a comma before the last item in a series, it seems to be a general academic convention to include it. The examples below demonstrate this trend.

> On her vacation, Lisa visited Greece, Spain, and Italy.

> In their speeches, many of the candidates promised to help protect the environment, bring about world peace, and end world hunger.

Use a comma to separate nonessential elements from a sentence. More specifically, when a sentence includes information that is not crucial to the message or intent of the sentence, enclose it in or separate it by commas.

> John's truck, a red Chevrolet, needs new tires.

> When he realized he had overslept, Matt rushed to his car and hurried to work.

Use a comma between coordinate adjectives (adjectives that are equal and reversible).

The irritable, fidgety crowd waited impatiently for the rally speeches to begin.

The sturdy, compact suitcase made a perfect gift.

Use a comma after a transitional element (*however, therefore, nonetheless, also, otherwise, finally, instead, thus, of course, above all, for example, in other words, as a result, on the other hand, in conclusion, in addition*).

For example, the Red Sox, Yankees, and Indians are popular baseball teams.

If you really want to get a good grade this semester, however, you must complete all assignments, attend class, and study your notes.

Use a comma with quoted words.

"Yes," she promised. Todd replied, saying, "I will be back this afternoon."

Use a comma in a date.

October 25, 1999
Monday, October 25, 1999
25 October 1999

Use a comma in a number.

15,000,000
1614 High Street

Use a comma in a personal title.

Pam Smith, MD
Mike Rose, Chief Financial Officer for Operations, reported the quarter's earnings.

Use a comma to separate a city name from the state.

West Lafayette, Indiana
Dallas, Texas

Avoid comma splices (two independent clauses joined only by a comma). Instead, separate the clauses with a period, with a comma followed by a coordinating conjunction, or with a semicolon.

Semicolon

Use a semicolon to join two independent clauses when the second clause restates the first or when the two clauses are of equal emphasis.

Road construction in Dallas has hindered travel around town; streets have become covered with bulldozers, trucks, and cones.

Use a semicolon to join two independent clauses when the second clause begins with a conjunctive adverb (however, therefore, moreover, furthermore, thus, meanwhile, nonetheless, otherwise) or a transition (*in fact, for example, that is, for instance, in addition, in other words, on the other hand, even so*).

Terrorism in the United States has become a recent concern; in fact, the concern for America's safety has led to an awareness of global terrorism.

Use a semicolon to join elements of a series when individual items of the series already include commas.

Recent sites of the Olympic Games include Athens, Greece; Salt Lake City, Utah; Sydney, Australia; Nagano, Japan.

Colon

Use a colon to join two independent clauses when you wish to emphasize the second clause.

> Road construction in Dallas has hindered travel around town: parts of Main, Fifth, and West Street are closed during the construction.

Use a colon after an independent clause when it is followed by a list, a quotation, an appositive, or other idea directly related to the independent clause.

> Julie went to the store for some groceries: milk, bread, coffee, and cheese.

> In his Gettysburg Address, Abraham Lincoln urges Americans to rededicate themselves to the unfinished work of the deceased soldiers: "It is for us the living rather to be dedicated here to the unfinished work which they who fought here have thus far so nobly advanced. It is rather for us to be here dedicated to the great task remaining before us — that from these honored dead we take increased devotion to that cause for which they gave the last full measure of devotion — that we here highly resolve that these dead shall not have died in vain, that this nation under God shall have a new birth of freedom, and that government of the people, by the people, for the people shall not perish from the earth."

> I know the perfect job for her: a politician.

Use a colon at the end of a business letter greeting.

> To Whom It May Concern:

Use a colon to separate the hour and minute(s) in a time notation.

> 12:00 p.m.

Use a colon to separate the chapter and verse in a Biblical reference.

> Matthew 1:6

Parentheses

Parentheses are used to emphasize content. They place more emphasis on the enclosed content than commas. Use parentheses to set off nonessential material, such as dates, clarifying information, or sources, from a sentence.

> Muhammed Ali (1942-present), arguably the greatest athlete of all time, claimed he would "float like a butterfly, sting like a bee."

Use parentheses to enclose numbered items in a sentence.

> He asked everyone to bring (1) a folding tent, (2) food and water for two days, and (3) a sleeping bag.

Also use parentheses for literary citations embedded in text or to give the explanation of an acronym.

> Research by Wegener and Petty (1994) supports...
> The AMA (American Medical Association) recommends regular exercise.

Dash

Dashes are used to set off or emphasize the content enclosed within dashes or the content that follows a dash. Dashes place more emphasis on this content than parentheses.

> Perhaps one reason why the term has been so problematic—so resistant to definition, and yet so transitory in those definitions—is because of its multitude of applications.

> In terms of public legitimacy—that is, in terms of garnering support from state legislators, parents, donors, and university administrators—English departments are primarily places where advanced literacy is taught.

The U.S.S. *Constitution* became known as "Old Ironsides" during the War of 1812—during which the cannonballs fired from the British H.M.S. *Guerriere* merely bounced off the sides of the *Constitution*.

To some of you, my proposals may seem radical—even revolutionary.

Use a dash to set off an appositive phrase that already includes commas. An appositive is a word that adds explanatory or clarifying information to the noun that precedes it.

The cousins—Tina, Todd, and Sam—arrived at the party together.

Quotation Marks

Use quotation marks to enclose direct quotations. Note that commas and periods are placed inside the closing quotation mark, and colons and semicolons are placed outside. The placement of question and exclamation marks depends on the situation.

He asked, "When will you be arriving?" I answered, "Sometime after 6:30."

Use quotation marks to indicate the novel, ironic, or reserved use of a word.

History is stained with blood spilled in the name of "justice."

Use quotation marks around the titles of short poems, song titles, short stories, magazine or newspaper articles, essays, speeches, chapter titles, short films, and episodes of television or radio shows.

"Self-Reliance," by Ralph Waldo Emerson
"Just Like a Woman," by Bob Dylan
"The Smelly Car," an episode of *Seinfeld*

Do not use quotation marks in indirect or block quotations. Indirect quotations are not exact wordings but rather rephrasings or summaries of another person's words. In this case, it is not necessary to use quotation marks. However, indirect quotations still require proper citations, and you will be committing plagiarism if you fail to do so.

Mr. Johnson, a local farmer, reported last night that he saw an alien spaceship on his own property.

Italics

Underlining and Italics are often used interchangeably. Before word-processing programs were widely available, writers would underline certain words to indicate to publishers to italicize whatever was underlined. Although the general trend has been moving toward italicizing instead of underlining, you should remain consistent with your choice throughout your paper. To be safe, you could check with your teacher to find out which he/she prefers. Italicize the titles of magazines, books, newspapers, academic journals, films, television shows, long poems, plays of three or more acts, operas, musical albums, works of art, websites, and individual trains, planes, or ships.

Time
Romeo and Juliet by William Shakespeare
The Metamorphosis of Narcissus by Salvador Dali
Amazon.com
Titanic

Italicize foreign words.

Semper fi, the motto of the U.S. Marine Corps, means "always faithful."

Italicize a word or phrase to add emphasis.

The *truth* is of utmost concern!

Italicize a word when referring to that word.

The word *justice* is often misunderstood and therefore misused.

Hyphen

Two words brought together as a compound may be written separately, written as one word, or connected by hyphens. For example, three modern dictionaries all have the same listings for the following compounds:

> hair stylist
> hairsplitter
> hair-raiser

Another modern dictionary, however, lists *hairstylist*, not *hair stylist*. Compounding is obviously in a state of flux, and authorities do not always agree in all cases, but the uses of the hyphen offered here are generally agreed upon.

1. Use a hyphen to join two or more words serving as a single adjective before a noun:

   > a one-way street
   > chocolate-covered peanuts
   > well-known author

   However, when compound modifiers come after a noun, they are not hyphenated:

   > The peanuts were chocolate covered.
   > The author was well known.

2. Use a hyphen with compound numbers:

   > forty-six
   > sixty-three
   > Our much-loved teacher was sixty-three years old.

3. Use a hyphen to avoid confusion or an awkward combination of letters:

   > re-sign a petition (vs. resign from a job)
   > semi-independent (but semiconscious)
   > shell-like (but childlike)

4. Use a hyphen with the prefixes *ex-* (meaning former), *self-*, *all-*; with the suffix *-elect*; between a prefix and a capitalized word; and with figures or letters:

   > ex-husband
   > self-assured
   > mid-September
   > all-inclusive
   > mayor-elect
   > anti-American
   > T-shirt
   > pre-Civil War
   > mid-1980s

5. Use a hyphen to divide words at the end of a line if necessary, and make the break only between syllables:

   > pref-er-ence
   > sell-ing
   > in-di-vid-u-al-ist

6. For line breaks, divide already hyphenated words only at the hyphen:

   > mass-
   > produced

Apostrophe

The apostrophe has three uses:

- to form possessives of nouns
- to show the omission of letters
- to indicate certain plurals of lowercase letters

Forming Possessives of Nouns

To see if you need to make a possessive, turn the phrase around and make it an "of the..." phrase. For example:

> the boy's hat = the hat of the boy
> three days' journey = journey of three days

If the noun after "of" is a building, an object, or a piece of furniture, then **no** apostrophe is needed!

> room of the hotel = hotel room
> door of the car = car door
> leg of the table = table leg

Once you've determined whether you need to make a possessive, follow these rules to create one.

- **add 's to the singular form of the word (even if it ends in -s):**

  the owner's car
  James's hat (James' hat is also acceptable. For plural, proper nouns that are possessive, use an apostrophe after the 's': "The Eggles' presentation was good." The Eggles are a husband and wife consultant team.)

- **add 's to the plural forms that do not end in -s:**

  the children's game
  the geese's honking

- **add ' to the end of plural nouns that end in -s:**

  houses' roofs
  three friends' letters

- **add 's to the end of compound words:**

  my brother-in-law's money

- **add 's to the last noun to show joint possession of an object:**

  Todd and Anne's apartment

Showing omission of letters

Apostrophes are used in contractions. A contraction is a word (or set of numbers) in which one or more letters (or numbers) have been omitted. The apostrophe shows this omission. Contractions are common in speaking and in informal writing. To use an apostrophe to create a contraction, place an apostrophe where the omitted letter(s) would go. Here are some examples:

> don't = do not
> I'm = I am
> he'll = he will
> who's = who is
> could've= could have (NOT "could of"!)
> '60 = 1960

Don't use apostrophes for possessive pronouns or for noun plurals.

Apostrophes should not be used with possessive pronouns because possessive pronouns already show possession — they don't need an apostrophe. *His, her, its, my, yours, ours* are all possessive pronouns. Here are some examples:

wrong: **his'** book
correct: **his** book

wrong: The group made **it's** decision.
correct: The group made **its** decision.

(Note: *Its* and *it' s* are not the same thing. *It' s* is a contraction for "it is" and *its* is a possessive pronoun meaning "belonging to it." It's raining out= it is raining out. A simple way to remember this rule is the fact that you don't use an apostrophe for the possessive *his* or *hers*, so don't do it with *its*!)

wrong: a friend of **yours'**
correct: a friend of **yours**

Proofreading for apostrophes

A good time to proofread is when you have finished writing the paper. Try the following strategies to proofread for apostrophes:

- If you tend to leave out apostrophes, check every word that ends in *-s* or *-es* to see if it needs an apostrophe.
- If you put in too many apostrophes, check every apostrophe to see if you can justify it with a rule for using apostrophes.

Ellipsis

An ellipsis (a row of three dots: ...) must be used whenever anything is omitted from within a quoted passage—word, phrase, line, or paragraph-- regardless of its source or use. It would, therefore, apply to all usage, including technical, non-technical, medical, journalistic, fiction, etc. The usual form is a "bare" ellipsis (just the three dots, preceded and followed by a space), although the MLA Handbook for Writers of Research Papers recommends that the writer enclose an ellipsis in brackets [...] when omitting part of an original quotation, to differentiate instances of deleted text from ellipses included in the original text. In all cases, the entire quoted passage, including ellipses, is preceded and followed by quotation marks and the source properly cited.

Two things to consider: 1) using ellipses is a form of "editing" the source material, so be certain that the final outcome does not change the original meaning or intent of the quoted passage; and 2) if quoted text ends up with more ellipses than words, consider paraphrasing rather than using direct quotes.

Brackets

Brackets are most often used to clarify the meaning of quoted material. If the context of your quote might be unclear, you may add a few words to provide clarity. Enclose the added material in brackets.

Added Material: The quarterback told the reporter, "It's quite simple. They [the other team] played a better game, scored more points, and that's why we lost."

Resources

SpringBoard Learning Strategies

READING STRATEGIES

STRATEGY	DEFINITION	PURPOSE
Close Reading	Accessing small chunks of text to read, reread, mark, and annotate key passages, word-for-word, sentence-by-sentence, and line-by-line	To develop comprehensive understanding by engaging in one or more focused readings of a text
Diffusing	Reading a passage, noting unfamiliar words, discovering meaning of unfamiliar words using context clues, dictionaries, and/or thesauruses, and replacing unfamiliar words with familiar ones	To facilitate a close reading of text, the use of resources, an understanding of synonyms, and increased comprehension of text
Double-Entry Journal	Creating a two-column journal (also called Dialectical Journal) with a student-selected passage in one column and the student's response in the second column (e.g., asking questions of the text, forming personal responses, interpreting the text, reflecting on the process of making meaning of the text)	To respond to a specific passage with comments, questions, or insights to foster active involvement with a text and to facilitate increased comprehension
Graphic Organizer	Using a visual representation for the organization of information	To facilitate increased comprehension and discussion
KWHL Chart	Setting up discussion with use of a graphic organizer. Allows students to activate prior knowledge by answering "What do I *know*?" sets a purpose by answering "What do I *want* to know?" helps preview a task by answering "*How* will I learn it?" and reflects on new knowledge by answering "What have I *learned?*"	To organize thinking, access prior knowledge, and reflect on learning to increase comprehension and engagement
Marking the Text	Selecting text by highlighting, underlining, and/or annotating for specific components, such as main idea, imagery, literary devices, and so on	To focus reading for specific purposes, such as author's craft, and to organize information from selections; to facilitate reexamination of a text
Metacognitive Markers	Responding to text with a system of cueing marks where students use a ? for questions about the text; a ! for reactions related to the text; and an * for comments about the text and underline to signal key ideas	To track responses to texts and use those responses as a point of departure for talking or writing about texts
Predicting	Making guesses about the text by using the title and pictures and/or thinking ahead about events which may occur based on evidence in the text	To help students become actively involved, interested, and mentally prepared to understand ideas
Previewing	Examining a text's structure, features, layout, and so on, prior to reading	To gain familiarity with the text, make connections to the text, and extend prior knowledge to set a purpose for reading
QHT	Expanding prior knowledge of vocabulary words by marking words with a Q, H, or T (Q signals words students do not know; H signals words students have heard and might be able to identify; T signals words students know well enough to teach to their peers.)	To allow students to build on their prior knowledge of words, to provide a forum for peer teaching and learning of new words, and to serve as a pre-reading exercise to aid in comprehension

STRATEGY	DEFINITION	PURPOSE
Questioning the Text*	Developing literal, interpretive, and universal questions about the text while reading a text	To engage more actively with texts, read with greater purpose and focus, and ultimately answer questions to gain greater insight into the text
Quickwrite	Responding to a text by writing for a short, specific amount of time about a designated topic or idea related to a text	To activate background knowledge, clarify issues, facilitate making connections, and allow for reflection
RAFT	Responding to and analyzing text by brainstorming various roles (e.g., self, characters from other texts), audiences (e.g., a different character, a real person), formats (e.g., letter, brochure, essay, travel guide), and topics; readers may choose one particular role, audience, format, and topic to create a new text	To initiate reader response; to facilitate an analysis of a text to gain focus prior to creating a new text
Rereading	Encountering the same text with more than one reading	To identify additional details; to clarify meaning and/or reinforce comprehension of texts
SIFT*	Analyzing a fictional text by examining stylistic elements, especially symbol, images, and figures of speech, in order to show how all work together to reveal tone and theme.	To focus and facilitate an analysis of a fictional text by examining the title and text for symbolism, identifying images and sensory details, analyzing figurative language and identifying how all these elements reveal tone and theme
Skimming/Scanning	Skimming by rapid or superficial reading of a text to form an overall impression or to obtain a general understanding of the material; scanning by focusing on key words, phrases, or specific details to provide speedy recognition of information	To quickly form an overall impression prior to an in-depth study of a text; to answer specific questions or quickly locate targeted information or detail in a text

*AP strategy

READING STRATEGIES (Continued)

STRATEGY	DEFINITION	PURPOSE
SMELL*	Analyzing a persuasive speech or essay by asking five essential questions: • **S**ender-receiver relationship—What is the sender-receiver relationship? Who are the images and language meant to attract? Describe the speaker of the text. • **M**essage—What is the message? Summarize the statement made in the text. • **E**motional Strategies—What is the desired effect? • **L**ogical Strategies—What logic is operating? How does it (or its absence) affect the message? Consider the logic of the images as well as the words. • **L**anguage—What does the language of the text describe? How does it affect the meaning and effectiveness of the writing? Consider the language of the images as well as the words.	To analyze a persuasive speech or essay by focusing on five essential questions
SOAPSTone*	Analyzing text by discussing and identifying *Speaker, Occasion, Audience, Purpose, Subject,* and *Tone*	To use an analytical process to understand the author's craft
Summarizing/ Paraphrasing	Restating in one's own words the main idea or essential information expressed in a text, whether it be narration, dialogue, or informational text	To facilitate comprehension and recall of a text
Think Aloud	Talking through a difficult passage or task by using a form of metacognition whereby the reader expresses how he/she has made sense of the text	To reflect on how readers make meaning of challenging texts
TP-CASTT*	Analyzing a poetic text by identifying and discussing *Title, Paraphrase, Connotation, Attitude, Shift, Theme,* and *Title* again	To use an analytical process to understand the author's craft
Visualizing	Forming a picture (mentally and/or literally) while reading a text	To increase reading comprehension and promote active engagement with text
Word Maps	Using a clearly defined graphic organizer such as concept circles or word webs to identify and reinforce word meanings	To provide a visual tool for identifying and remembering multiple aspects of words and word meanings

*AP strategy

WRITING STRATEGIES

STRATEGY	DEFINITION	PURPOSE
Adding	Making conscious choices to enhance a text by adding additional words, phrases, sentences, or ideas	To refine and clarify the writer's thoughts during revision and/or drafting
Brainstorming	Using a flexible but deliberate process of listing multiple ideas in a short period of time without excluding any idea from the preliminary list	To generate ideas, concepts, or key words that provide a focus and/or establish organization as part of the prewriting or revision process
Deleting	Providing clarity and cohesiveness for a text by eliminating words, phrases, sentences, or ideas	To refine and clarify the writer's thoughts during revision and/or drafting
Double-Entry Journal	Creating a two-column journal (also called Dialectical Journal) with a student-selected passage in one column and the student's response in the second column (e.g., asking questions of the text, forming personal responses, interpreting the text, reflecting on the process of making meaning of the text)	To assist in organizing key textual elements and responses noted during reading in order to generate textual support that can be incorporated into a piece of writing at a later time
Drafting	Composing a text in its initial form	To incorporate brainstormed or initial ideas into a written format
Free writing	Using a fluid brainstorming process to write without constraints in order to solidify and convey the writer's purpose	To refine and clarify the writer's thoughts, spark new ideas, and/or generate content during revision and/or drafting
Generating Questions	Clarifying and developing ideas by asking questions of the draft. May be part of self-editing or peer editing	To clarify and develop ideas in a draft. Used during drafting and as part of writer response
Graphic Organizer	Representing ideas and information visually (e.g., Venn diagrams, flowcharts, cluster maps)	To provide a visual system for organizing multiple ideas, details, and/or textual support to be included in a piece of writing
Looping	Focusing on one section of a text and using that section to generate new ideas and then repeating the process with the newly generated segments	To refine and clarify the writer's thoughts, spark new ideas, and/or generate new content during revision and/or drafting
Mapping	Creating a graphic organizer that serves as a visual representation of the organizational plan for a written text	To generate ideas, concepts, or key words that provide a focus and/or establish organization during the prewriting, drafting, or revision process

WRITING STRATEGIES (Continued)

STRATEGY	DEFINITION	PURPOSE
Marking the Draft	Interacting with the draft version of a piece of writing by highlighting, underlining, color-coding, and annotating to indicate revision ideas.	To encourage focused, reflective thinking about revising drafts
Outlining	Using a system of numerals and letters in order to identify topics and supporting details and ensure an appropriate balance of ideas	To generate ideas, concepts, or key words that provide a focus and/or establish organization prior to writing an initial draft and/or during the revision process
Quickwrite	Writing for a short, specific amount of time about a designated topic related to a text	To generate multiple ideas in a quick fashion that could be turned into longer pieces of writing at a later time (May be considered as part of the drafting process)
RAFT	Generating and/or transforming a text by identifying and/or manipulating its component parts of Role, Audience, Format, and Topic	To consider the main elements of the writer's own work in order to generate a focus and purpose during the prewriting and drafting stages of the writing process
Rearranging	Selecting components of a text and moving them to another place within the text and/or modifying the order in which the author's ideas are presented	To refine and clarify the writer's thoughts during revision and/or drafting
Revisiting Prior Work	Looking through a collection of previously completed work to identify successes and challenges that may have been encountered with particular formats, conventions, style, word choice, and so on	To build on prior experience in preparation for a new piece of writing and/or to revise a previous piece of writing
Self-Editing/Peer Editing	Working with a partner to examine a text closely in order to identify areas that might need to be corrected for grammar, punctuation, spelling	To provide a systematic process for editing a written text to ensure correctness of identified components such as conventions of standard English
Sharing and Responding	Communicating with another person or a small group of peers who respond to a piece of writing as focused readers (not necessarily as evaluators)	To make suggestions for improvement to the work of others and/or to receive appropriate and relevant feedback on the writer's own work, used during the drafting and revision process
Sketching	Drawing or sketching ideas or ordering of ideas. Includes storyboarding, visualizing	To generate and/or clarify ideas by visualizing them; may be part of prewriting
Substituting	Replacing original words or phrases in a text with new words or phrases that achieve the desired effect	To refine and clarify the writer's thoughts during revision and/or drafting
Transformation of Text	Providing opportunities for students to create new text from a studied text by changing the genre, vernacular, time period, culture, point of view, and so on	To highlight the elements of a genre, point of view and so on; to illustrate how elements of style work together
TWIST*	Arriving at a thesis statement that incorporates the following literary elements: tone, word choice (diction), imagery, style and theme	To craft an interpretive thesis in response to a prompt about a passage
Webbing	Developing a graphic organizer that consists of a series of circles connected with lines to indicate relationships among ideas	To generate ideas, concepts, or key words that provide a focus and/or establish organization prior to writing an initial draft and/or during the revision process

SPEAKING AND LISTENING STRATEGIES

STRATEGY	DEFINITION	PURPOSE
Notetaking	Creating a record of information while listening to a speaker	To facilitate active listening; to record and organize ideas that assist in processing information
Oral Interpretation	Reading a text orally while providing the necessary inflection and emphasis that demonstrate an understanding of the meaning of the text	To share with an audience the reader's personal insight into a text through voice, fluency, tone, and purpose
Oral Reading	Reading aloud one's own text or the texts of others (e.g., echo reading, choral reading, paired readings).	To share one's own work or the work of others; build fluency and increase confidence in presenting to a group
Role Playing	Assuming the role or persona of a character	To develop the voice, emotions, and mannerisms of a character to facilitate improved comprehension of a text
Rehearsal	Encouraging multiple practices of a piece of text prior to a performance	To provide students with an opportunity to clarify the meaning of a text prior to a performance as they refine the use of dramatic conventions (e.g., gestures, vocal interpretations, facial expressions)

COLLABORATIVE STRATEGIES

STRATEGY	DEFINITION	PURPOSE
Think-Pair-Share	Considering and thinking about a topic or question and then writing what has been learned; pairing with a peer or a small group to share ideas; sharing ideas and discussion with a larger group	To construct meaning about a topic or question; to test thinking in relation to the ideas of others; to prepare for a discussion with a larger group
Discussion Groups	Engaging in an interactive, small group discussion, often with an assigned role; to consider a topic, text, question, and so on	To gain new understanding or insight of a text from multiple perspectives

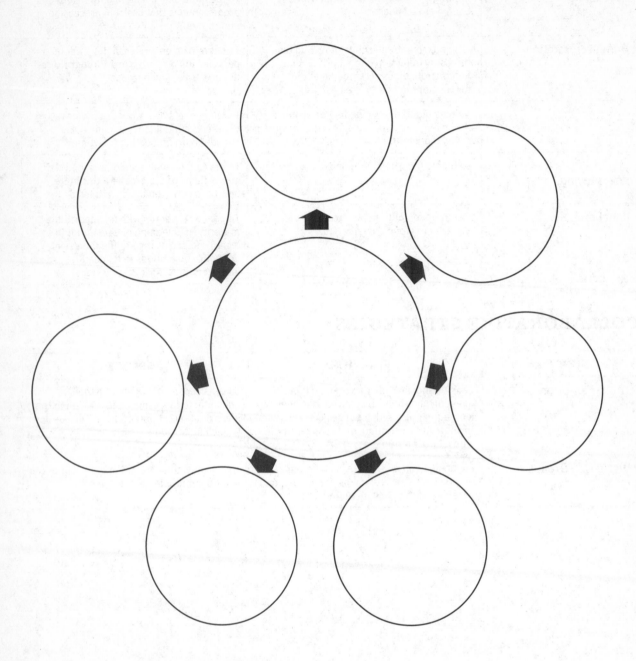

Word Map

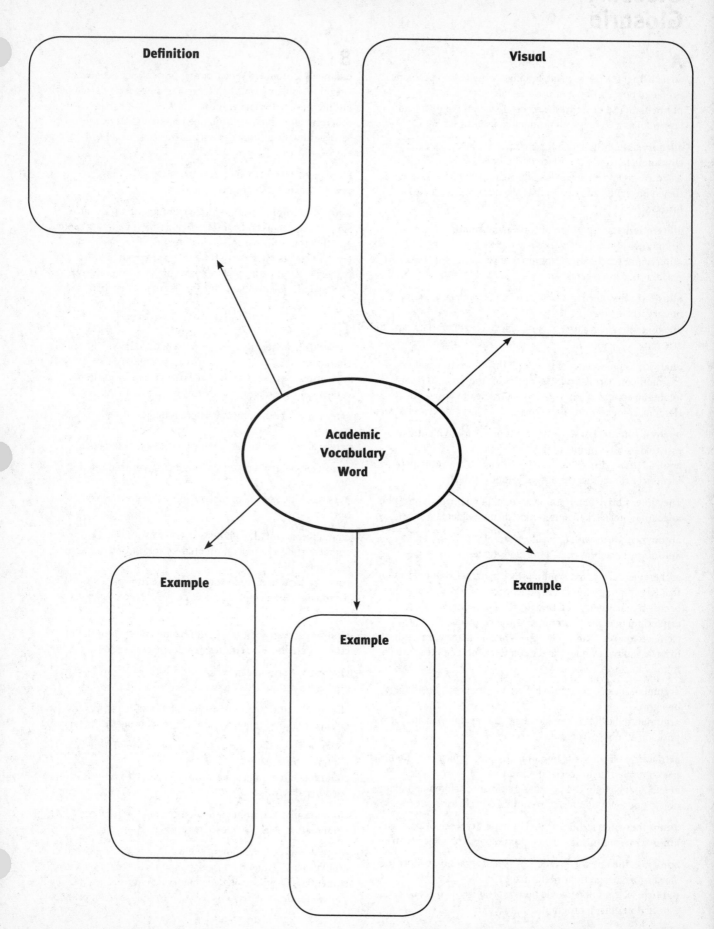

Definition

Visual

Academic
Vocabulary
Word

Example

Example

Example

Glossary
Glosario

A

advertising: the use of print, graphics, or videos to persuade people to buy a product or use a service
publicidad: uso de impresos, gráfica o videos para persuadir a las personas a comprar un producto o usar un servicio

allegory: a story in which the characters, objects, or actions have a meaning beyond the surface of the story
alegoría: cuento en el que los personajes, objetos o acciones tienen un significado que va más allá de la superficie de la historia

alliteration: the repetition of consonant sounds at the beginnings of words that are close together
aliteración: repetición de sonidos consonánticos al comienzo de palabras que están cercanas

allusion: a reference to a well-known person, place, event, literary work, or work of art
alusión: referencia a una persona, lugar, obra literaria u obra de arte muy conocidos

analogy: a comparison of the similarity of two things; for example, comparing a *part to a whole* or the *whole to a part*
analogía: comparación de la semejanza de dos cosas; por ejemplo, comparar una *parte con un todo* o el *todo con una parte*

analysis (literary): a study of details of a work to identify essential features or meaning
análisis (literario): estudio de los detalles de una obra para identificar características o significados esenciales

anecdote: a brief, entertaining account of an incident or event
anécdota: breve relato entretenido de un incidente o suceso

antonyms: words with opposite meanings
antónimos: palabras con significados opuestos

archetype: a character, symbol, story pattern, or other element that is common to human experience across cultures and that occurs frequently in literature, myth, and folklore
arquetipo: personaje, símbolo, patrón de un cuento u otro elemento que es común a la experiencia humana a través de diversas culturas y que aparece con frecuencia en literatura, mitos y folclor

argument: facts or reasoning offered to support a position as being true
argumento: hechos o razonamiento entregados para apoyar una posición como verdadera

artifact: an object made by a human being, typically an item that has cultural or historical significance
artefacto: objeto hecho por un ser humano, habitualmente un objeto que tiene significación cultural o histórica

atmosphere: the feeling created by a literary work or passage
atmósfera: sentimiento creado por una obra o pasaje literario

audience: the intended readers of specific types of texts or the viewers of a program or performance
público: lectores objetivo de tipos específicos de textos o espectadores de un programa o actuación

B

balanced sentence: a sentence that presents ideas of equal weight in similar grammatical form to emphasize the similarity or difference between the ideas
oración balanceada: oración que presenta ideas de igual peso en forma gramatical similar para enfatizar la semejanza o diferencia entre las ideas

blank verse: unrhymed verse
verso blanco: verso que no tiene rima

body paragraph: a paragraph that contains a topic sentence, supporting details and commentary, and a concluding sentence and that is usually part of a longer text
párrafo representativo: párrafo que contiene una oración principal, detalles de apoyo y comentarios, y una oración concluyente que normalmente forma parte de un texto más extenso

C

caricature: a visual or verbal representation in which characteristics or traits are distorted for emphasis
caricatura: representación visual o verbal en la que las características o rasgos son distorsionados para dar énfasis

cause: an initial action; an event that makes something else happen
causa: acción inicial; suceso que hace que otra cosa ocurra

character: a person or animal that takes part in the action of a literary work
personaje: persona o animal que participa en la acción de una obra literaria

characterization: the methods a writer uses to develop characters; for example, through description, actions, and dialogue
caracterización: métodos que usa un escritor para desarrollar personajes; por ejemplo, a través de descripción, acciones y diálogo

citation: giving credit to the authors of source information
cita: dar crédito a los autores de información usada como fuente

cliché: an overused expression or idea
cliché: expresión o idea usada en exceso

climax: the turning point or the high point of a story
clímax: punto de inflexión o momento culminante de un cuento

coherence: the clear and orderly presentation of ideas in a paragraph or essay
coherencia: presentación clara y ordenada de las ideas en un párrafo o ensayo

comedy: an entertainment that is amusing or humorous
comedia: espectáculo que es divertido o cómico

commentary: explanation of the way the facts, details and/or examples in a paragraph or essay support the topic sentence
comentario: explicación de la manera en que los hechos, detalles y ejemplos de un párrafo o ensayo apoyan la oración principal

commercialism: an emphasis on gaining profits through advertising or sponsorship
mercantilismo: énfasis en obtener utilidades por medio de la publicidad o el auspicio

communication: the process of giving or exchanging information
comunicación: proceso de dar o intercambiar información

compare: to identify similarities in two or more items
comparar: identificar semejanzas en dos o más elementos

concluding sentence: a final sentence that pulls together the ideas in a paragraph by restating the main idea or by summarizing or commenting on the ideas in the paragraph
oración concluyente: oración final que reúne las ideas de un párrafo, reformulando la idea principal o resumiendo o comentando las ideas del párrafo

conclusion: the ending of a paragraph or essay, which brings it to a close and leaves an impression with the reader
conclusión: fin de un párrafo o ensayo, que lo lleva a su término y deja una impresión en el lector

conflict: a struggle between opposing forces. In an **external conflict**, a character struggles with an outside force, such as another character or something in nature. In an **internal conflict**, the character struggles with his or her own needs, desires, or emotions.
conflicto: lucha entre fuerzas opuestas. En un **conflicto externo**, un personaje lucha contra una fuerza externa, como por ejemplo otro personaje o algo de la naturaleza. En un **conflicto interno**, el personaje lucha contra sus propias necesidades, deseos o emociones.

connotation: the suggested or implied meaning or emotion associated with a word—beyond its literal definition
connotación: significado o emoción sugerida o implícita que se asocia con una palabra—más allá de su definición literal

consumer: a buyer; a person who acquires goods and services
consumidor: comprador, persona que adquiere bienes y servicios

consumerism: the buying and consuming of goods and products; the belief that it is good to buy and consume goods and services
consumismo: compra y consumo de bienes y productos; creencia de que es bueno comprar y consumir bienes y servicios

context clue: information in words and phrases surrounding an unfamiliar word that hint at the meaning of the unfamiliar word.
clave de contexto: información en las palabras y frases que rodean una palabra no conocida y que dan una pista acerca del significado de esa palabra.

contrast: to identify differences in two or more items
contrastar: identificar las diferencias entre dos o más elementos

copy: the actual text in an advertisement
texto publicitario: información actual en un anuncio publicitario

counter-argument: reasoning or facts given in opposition to an argument
contraargumento: razonamiento o hechos dados en oposición a un argumento

criteria: the facts, rules, or standards on which judgments are based
criterios: hechos, reglas o estándares sobre las cuales están basadas las opiniones

D

debate: *n.* a discussion involving opposing points of view; *v.* to present the sides of an argument by discussing opposing points
debate: *s.* discusión que involucra puntos de vista opuestos; *v.* presentar los lados de un argumento discutiendo puntos opuestos

definition: the process of making clear the meaning or nature of something
definición: proceso de aclarar el significado o naturaleza de algo

denotation: the exact, literal meaning of a word
denotación: significado exacto y literal de una palabra

detail: in writing, evidence (facts, statistics, examples) that supports the topic sentence
detalle: en la escritura, evidencia (hechos, estadística, ejemplos) que apoya la oracón principal

dialogue: conversation between characters
diálogo: conversación entre personajes

diction: a writer's or speaker's choice of words
dicción: selección de palabras por parte del escritor u orador

dissolve: the slow fading away of one image in a film as another fades in to take its place
desvanecimiento: desaparición lenta de una imagen en una película a medida que otra aparece progresivamente para tomar su lugar

drama: a genre of literature that is intended to be performed before an audience; a play
drama: género literario destinado a ser representado ante un público; obra teatral

dystopia: an imagined place or state in which the condition of life is imperfect or bad
distopía: lugar o estado imaginario en el que las condiciones de vida son imperfectas o malas

E

editorial: a short essay in which a publication, or someone speaking for a publication, expresses an opinion or takes a stand on an issue
editorial: ensayo corto en el que una publicación, o alguien que representa una publicación, expresa una opinión o toma partido acerca de un tema

effect: the result of an event or action
efecto: resultado de un suceso o acción

epic: a long narrative poem about the deeds of heroes or gods
épica: poema narrativo largo acerca de las proezas de héroes o dioses

epilogue: a section at the end of a book or play that extends or comments on the ending
epílogo: sección al final de un libro u obra teatral, que extiende o comenta el final

essay: a short literary composition on a single subject
ensayo: composición literaria corta acerca de un único tema

ethos: a rhetorical appeal that focuses on the character or qualifications of the speaker
ethos: recurso retórico centrado en el carácter o las capacidades del orador

euphemism: an inoffensive expression that is used in place of one that is considered harsh or blunt
eufemismo: expresión inofensiva usada en lugar de una considerada cruel o ruda

exposition: *(1)* a type of writing that explains, clarifies, defines, or gives information; *(2)* events that give a reader background information needed to understand a story
exposición: *(1)* tipo de escrito que explica, clarifica, define o entrega información; *(2)* sucesos que entregan al lector los antecedentes necesarios para comprender un cuento

expository essay: an essay that makes an assertion and explains it with details, reasons, textual evidence, and commentary
ensayo expositivo: ensayo que hace una afirmación y la explica con detalles, razones, evidencia textual y comentarios

expository paragraph: a paragraph that makes an assertion and supports it with details and commentary
párrafo expositivo: párrafo que hace una afirmación y la apoya con detalles y comentarios

F

fable: a brief story that teaches a lesson or moral, usually through animal characters that take on human qualities
fábula: cuento breve que enseña una lección o moraleja, normalmente por medio de personajes animales que asumen cualidades humanas

fact: a statement that can be proven
hecho: enunciado que puede demostrarse

fairy tale: a story that involves fantasy elements such as witches, goblins, and elves. These stories often involve princes and princesses and today are generally told to entertain children.
cuento de hadas: cuento que involucra elementos fantásticos como brujas, duendes y elfos. A menudo, estos cuentos involucran a príncipes y princesas y hoy se cuentan generalmente para entretener a los niños.

falling action: events after the climax of a story but before the resolution
acción descendente: sucesos posteriores al clímax de un cuento, pero antes de la resolución

fantasy: a story based on things that could not happen in real life
fantasía: cuento basado en cosas que no podrían ocurrir en la vida real

figurative language: imaginative language that is not meant to be interpreted literally
lenguaje figurativo: lenguaje imaginativo que no pretende ser interpretado literalmente

flashback: a sudden and vivid memory of an event in the past; also, an interruption in the sequence of events in the plot of a story to relate events that occurred in the past
narración retrospectiva: recuerdo repentino y vívido de un

suceso del pasado; además, interrupción en la secuencia de los sucesos del argumento de un cuento para relatar sucesos ocurridos en el pasado

fluency: the ability to use language clearly and easily
fluidez: capacidad de usar el lenguaje fácilmente y de manera clara

folk literature: the traditional literature of a culture, consisting of a variety of myths and folk tales
literatura folclórica: literatura tradicional de una cultura, consistente en una variedad de mitos y cuentos folclóricos

folklore: the stories, traditions, sayings, and customs of a culture or a society
folclor: historias, tradiciones, dichos y costumbres de una cultura o sociedad

folk tale: an anonymous traditional story passed on orally from one generation to another
cuento folclórico: cuento tradicional anónimo pasada oralmente de generación en generación

foreshadowing: clues or hints signaling events that will occur later in the plot
presagio: claves o pistas que señalan sucesos que ocurrirán mas adelante en el argumento

free verse: a kind of poetry that does not follow any regular pattern, rhythm, or rhyme
verso libre: tipo de poesía que no sigue ningún patrón, ritmo o rima regular

G

genre: a category or type of literature, such as short story, folk tale, poem, novel, play
género: categoría o tipo de literatura, como el cuento corto, cuento folclórico, poema, novela, obra teatral

global revision: the process of deeply revising a text to improve organization, development of ideas, focus, and voice
revisión global: proceso de revisar en profundidad un texto para mejorar su organización, desarrollo de ideas, enfoque y voz

graphic novel: a narrative told through visuals and captions
novela gráfica: narrativa que se cuenta por medio de efectos visuales y leyendas

H

headline: a short piece of text at the top of an article, usually in larger type, designed to be the first words the audience reads
titular: trozo corto de texto en la parte superior de un artículo, habitualmente en letra más grande, diseñado para ser las primeras palabras que el público lea

humor: the quality of being comical or amusing
humor: cualidad de ser cómico o divertido

hook *n.:* a compelling idea or statement designed to get readers' attention in an introduction
gancho *n.:* idea o afirmación atractiva diseñada para captar la atención del lector en una introducción

hyperbole: extreme exaggeration used for emphasis, often used for comic effect
hypérbole: exageración extrema usada para dar énfasis, habitualmente usada para dar efecto cómico

I

idiom: a figure of speech that cannot be defined literally
expresión idiomatica: figura del discurso que no puede definirse literalmente

image: a picture, drawing, photograph, illustration, chart, or other graphic that is designed to affect the audience in some purposeful way
imagen: pintura, dibujo, fotografía, ilustración, cuadro u otra gráfica diseñada para producir algún efecto intencional sobre el público

imagery: descriptive or figurative language used to create word pictures; imagery is created by details that appeal to one or more of the five senses
imaginería: lenguaje descriptivo o figurativo utilizado para crear imágenes verbales; la imaginería es creada por detalles que apelan a uno o más de los cinco sentidos

improvise: to respond or perform on the spur of the moment
improvisar: reaccionar o representar impulsivamente

incident: a distinct piece of action as in an episode in a story or a play. More than one incident may make up an event.
incidente: trozo de acción distintivo como un episodio de un cuento o de una obra teatral. Más de un incidente puede conformar un suceso.

inference: a logical guess or conclusion based on observation, prior experience, or textual evidence
inferencia: conjetura o conclusión lógica basada en la observación, experiencias anteriores o evidencia textual

inflection: the emphasis a speaker places on words through change in pitch or volume
inflexión: énfasis que pone un orador en las palabras por medio del cambio de tono o volumen

interpretation: a writer's or artist's representation of the meaning of a story or idea
interpretación: representación que hace un escritor o artista del significado de un cuento o idea

interview: a meeting between two people in which one, usually a reporter, asks the other questions to get that person's views on a subject
entrevista: reunión entre dos personas, en la que una, normalmente un reportero, hace preguntas a la otra para conocer sus opiniones acerca de un tema

introduction: the opening paragraph of an essay, which must get the reader's attention and indicate the topic
introducción: párrafo inicial de un ensayo, que debe captar la atención del lector e indicar el tema

L

legend: a traditional story believed to be based on actual people and events. Legends, which typically celebrate heroic individuals or significant achievements, tend to express the values of a culture.
leyenda: cuento tradicional que se considera basado en personas y sucesos reales. Las leyendas, que típicamente celebran a individuos heroicos o logros importantes, tienden a expresar los valores de una cultura.

limerick: a light, humorous, nonsensical verse of few lines, usually with a rhyme scheme of a-a-b-b-a
quintilla: verso liviano, humorístico, disparatado y de pocas líneas, normalmente con un esquema a-a-b-b-a

listening: the process of receiving a message and making meaning of it from verbal and nonverbal cues
escuchar: proceso de recibir el mensaje y comprender su significado a partir de claves verbales y no verbales

literary analysis: the process of examining closely and commenting on the elements of a literary work
análisis literario: proceso de examinar atentamente y comentar los elementos de una obra literaria

local revision: revising a text on a word or sentence level
revisión local: revisar un texto a nivel de palabras o de oraciones

logo: a unique design symbol used to identify a company visually
logotipo: símbolo único de diseño, utilizado para identificar visualmente una empresa

logos: a rhetorical appeal to reason or logic through statistics, facts, and reasonable examples
logos: apelación retórica a la razón o la lógica por medio de estadísticas, hechos y ejemplos razonables

M

media: the various means of mass communication, such as radio, television, newspapers, and magazines
medios de comunicación: los diversos medios de comunicación masiva, como radio, televisión, periódicos y revistas

media channel: a type of media, such as television or newspaper
canal mediático: tipo de medios de comunicación, como televisión o periódicos

metaphor: a comparison between two unlike things in which one thing is said to be another
metáfora: comparación entre dos cosas diferentes en la que una cosa se convierte en otra

monologue: a speech or written expression of thoughts by a character
monólogo: discurso o expresión escrita de pensamientos por parte de un personaje

mood: the overall emotional quality of a work, which is created by the author's language and tone and the subject matter
carácter: la calidad emocional general de una obra, que es creada por el lenguaje y tono del autor y por el tema

motif: a recurring element, image, or idea in a work of literature
motivo: elemento, imagen o idea recurrente en una obra literaria

multiple intelligences: the variety of learning styles that everyone has in varying degrees. In each individual, different intelligences predominate.
inteligencias múltiples: diversidad de estilos de aprendizaje que todos tienen en diversos grados. En cada individuo

predominan diferentes inteligencias.

myth: a traditional story that explains the actions of gods or heroes or the origins of the elements of nature
mito: cuento tradicional que explica las acciones de dioses o héroes o los orígenes de los elementos de la naturaleza

N

narrative: a type of writing that tells a story or describes a sequence of events in an incident
narrativa: tipo de escritura que cuenta un cuento o describe una secuencia de sucesos de un incidente

narrative poem: a story told in verse
poema narrativo: historia contada en verso

news article: an article in a news publication that objectively presents both sides of an issue
artículo noticioso: artículo de una publicación noticiosa que presenta objetivamente ambos lados de un asunto

nonprint text: a text, such as film or graphics, that communicates ideas without print
texto no impreso: texto, como una película o gráfica, que comunica ideas sin imprimir

nonverbal communication: gestures, facial expressions, and inflection that form unspoken communication
comunicación no verbal: gestos, expresiones faciales e inflexión que forman la comunicación no hablada

novel: a type of literary genre that tells a fictional story
novela: tipo de género literario que cuenta una historia ficticia

O

objective: supported by facts and not influenced by personal opinion
objetivo: apoyado por hechos y no influenciado por la opinión personal

objective camera view: in film, when the camera takes a neutral point of view
visión objetiva de la cámara: en el cine, cuando la cámara toma un punto de vista neutro

omniscient: a third-person point of view in which the narrator is all knowing
omnisciente: punto de vista de una tercera persona, en la que el narador lo sabe todo

onomatopoeia: the use of words that imitate the sounds of what they describe
onomatopeya: el uso de palabras que imitan los sonidos de lo que describen

one-liner: a short joke or witticism expressed in a single sentence
agudeza: chiste u comentario ingenioso que se expresa en una sola oración

opinion: a perspective that can be debated
opinión: perspectiva que es debatible

oral interpretation: reading aloud a literary text with expression
interpretación oral: leer en voz alta un texto literario con expresión

oxymoron: a figure of speech in which the words seem to contradict each other; for example, "dark light"
oxímoron: figura del discurso en la que las palabras parecen contradicirse mutuamente; por ejemplo, "oscuridad brillante"

P

pantomime: a form of acting without words, in which motions, gestures, and expressions convey emotions or situations
pantomima: forma de actuación sin palabras, en la que los movimientos, gestos y expresiones transmiten emociones o situationes

paraphrase: to restate in one's own words
parafrasear: reformular en nuestras propias palabras

parody: a humorous imitation of a literary work
parodia: imitación humorística de una obra literaria

pathos: a rhetorical appeal to the reader's or listener's senses or emotions through connotative language and imagery
pathos: apelación retórica a los sentidos o emociones del lector u oyente por medio de un lenguaje connotativo y figurado

performance: presenting or staging a play
actuación: presentar o poner en escena una obra teatral

persona: the voice or character speaking or narrating a story
persona: voz o personaje que habla o narra una historia

personal letter: a written communication between friends, relatives, or acquaintances that shares news, thoughts, or feelings
carta personal: comunicación escrita entre amigos, parientes o conocidos, que comparte noticias, pensamientos o sentimientos

personal narrative: a piece of writing that describes an incident and includes a personal response to and reflection on the incident
narrativa personal: texto escrito que describe un incidente e incluye una reacción personal ante el incidente y una reflexión acerca de él

personification: a kind of metaphor that gives objects or abstract ideas human characteristics
personificación: tipo de metáfora que da características humanas a los objetos o ideas abstractas

perspective: the way a specific character views a situation or other characters
perspectiva: manera en que un personaje específico visualiza una situación o a otros personajes

persuasion: the act or skill of causing someone to do or believe something
persuasión: acto o destreza de hacer que alguien haga o crea algo

persuasive essay: an essay that attempts to convince the reader to take an action or believe an idea
ensayo persuasivo: ensayo que intenta convencer al lector de que realice una acción o crea una idea

phrasing: dividing a speech into smaller parts, adding pauses for emphasis
frasear: dividir un discurso en partes más pequeñas, añadiendo pausas para dar énfasis

pitch: the highness or lowness of a sound, particularly the voice in speaking
tono: altura de un sonido, especialmente de la voz al hablar

plagiarism: taking and using as your own the words and ideas of another
plagio: tomar y usar como propias las palabras e ideas de otro

plot: the sequence of related events that make up a story or novel
trama: secuencia de sucesos relacionados, que conforman un cuento o novela

pun: the humorous use of a word or words to suggest another word with the same sound or a different meaning
retruécano: uso humorístico de una o varias palabras para sugerir otra palabra que tiene el mismo sonido o un significado diferente

point of view: the perspective from which a story is told. In **first-person** point of view, the teller is a character in the story telling what he or she sees or knows. In **third-person** point of view, the narrator is someone outside of the story.
punto de vista: perspectiva desde la cual se cuenta una historia. En el punto de vista de la **primera persona**, el relator es un personaje del cuento que narra lo que ve o sabe. En el punto de vista de la **tercera persona**, el narrador es alguien que está fuera del cuento.

prediction: a logical guess or assumption about something that has not yet happened
predicción: conjetura lógica o suposición acerca de algo que aún no ha ocurrido

presentation: delivery of a formal reading, talk, or performance
presentación: entrega de una lectura, charla o representación formal

prose: the ordinary form of written language, using sentences and paragraphs; writing that is not poetry, drama, or song
prosa: forma común del lenguaje escrito, usando oraciones y párrafos; escritura que no es poesía, drama ni canción

purpose: the reason for writing; what the writer hopes to accomplish
propósito: razón para escribir; lo que el escritor espera lograr

Q

quatrain: a four-line stanza in poetry
cuarteta: en poesía, estrofa de cuatro versos

R

rate: the speed at which a speaker delivers words
rapidez: velocidad a la que el orador pronuncia las palabras

reflection: a kind of thinking and writing which seriously explores the significance of an experience, idea, or observation
reflexión: tipo de pensamiento y escritura que explora seriamente la importancia de una experiencia, idea u observación

reflective essay: an essay in which the writer explores the significance of an experience or observation
ensayo reflexivo: ensayo en que el autor explora la importancia de una experiencia u observación

refrain: a regularly repeated word, phrase, line, or group of lines in a poem or song
estribillo: palabra, frase, verso o grupo de versos de un poema o canción que se repite con regularidad

repetition: the use of the same words or structure over again
repetición: uso de las mismas palabras o estructura una y otra vez

research: (v.) the process of locating information from a variety of sources; (n.) the information found from investigating a variety of sources
investigar: (v.) proceso de buscar información en una variedad de fuentes; *también*, investigación (n.) información que se halla al investigar una variedad de fuentes

resolution: the outcome of the conflict of a story, when loose ends are wrapped up
resolución: resultado del conflicto de un cuento, cuando se atan los cabos sueltos

revision: a process of evaluating a written piece to improve coherence and use of language; *see also,* local revision, global revision
revisión: proceso de evaluar un texto escrito para mejorar la coherencia y el uso del lenguaje; *ver también*, revisión local, revisión global

rhetorical question: a question asked to emphasize a point or create an effect; no answer is expected
pregunta retórica: pregunta que se hace para enfatizar un punto o crear un efecto; no se espera una respuesta

rhyme: the repetition of sounds at the ends of words
rima: repetición de sonidos al final de las palabras

rhyme scheme: a consistent pattern of end rhyme throughout a poem
esquema de la rima: patrón consistente de una rima final a lo largo de un poema

rhythm: the pattern of stressed and unstressed syllables in spoken or written language, especially in poetry
ritmo: patrón de sílabas acentuadas y no acentuadas en lenguaje hablado o escrito, especialmente en poesía

rising action: major events that develop the plot of a story and lead to the climax
acción ascendente: sucesos importantes que desarrollan la trama de un cuento y conducen al clímax

S

science fiction: a genre in which the imaginary elements of the story could be scientifically possible
ciencia ficción: género en que los elementos imaginarios del cuento podrían ser científicamente posibles

sensory details: words or information that appeal to the five senses
detalles sensoriales: palabras o información que apelan a los cinco sentidos

sequence of events: the order in which events happen
secuencia de los sucesos: orden en que ocurren los sucesos

setting: the time and the place in which a narrative occurs
ambiente: tiempo y lugar en que ocurre un relato

short story: a work of fiction that presents a sequence of events, or plot, that deals with a conflict
cuento corto: obra de ficción que presenta una secuencia de sucesos, o trama, que tratan de un conflicto

simile: a comparison between two unlike things, using the word *like* or *as*
símil: comparación entre dos cosas diferentes usando las palabras *como* o *tan*

slogan: a catchphrase that evokes a particular feeling about a company and its product
eslogan: frase o consigna publicitaria que evoca un sentimiento en particular acerca de una empresa y su producto

speaker: the voice that communicates with the reader of a poem
hablante: la voz que se comunica con el lector de un poema

speaking: process of sharing information, ideas, and emotions using verbal and nonverbal means of communication
hablar: proceso de compartir información, ideas y emociones usando medios de comunicación verbales y no verbales

stanza: a group of lines, usually similar in length and pattern, that form a unit within a poem
estrofa: grupo de versos, normalmente similares en longitud y patrón, que forman una unidad dentro de un poema

stereotype: a fixed, oversimplified image of a person, group, or idea; something conforming to that image
estereotipo: imagen fija y demasiado simplificada de una persona, grupo o idea; algo que cumple esa imagen

subjective: influenced by personal opinions or ideas
subjectivo: influenciado por opiniones o ideas personales

subjective camera view: in film, when the camera seems to show the events through a character's eyes
visión subjetiva de la cámara: en el cine, cuando la cámara parece mostrar los sucesos a través de los ojos de un personaje

subplot: a secondary plot that occurs along with a main plot
trama secundaria: argumento secundario que ocurre conjuntamente con un argumento principal

summarize: to briefly restate the main ideas of a piece of writing
resumir: reformular brevemente las ideas principales de un texto escrito

symbol: an object, a person, or a place that stands for something else
símbolo: objeto, persona o lugar que representa otra cosa

symbolism: the use of symbols
simbolismo: el uso de símbolos

synonyms: words with similar meanings
sinónimos: palabras con significados semejantes

T

talking points: important points or concepts to be included in a presentation
puntos centrales: puntos o conceptos importantes a incluirse en una presentación

tall tale: a highly exaggerated and often humorous story about folk heroes in local settings
cuento increíble: cuento muy exagerado y normalmente humorístico acerca de héroes folclóricos en ambientes locales

target audience: the specific group of people that advertisers aim to persuade to buy
público objetivo: grupo específico de personas a quienes los publicistas desean persuadir de comprar

tempo: the speed or rate of speaking
ritmo: velocidad o rapidez al hablar

textual evidence: quotations, summaries, or paraphrases from text passages to support a position
evidencia textual: citas, resúmenes o paráfrasis de pasajes de texto para apoyar una position

theme: the central idea, message, or purpose of a literary work
tema: idea, mensaje o propósito central de una obra literaria

thesis statement: a sentence, in the introduction of an essay, that states the writer's position or opinion on the topic of the essay
enunciado de tesis: oración, en la introducción de un ensayo, que plantea el punto de vista u opinión del autor acerca del tema del ensayo

tone: a writer's or speaker's attitude toward a subject
tono: actitud de un escritor u orador hacia un tema

topic sentence: a sentence that states the main idea of a paragraph; in an essay, it also makes a point that supports the thesis statement
oración principal: oración que plantea la idea principal de un párrafo; en un ensayo, también plantea un punto que apoya el enunciado de tesis

transitions: words or phrases that connect ideas, details, or events in writing
transiciones: palabras o frases que conectan ideas, detalles o sucesos de un escrito

TV news story: a report on a news program about a specific event
documental de televisión: reportaje en un programa noticioso acerca de un suceso específico

U

utopia: an ideal or perfect place
utopía: lugar ideal o perfecto

V

verse: a unit of poetry, such as a line or a stanza
verso: unidad de la poesía, como un verso o una estrofa

voice: a writer's distinctive use of language
voz: uso distintivo del lenguaje por parte de un escritor

voice-over: the voice of an unseen character in film expressing his or her thoughts
voz en off: voz de un personaje de una película, que no se ve pero que expresa sus pensamientos

volume: the degree of loudness of a speaker's voice or other sound
volumen: grado de intensidad sonora de la voz de un orador o de otro sonido

W

wordplay: a witty or clever verbal exchange or a play on words
juego de palabras: intercambio verbal ingenioso u ocurrente o un juego con palabras

Index of Skills

Literary Skills

Allusions, 219
Analogies, 23, 55, 100, 161, 164, 203, 210, 259, 261, 282, 336
Analyses, 123
Annotated bibliographies, 234
Atmosphere, 181
Book covers, 223
Clichés, 261
Climax, plot, 57
Conflict, 209, 229
Creation stories, 76–77
Critiques, 223
Discussion groups, 155
Domain suffixes, 233
Editorials, 147, 152, 153, 161
Ethos, 159
Exposition, 57
Fables, 42, 43
Fairy tales, 42, 43
Falling action, 57
Films, characterization in, 188
5 Ws, 194
Flashbacks, 186
Folk literature, 43
Folklore, 42, 43
Folk tales, 43
Foreshadowing, 174, 187, 318
Free verse, 315
Hyperbole, 206
Imagery, 176, 317, 321
Inferences, 177
Interpretive level of questioning, 181
Interviews, 335–337
KWHL charts, 178
Lead paragraphs, 152
Legends, 42, 43
Lettering, 177
Literal level of questioning, 181
Literary analysis, 174
Logos, 159
Metaphors, 176, 317
Mood, 181
Morals, 42
Motifs, 204
Motivation, 174
Myth(s)
    creation stories, 76
    definition of, 43, 50
    Greek mythology, 50–51
    illustrated, 81–83
    plot elements in, 57, 82
    purpose of, 42
    symbols in, 72
    theme in, 58
Narrative, meaning of term, 5

News articles, 147, 152, 153, 193
Novels
    conflict and plot in, 209
    design of, 177–178
    KWHL charts of, 178
    previewing, 179
    prologue in, 180
    questioning levels, 181
Oral appeals, 131
Oral tradition, 274
Parody, 319
Pathos, 159
Persuasive advertising, 92
Persuasive arguments, 159
Persuasive techniques, 112–114
Plot structure, 57
Poetry
    drawing images from, 321
    free verse, 315
    inflection in, 286
    narrative, 315
    poetic devices, 317–318
    prose transformations into, 341–342
    punctuation in, 10, 284
    TP-CASTT interpretation of, 285, 292, 322
Point of view, 180, 229
Predictions, 177
Prologues, 180
Prose, 315
Question-answer format, 335
Refrain, 318
Resolution, plot, 57
Rhetorical questions, 115
Rhyme schemes, 10, 315
Rhythm, 318
Rising action, 57
Similes, 176, 317
Stanzas, 317
Subplots, 209
Symbols, 71–72, 317
Tall tales, 43
Theme, 58
Tone, 16, 138, 274, 318
TP-CASTT strategy, 285, 292, 322
Transitions, 20, 26
Universal level of questioning, 181
Venn diagrams, 153, 186, 202

Reading Skills

Anticipation guides, 103, 134, 139
Book covers, 223
Close reading, 11, 60, 93, 177, 180, 186, 192, 201, 203, 204, 211, 219, 316
Double-entry journals, 179, 185, 191
Editorials, 161

Emphasis, 274, 283
Independent reading, 4, 92, 245, 274
Inflection, 274
Intonation, 274
Marking the text, 5, 10, 11, 16, 18, 29, 36, 52, 60, 73, 93, 94, 121, 147, 159, 161, 175, 206, 211, 219, 246, 259, 275, 284, 287, 295, 300, 310, 321, 328, 330, 335, 339
Monologues, 274, 297, 308
Oral interpretation, 274, 283
Post-reading analysis, 137–138
Predicting, 210, 246, 275
Previewing the text, 44, 179, 223
Questioning levels, 181, 210
RAFT strategy, 218, 245, 256, 297
Scanning, skimming, 5, 93, 94, 118, 121, 137, 139, 159, 175, 210, 230, 246, 275, 323, 339
SOAPSTone strategy, 137–138, 139, 146
Summarizing, 32, 37, 180, 210

Writing Skills

Accuracy of sources, 229, 231, 232
Annotated bibliographies, 234
Argument(s)
    counter-arguments, 161
    in editorials, 161
    examining and evaluating, 159
    in letters to the editor, 160, 165
    opinions in, 158
    position statements, 158
    purpose of, 131
    types of appeals in, 159
Audience
    for advertising, 117, 120, 124
    analysis of, 137
    for police reports, 222
    voice and, 254–255
    as writer's choice, 245
Authority of sources, 229, 231, 232
Avant-garde technique, 112
Bandwagon technique, 112
Bar graphs, 99
Brainstorming
    charts in, 81, 94, 123
    cluster diagrams in, 8
    in RAFT technique, 256
    for research projects, 230
    web, 6
    word sorts in, 9
    in writing process, 4
Cause and effect, 112
Characterization, 19
Characters
    in films, 188

Index of Authors and Titles

Text credits:

From "You" by Edgar A. Guest. Reproduced by permission of the Estate of Edgar A. Guest.

From *Staying Fat for Sarah Byrnes* by Chris Crutcher. Text copyright © 1991 Chris Crutcher. Used by permission of HarperCollins Publishers.

From *Dust Tracks on a Road* by Zora Neale Hurston. Copyright 1942 by Zora Neale Hurston; renewed © 1970 by John C. Hurston. Reprinted by permission of HarperCollins Publishers.

"A Hundred Bucks of Happy" by Susan Beth Pfeffer from *Visions* by Donald R. Gallo, Editor. Copyright © 1987 by Susan Beth Pfeffer. Used by permission of Random House Children's Books, a division of Random House, Inc.

"The Classroom of Life" by Alan Lawrence Sitomer from *Reader*, Issue 1, Vol. 55, 2005. Used by permission of Weekly Reader Publishing.

Excerpt from *A Single Shard* by Linda Sue Park. Copyright © 2001 by Linda Sue Park. Reprinted by permission of Clarion Books, an imprint of Houghton Mifflin Harcourt Publishing Company. All rights reserved.

"Daedalus and Icarus" from *Greek Myths* by Geraldine McCaughrean. Text copyright © 1992 Geraldine McCaughrean. Reproduced with the permission of Margaret K. McElderry Books, an imprint of Simon & Schuster Childrens Publishing Division.

"Phaethon" from *Heroes, Gods and Monsters of Greek Mythology* by Bernard Evslin. Published by permission of Writers House, LLC as Agent for the Estate of Bernard Evslin.

"Arachne" from *Greek Myths* by Olivia E. Coolidge. Copyright 1949; copyright renewed © 1977 by Olivia E. Coolidge. Reprinted by permission of Houghton Mifflin Harcourt Publishing Company. All rights reserved.

"Raven and the Sources of Light" by Donna Rosenberg from *World Mythology*. Reproduced by permission of Glencoe/McGraw-Hill Company.

"Today's Youth Look to Advertising as Much as Their Friends When Making Purchase Decisions," Harris Interactive, August 21, 2006.

"From Ramp to Riches" by Lea Goldman from *Forbes*, July 5, 2004. Reprinted by permission of Forbes Media LLC © 2010.

"Facts About Marketing to Children" by Betsy Taylor on behalf of the Center for a New American Dream. Reproduced by permission.

"America the Not-So-Beautiful" from *Not That You Asked* by Andrew A. Rooney, copyright © 1989 by Essay Productions, Inc. Used by permission of Random House, Inc.

"Buying Into The Green Movement" from *The New York Times*, Style Section, July 1, 2007. Copyright © 2007 The New York Times. All rights reserved. Used by permission and protected by the Copyright Laws of the United States. The printing, copying, redistribution, or retransmission of the Material without express written permission is prohibited. www.nytimes.com

"City Schools Cut Parents' Lifeline (the Cellphone) from *The New York Times*, Style Section, April 27, 2006. Copyright © 2006 The New York Times. All rights reserved. Used by permission and protected by the Copyright Laws of the United States. The printing, copying, redistribution, or retransmission of the Material without express written permission is prohibited. www.nytimes.com

"Hang It Up" by Jesse Scaccia from *The New York Times*, May 23, 2006, OP-ED. Copyright 2006 The New York Times. Reprinted by permission.

"Ironing Out Policies on School Uniforms" by Carol Motsinger from *USA Today*, August 5, 2007. Reproduced with permission.

"Balancing Act on Cell Phones" from *The Commercial Appeal*, September 3, 2008. Used by permission of *The Commercial Appeal*, Memphis, Tennessee.

"Bullying in Schools" by Hilda Clarice Quiroz, June Lane Arnette, Ronald D. Stephens, National School Safety Center. Copyright © 2006. Used by permission of the National School Safety Center. www.schoolsafety.us.

"Taming Wild Girls" by Jeanne McDowell from *Time*, April 24, 2006. Copyright © 2006, Time Inc. All rights reserved. Used by permission of Rightslink.

"Choices" from *Cotton Candy on a Rainy Day* by Nikki Giovanni. Copyright © 1978. Reprinted by permission of HarperCollins Publishers/William Morrow.

"Stopping by the Woods on a Snowy Evening" from *The Poetry of Robert Frost* edited by Edward Connery Lathem. Copyright © 1923, 1969 by Henry Holt and Company. Copyright 1951 by Robert Frost. Reprinted by arrangement with Henry Holt and Company, LLC.